Making Stuffed **TOYS**

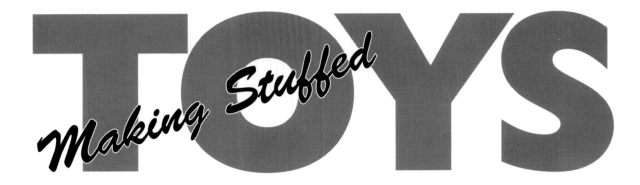

Making Stuffed TOYS

35 cuddly dolls and animals to make, complete
with sewing instructions and patterns

Jane Gisby and Sue Quinn

Published by Salamander Books Limited
LONDON

Published by Salamander Books Limited
129-137 York Way
London N7 9LG
United Kingdom

© Salamander Books Ltd., 1995

Distributed by Random House Value Publishing, Inc.
40 Engelhard Avenue
Avenel, New Jersey 07001

ISBN 0-517-14088-8

1 3 5 7 9 8 6 4 2

Printed in Italy

A CIP catalog record for this book is available
from the Library of Congress

All correspondence concerning the content of this volume
should be addressed to Salamander Books Ltd.

CONTENTS

INTRODUCTION

Making stuffed toys is an enjoyable and rewarding pastime and the toys and dolls in this book will give a great deal of fun and pleasure to their recipients as well as to their makers. The appeal of a toy relies largely on its design and character, and within this book Sue Quinn and Jane Gisby have created a menagerie of charming and beautifully designed characters, from toys for babies, such as Cheeky Squeeky Mice and Chiming Chicks, to more complex animal toys, such as Morris the Monkey and Beatrice the Cow, and beautiful dolls for little girls, such as Kyrstal the Snow Queen and Pretty Petula. Please remember, though, that you don't have to follow every given detail for a particular toy or doll; a different hair style, features or clothes will make a doll that is truly your own creation. A child can draw a doll's face to a given size, which will have great appeal; you can then paint or embroider these features.

Some knowledge of simple sewing skills is useful but not essential. The opening pages of this book contain important information on the equipment and its use; the various types of materials available and which to choose; how to prepare the pattern and cut the fabric; plus the numerous sewing techniques referred to throughout the book, such as those required for sewing, turning and stuffing a toy. Following this are detailed instructions on how to make 34 delightful toys, each design accompanied by a cutting pattern and a series of easy-to-follow step-by-step instructions and photographs. In each case the finished toy is illustrated in a colour photograph. This is a book that will delight all and will encourage even the most cautious toymaker, as well as those with more experience, to enjoy making stuffed toys and dolls. There is much to delight both the eye and the hand.

EQUIPMENT

Before you begin to sew, you must assemble the right equipment. Having the correct tool for the job makes the work easier and ensures that the final result is as attractive as possible.

SCISSORS

One of the most important pieces of equipment is a good sharp pair of scissors. You should actually have at least two pairs; one for cutting out the cardboard used for making the patterns and one for cutting the fabric. A small pair of embroidery scissors with very sharp points are also a must. These are used for piercing the tiny eye holes, for cutting the ear slits and for unpicking thread.

PINS AND NEEDLES

It is very easy to lose pins in the pile of fur fabric, so it is advisable to count the number you use before starting and again when the work is completed. Never leave a pin inside a toy that a child will play with.

Have a wide selection of handsewing needles available. You will soon find the length of needle that suits you best. Have some long darning needles on hand, too, for sewing on the heads of the toys and for embroidering the nose and mouth (see page 13).

BRUSHES

Fur fabrics can quickly lose their fluffiness from all the handling. Brushes are used to bring up the pile and to restore the fabric to its original shape. Teazle brushes are especially good for brushing out fur that has become trapped in the seams. For a large toy, though, a dog brush with similar teeth is much easier to use and covers a larger area. The tiny wire teeth in brushes work loose after a time and become struck in the fabric, so remove any loose teeth from the brush each time it is used. Also, never use the brush too near the plastic eyes of the toys, as the surface of the eye can easily become scratched.

SCREWDRIVERS

Screwdrivers are very useful tools for turning the finished toy the right way out. Use a screwdriver with a blunt end to avoid damaging the fabric. A knitting needle can also be used, but always use the blunt end. Likewise, wooden spoon handles are suitable.

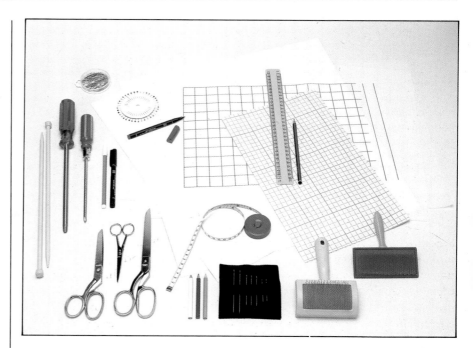

Be sure to use the right tool for each job. Assemble all the equipment before you begin to sew, making sure you have everything you need.

CARDBOARD AND PAPER

Pieces of medium-thickness cardboard are necessary for marking out the pattern pieces. You can buy packages of cardboard in stationery stores, or you can improvise using old cereal packages. Dressmaker's squared paper, used for making the patterns, is available from fabric stores. Alternatively, you can make your own, for which you will need large sheets of thin paper and a ruler and pen to draw up the grid.

PENS AND PENCILS

A quick-drying felt-tip pen is the best type for marking out patterns and for making the cardboard pattern pieces. A soft lead pencil is usually preferred for marking the eye and ear positions, as well as for marking out any other guidelines that must be transferred from the pattern onto the fabric. For dark fabrics, a white chalk pencil is needed to be sure that the outline shows up. There are numerous ones on the market, some of them specifically made for dressmakers.

MATERIALS

Before making your stuffed toy or doll, decide if it needs to be completely washable or if it is to be a decorative toy and then choose suitable fabrics.

CALICO

Calico is perhaps the most popular material for 'rag' doll making, being strong, closely woven and washable. It can be bought from craft stores and specialist craft mail order suppliers in colours suitable for a wide range of dolls. Calico creases readily and needs to be pressed before making and then again before filling.

STOCKINETTE

Stockinette is a stretch knitted interlock fabric, made in white or flesh pink. It makes a very soft cuddly and attractive doll's body when filled with a light bouncy fibre, but care must be taken with the filling since the body shape can be over stretched. To avoid this the fabric is often used in a double thickness. The seams can be almost invisible and it is excellent for modelling the features with a needle and thread.

FUR FABRIC

It is always best to buy high quality fur fabric, if possible. A fur fabric with a woven backing is usually the best, as it has a pleasant, realistic feel. The fabric does not stretch very much, though, and can be difficult to work with. If you are a beginner, choose a fur fabric with a knitted backing. These do not fray and will stretch slightly, making them easier to work with.

When choosing fur, look at the pile of the material. If too much of the knitted backing can be detected through the fur, it will be disappointing to work with. Feel the knitted side of the fabric. If it is too harsh and hard, again it will be difficult to sew, turn and stuff.

FELT

Felt does not fray, it stretches slightly and comes in a wonderful selection of colours. Felt is usually made of man-made fibres; occasionally a pure wool felt is available but these are very expensive. Felt is not washable, though, and does not have the strength that other fabrics have. Self-adhesive felts are available but they come in a limited range of colours. Black self-adhesive felt is extremely useful for eyes.

FILLING

Dacron and polyester, which is a man-made fibre, is the best. It is springy, washable, and non-allergic. It is sold in different grades so choose the best you can afford. This filling also comes in different colours, but only buy coloured filling if a dark toy is being made.

Kapok is a natural fibre and very fluffy. It is not washable, it is messy to use and not very springy. It does have a beautiful soft feel, though, and could be used for certain types of toys.

Foam Chips are not recommended as filling for toys.

THREADS

A sewing thread with man-made fibres is suitable for all seams and will give a little when body parts are turned to right side out and filled. Choose a strong matching thread to sew limbs to the body and to close the gap after filling. A soft cotton embroidery thread can be used for the hair of small dolls, and a stranded silk embroidery thread which can be divided into one or two strands is best for eyes, nose and mouth.

PATTERN PREPARATION

The patterns in this book have all been reduced in size to fit the page. If you look at one of the patterns, you will see that it has been drawn on a grid. Each square on that grid represents 2.5cm (1in). To enlarge the patterns you will need scissors, cardboard, dressmaker's squared paper, a felt-tip pen and a soft lead pencil. The dressmaker's paper must be divided into 2.5cm (1in) squares in order to reproduce the pattern at its full size. If such paper is not readily available, or simply if you wish to save money, you can easily draw up your own grids on some large sheets of thin paper. A long ruler and set square will prove useful for this purpose.

To begin, first lay out a large sheet of the squared paper, flattening it out if it has been folded. Select a starting point on the pattern and look at the square that part of the pattern occupies. Note where the pattern line enters that square and mark the position on one of the larger squares of your grid, making sure you have left lots of space all around. Now examine the same square on the pattern in the book, and note where the line leaves the square. Again, mark that spot on your paper. Next, join the two marks together, noting what happens to the line in between the two points. Follow the line exactly, copying it onto the larger square.

Work around the whole pattern shape in this way, constantly checking and rechecking the general shape of each piece. With a little practice and patience it becomes much easier. Remember, too, to mark the eye positions and slits for the ears, as well as any letters or arrows on the pattern. When you have completed the whole pattern, cut it out very carefully. Now mark around this outline onto pieces of cardboard, copying down all the relevant points. Cut out the cardboard

templates. These will be firm enough to draw around without buckling or tearing, and can be used several times. Keep the paper copy in an envelope in case any of the cardboard pieces are lost.

MARKING AND CUTTING OUT

Lay out the piece of fabric you have selected and check which way the pile goes; mark an arrow on the reverse side of the fabric to remind yourself of the direction of pile. (This is important, as the direction of pile will affect the whole appearance of the toy.)

Lay the cardboard pattern pieces onto the reverse of the fabric, putting the pieces against a fold where indicated. Make sure that the arrows on the pattern pieces point in the same direction as the arrow marked on the fabric. Hold the pattern down with one hand and draw around the shape of the pattern onto the fabric with the other hand. If two asymmetrical fur pieces are required, for instance two body sides, turn the pattern over to get a mirror image for the second piece, but still making sure that the arrow is pointing in the same direction.

Once all the pattern pieces have been marked out, check to make sure that nothing has been omitted. Carefully cut around the outline using your fabric scissors. Where slits or holes are noted, use the small pointed scissors instead.

When using very long fur fabric, for Santa's beard for instance, snip the back carefully without cutting through the actual pile of the fabric so that the fur maintains its length. Felt, velvet and ordinary fabrics can be marked out and cut double thickness; fur fabric should always be marked and cut using a single thickness only.

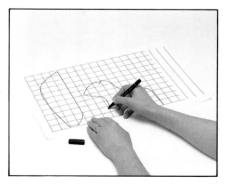

Following the book pattern, draw the full-sized pieces onto the grid.

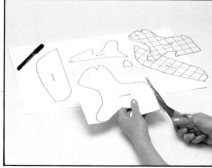

After drawing the pattern onto cardboard, cut out the pieces.

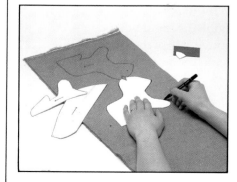

Outline the pattern pieces onto the fabric using a felt-tip pen.

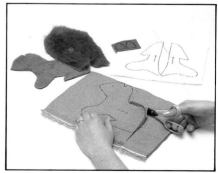

Cut out the material, making sure to use the fabric scissors.

SEWING TECHNIQUES

When sewing a seam, begin by pinning together the two pieces to be joined. Then tack along the seam line, using plain sewing thread and a standard needle. Once the tacking has been completed, take out the pins. Then machine sew along the seam; a 5mm- (^{1}/$_5$in) seam allowance has been allowed for on the pattern. At the start and end of each seam, reverse stitch twice to ensure that the ends will not open.

A running stitch is used for gathering the raw edges of the head at the neck, for gathering lace or ribbon, and for making noses. Using strong thread and a handsewing needle, sew small straight stitches around the edge of the item to be gathered, then pull the thread gently. Fasten off firmly or the gathering will come loose.

The ladder stitch is used for closing the gap after stuffing the toy.

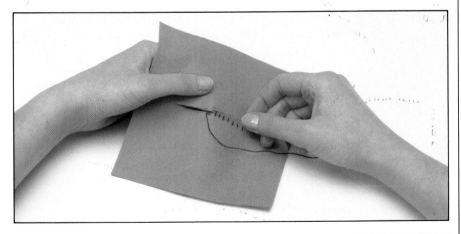

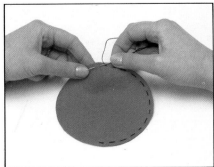

A running stitch is used to gather fabric, lace and ribbon.

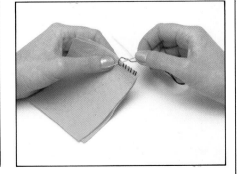

Oversewing can be used to join two fabric pieces together.

A ladder stitch is used for closing gaps after the toy has been stuffed and for attaching heads and limbs. When finished, this stitch should be almost invisible. To close a gap, start sewing at the very end and to one side of the gap. Push the needle through from the underside of the fabric so that the knot is underneath. Bring the needle and thread over the gap and make a stitch about 5mm (^{1}/$_5$in) long on the other side, beginning level with the original stitch and running parallel to the gap. Then take the needle and thread back across the gap and make a stitch on that side. Continue working ladder stitches in this way all the way down the gap, pulling in the raw edges as you go. At the end of the gap, finish off firmly.

To attach the head, begin by holding it firmly onto the body. Then, using strong thread, make a small stitch in the body where the head meets the neck. Next make a small stitch in the head, keeping the entrance hole for the needle level with the exit hole on the body. Continue in this way all around the head and neck, keeping the holes aligned. Sew around the head once or twice and finish off firmly. The same method is used for attaching the arms and legs to the body.

Oversewing is sometimes used to join together the raw edges of two pieces of fabric. Place the two pieces to be joined with the edges level. Starting at one end, push needle and thread through both layers of fabric. Bring the needle through to the other side, then bring the thread over the top of the fabric edges. Insert the needle through the same side of the fabric as the first stitch, about 5mm (^{1}/$_5$in) away, keeping it level with the first hole. Take needle and thread through the other side. Continue making stitches in this way, bringing needle and thread over the fabric edge each time.

TURNING, STUFFING AND FINISHING

When the toy is sewn up completely, it is time to turn it the right way out. First inspect all seams carefully to make sure there are no holes. Start turning with the ends of the legs and arms, pushing the tips in with the fingers and thumbs, and using a blunt instrument to help where necessary. Turn the body through the gap, easing out a bit at a time.

Once the eyes are inserted, you can procede to stuff the animal. Fluff out the filling between the fingers to be sure there are no lumps. Push small amounts of filling into the ends of the legs and arms, working slowly. Stuff the body cavity, making sure the legs are not wobbly where they meet the body. Push a little more filling into that space if necessary. Heads and bodies can be moulded into shape with filling. Only when you are completely satisfied with the shape should the gap be closed. Once the stuffing is completed, brush the seams with care, pulling out any trapped fibres from the stitches.

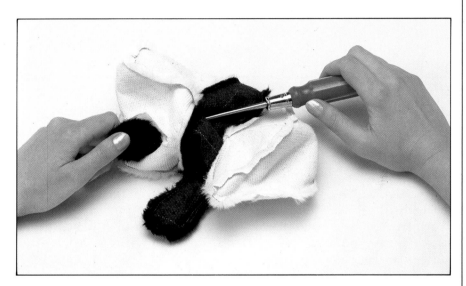

After sewing is completed, start turning the toy at the arms or legs. Use a blunt instrument such as blunt-ended screwdriver to help.

EYES AND NOSES

There are several different types of eyes available. The best are safety eyes which come with metal or plastic washers. Fixed in the correct manner they are impossible to remove. The stalk of the eye should be pushed through the tiniest of holes in the fabric. The washer should be pushed onto the stalk on the reverse of the fabric as far as it will go. If a fabric has a loose weave or knitted backing it will be necessary to reinforce or strengthen the fabric when using safety eyes. Stick small circles of felt to the back of the material over the holes, or sew around the hole to prevent stretching. An embroidered eye is the best type to use if the toy is for a young child. Round felt eyes can also look effective and should be sewn into place with tiny stitches.

Plastic noses can be purchased and fixed into place using the same method as for safety eyes. Black pom poms can also look good, as can balls made from circles of felt gathered with a running stitch. A number of the noses in this book have been embroidered.

FACIAL FEATURES

A calico doll can have the features embroidered before making. The satin stitch used for the embroidery consists of short straight stitches worked so close together that they touch. A simple mouth is formed by a straight stitch or one that is caught in the centre by a small single stitch to form a curve. Fabric paints or permanent marker pens also make excellent features – they are easy to use and are washable. Draw

the front head onto an oversize piece of fabric since it will be easier to handle while working the features and can be cut to the pattern shape later when you are satisfied. It is a good idea to practise on paper or fabric with several faces before marking the position onto the doll with a soft pencil. Felt features are sewn in place after the toy is finished. Small circles for eyes can be cut with a paper or leather punch.

For added expression, a few modelling stitches can be used. You need a long needle and double matching sewing thread. For these, fasten the thread end at the centre back of the head, take the needle through the head to the inner corner of the eye, then take a second stitch very close to the first one beside the eye and back through the head. Pull the thread and see if you like the way the face is dented then fasten the thread.

Fingers and thumbs can also be modelled, see below.

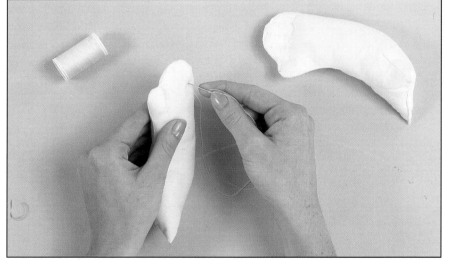

After making the arms, the fingers and thumb can be modelled with stitches. Take the needle and thread vertically through the arm, to make small stab stitches. Pull the thread to mould the fabric and filling.

HAIR STYLES

Yarn, fur fabric and artifical doll's hair have been used in the book. Yarn is washable and can be styled in many ways. Embroidered eyes should tone with the hair colour. Yarn hair must be sewn firmly in place and can also be glued to the head. Fur fabric of a medium-length pile will make excellent hair for a boy or baby doll. The pile should brush towards the face and the fabric is sewn to the head.

Artificial hair is not washable and will shed individual strands, but it is realistic. Do not use on a small child's toy.

SAFETY

Toys made for sale must conform to safety standards and most countries have their own code. However, the doll maker has an equal responsibility for toys made as gifts. For young children the doll should be suitable for the child's age, with all small parts sewn firmly in place. Filling and fabrics where possible should be flame-proof and any paints, pens, crayons or glues that are used must be non-toxic.

Sewing the Nose and Mouth

To begin, insert the needle and the embroidery thread through the toy from the base of the head to a point approximately 7mm (¼in) to the left of the nose tip. Be sure to keep the seam in the centre. Pull the needle and thread all the way through the fabric.

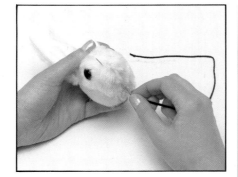

Pull the thread over to the other side of the centre seam. Insert the needle through the fabric so that it exits through the seam line approximately 4mm (⅙in) down from the first stitch.

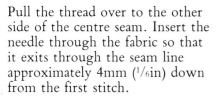

Pull the needle through the fabric and loop the thread through the top straight stitch. Pull it down into a V-shape. Push the needle through the head at a point below the V, still on the seam line. It should reappear to the right of the seam line and down a little.

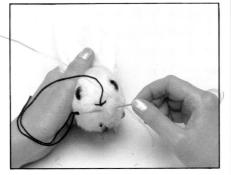

Take the needle back up to the base of the Y. Insert it through the fabric and bring it out of the fabric at a point on the left side.

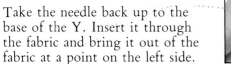

Take the needle back up to the centre again and push it through so that it makes an exit underneath the head. This way the thread can be fastened off without being seen.

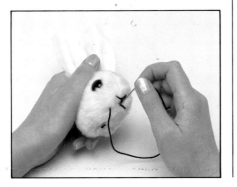

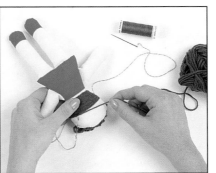

Making Hair Styles

To make fringe for either a boy or girl doll, wind yarn around a piece of card to form loops. Place card to centre front of head and sew each loop to head seam. Remove card and sew across loops to hold them close to front head.

The back hair, for a doll with plaits, can be made by covering the head with a continous length of yarn. Thread two needles and sew end of yarn to head side seam on lower hair line. Take yarn across back head to corresponding point on opposite head seam and sew to the head with the second needle. Continue until whole head is covered.

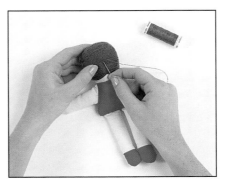

To complete the back hair, with matching thread sew yarn strands to back head along a centre parting.

For front hair of a boy or girl doll, cut strands of yarn of required number and length. Place yarn onto head to cover join of fringe and back hair. Sew each strand to head along a centre parting from front to back of head. Sew each group of strands to front head on seam at lower edge of back hair. Plait hair and tie with ribbon.

A boy doll has back hair made by winding yarn around a larger piece of card. The yarn loops are sewn around back head, the card removed and the loops are flattened and sewn to back head just above hair line to keep them close to head. The gap between back hair and fringe is covered by front hair sewn to head on a centre parting and side seams. Trim yarn to a boy's hair style.

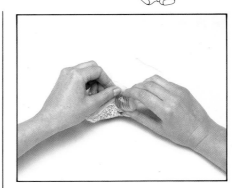

Turn the mouse the right way out. Place a small amount of filling inside, easing it into the nose and one side of the mouse. Push the squeeker into the mouse in a central position. Pack a little more filling around the squeeker so that it is padded on all sides. Neatly ladder stitch the opening.

Position the white felt ears onto the head. Firmly oversew to the body along the straight edge. Stitch the black felt eyes to the head below the ears. Pass the threaded needle through from one eye to the other, gently pulling it until you are completely satisfied with the mouse's expression.

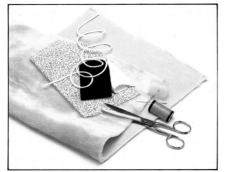

MATERIALS

Small piece of pastel fur fabric
Small scrap of cotton fabric in
   contrasting colour
Small scraps of black and
   white felt
Length of white cord
1 squeeker
Filling

Tack and sew the side body pieces together, leaving the straight edge open. Catch the white cord in the seam, about 15mm (¾in) from the bottom at the position marked on the pattern. Put a knot in the end of the cord to finish off the tail.

With right sides together, tack and sew the cotton base piece to the body, leaving a small gap at the side for turning and filling.

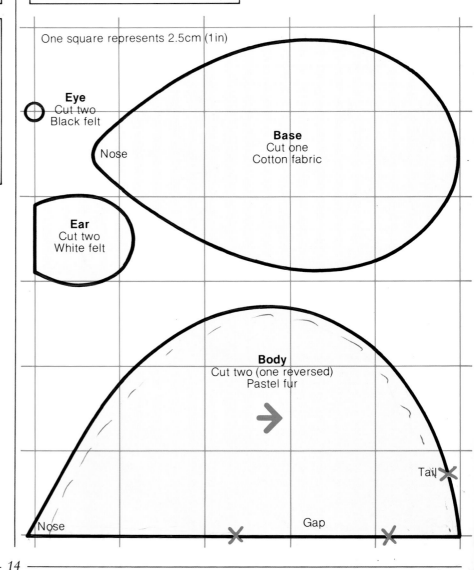

One square represents 2.5cm (1in)

Eye
Cut two
Black felt

Nose

Base
Cut one
Cotton fabric

Ear
Cut two
White felt

Body
Cut two (one reversed)
Pastel fur

Nose

Tail

Gap

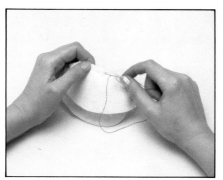

MATERIALS

Small piece of lemon fur fabric
Small piece of white fur fabric
Scrap of black felt
Scrap of orange felt
1 jingle bell about 5cm (2in)
  in diameter
Ribbon
Filling

With right sides together, sew the top of the two side body pieces around the head and back along seam A-B. Then sew the under body to the bottom of the side body, starting at point A, matching point B and then back to point A. Cut a small slit in the tummy where indicated and turn the chick the right way out, carefully poking out the tail.

Fill the chick with stuffing, starting with the head. Place a little filling in the body, spreading it evenly along one side. Push the jingle bell inside the body and continue to add stuffing until the bell is well padded on all sides.

Close the gap with a ladder stitch. Place the wings in position at the neck and oversew along the straight edge to hold them in place. Sew the eye circles in position on the side of the head with a couple of tiny stitches. Place the beak centrally under the eyes and oversew at either side in the corners. Finally, tie a ribbon around the chick's neck, forming a bow.

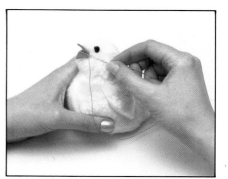

One square represents 2.5cm (1in)

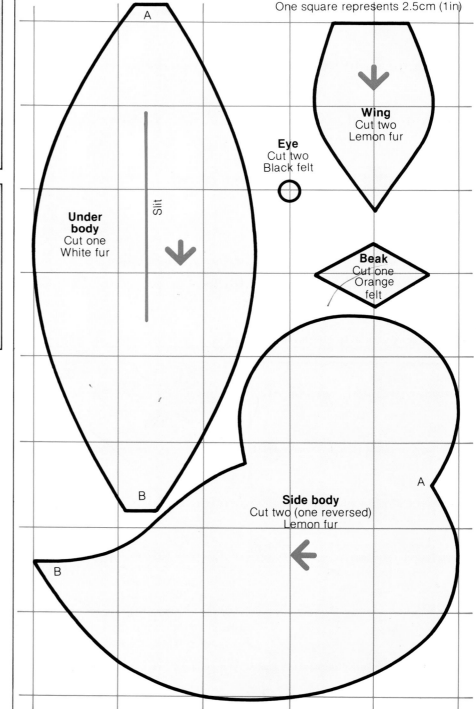

A

Under body
Cut one
White fur

Slit

Wing
Cut two
Lemon fur

Eye
Cut two
Black felt

Beak
Cut one
Orange felt

B

Side body
Cut two (one reversed)
Lemon fur

A

B

With right sides together, tack and sew the top and bottom gusset pieces together between points E and F.

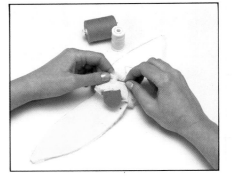

Sew the completed body gusset to the side body, starting at H. Make sure seam E-F on gusset matches that point on body. Finish up at G. Repeat for other side. Tack and sew from J to H. Turn the duck the right way out, pushing out the beak and tail.

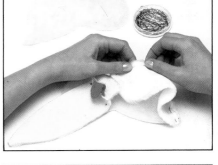

Insert safety eyes through the holes made earlier, securing them on the reverse side with washers. Stuff the toy carefully, starting with the beak and head. When nicely rounded, fill the body in the same way. Ladder stitch the back opening and fasten off firmly.

MATERIALS

20cm (8in) lemon fur fabric
Small piece white fur fabric
1 pair safety eyes with washers
35cm (14in) red and white
   striped jersey fabric
3 white pom poms, about 35mm
   (1 ½in) in width
Filling

With right sides together, sew the linings onto the wing pieces, leaving the straight edge K-L open for turning. Turn the wings the right side out, poking out the tips. Oversew the tops of the wings and ladder stitch to the side of the body at the neck, with the points of the wings facing toward the back.

Cut out all the pieces except for the feet. Pierce the fabric at the eye positions. Then tack and sew each section of orange beak to the top gusset pieces between points A and B. Place the two sections right sides together. Tack and sew from C to A, then around the orange beak to point B, then from points B to D.

Mark out the foot pattern twice onto two layers of orange felt. Stitch carefully around this outline. Trim away the felt close to the stitches. Make a small slit at the base of each foot and place a tiny amount of filling inside. Oversew the slits, then ladder stitch the feet to the body.

Top gusset
Cut one
Lemon fur

F ↑ E

D B A C

D B A C

Eye Eye

Top gusset
Cut one
Lemon fur

E F

Bottom gusset
Cut one
White fur

K L

Wing
Cut four (two reversed)
Lemon fur

For the scarf and hat, cut two rectangles of jersey, one 35cm x 7cm (14in x 3in) for the scarf and the other 15cm x 30cm (6in x 12in) for the hat. Fold both lengthwise, then tack and sew down the long edge. Turn both pieces the right way out. For the scarf, gather the ends of the tube with a running stitch and attach pom poms to each end.

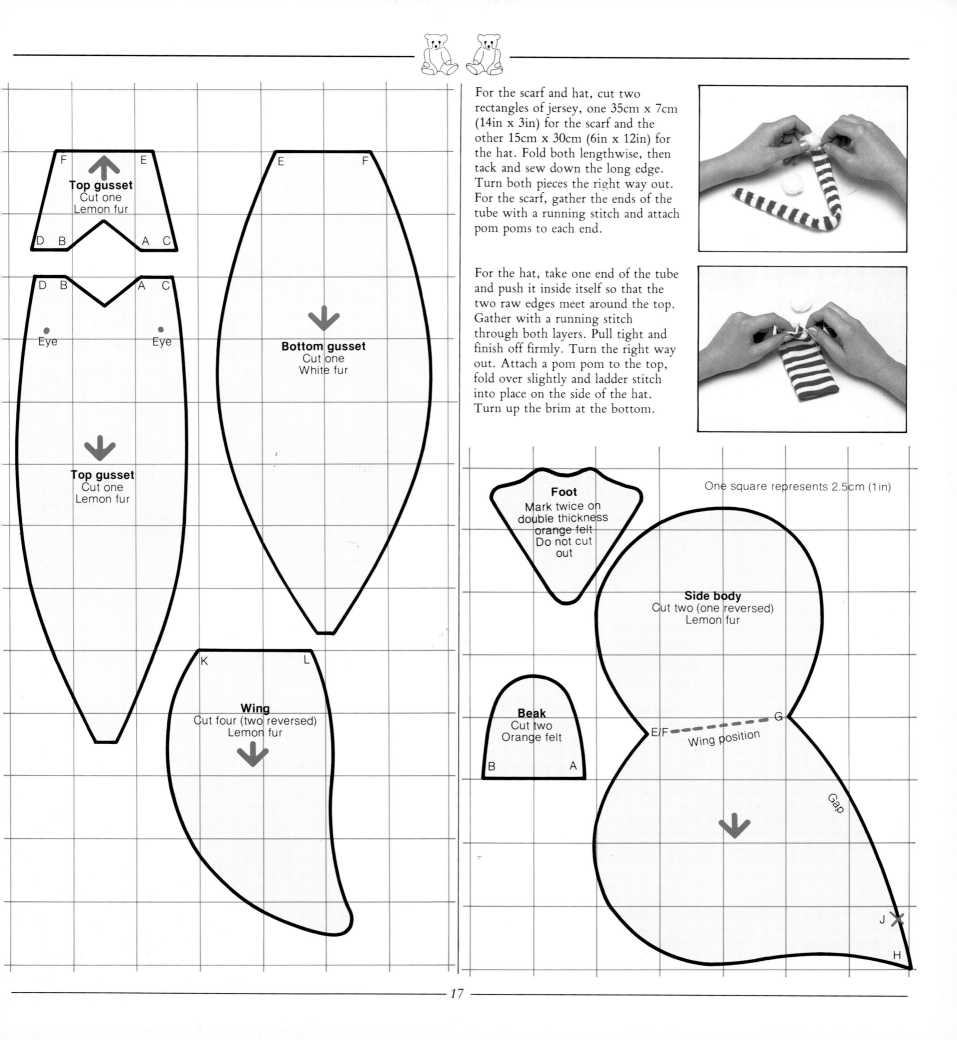

For the hat, take one end of the tube and push it inside itself so that the two raw edges meet around the top. Gather with a running stitch through both layers. Pull tight and finish off firmly. Turn the right way out. Attach a pom pom to the top, fold over slightly and ladder stitch into place on the side of the hat. Turn up the brim at the bottom.

One square represents 2.5cm (1in)

Foot
Mark twice on double thickness orange felt
Do not cut out

Side body
Cut two (one reversed)
Lemon fur

Beak
Cut two
Orange felt

B A

E/F G
Wing position

Gap

J

H

Tack and sew the side head pieces together from C to D, leaving the straight edge open. Push the ear into the head and, with the white ear lining pointing forward towards the nose, ease the raw edge of the ear into the slit. Firmly sew all the layers together. Repeat with the other side.

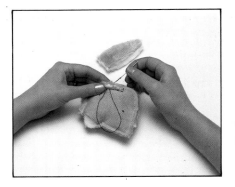

Turn the head, pushing out the nose tip. Push the safety eyes through the holes made earlier and secure with metal washers. Stuff the head, moulding it into a round shape. Pay particular attention to the bunny's cheeks to give the toy a good expression.

Make a running stitch around raw edge of the neck and pull tight. Oversew several times and secure. Using black embroidery thread, stitch the nose referring to the instructions on page 13.

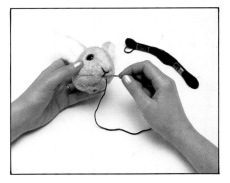

MATERIALS

25cm (10in) gold fur fabric
Small piece of white fur fabric
Scraps of green and orange felt
1 pair 16.5mm brown safety
* eyes with washers*
Filling
Black embroidery thread
14cm x 60cm (5½ in x 24in) strip
* of gingham*
Narrow elastic

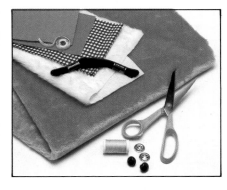

Sew up the darts on either side of the back body. Place the front and back body pieces right sides together. Tack and sew all around, leaving the straight edge open at the top for turning. Turn the body the right way out. Starting with the legs, fill and mould the toy into a semi-sitting position. Sew a running stitch to gather the top raw edge, then finish off securely.

Pierce the fabric carefully at the eye positions and cut along the slit line on head pieces. Tack and sew the gold and white ear pieces together, leaving the straight edges A-B open. Turn the ears, pushing out the points. Oversew edges A-B at the base.

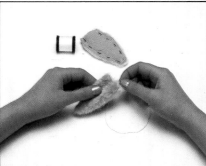

Ladder stitch the head to the body several times. Gather the edge of the round tail piece with a running stitch. Place a small amount of filling in centre, then pull the stitching tight. Finish off tightly, then ladder stitch the tail to the bottom of the bunny's back.

Cut felt for the carrot. Fold the triangular piece lengthwise and sew along the straight edge. Tack and sew the circular piece to the top. Snip a small slit across the top and turn the carrot. Stuff and oversew the slit. Gather the centre of the green leaf and oversew it several times to the top of the carrot. Ladder stitch the carrot to the bunny's arm.

For the skirt, tack and sew the short edges of gingham together. Hem the bottom of the skirt. Turn over the top of the skirt on the wrong side 5mm (¼in) and then 15mm (¾in). Machine sew this casing, leaving a gap of 15mm (¾in) at the back of the skirt. Thread narrow elastic through the gap and adjust to fit the bunny's waist.

One square represents 2.5cm (1in)

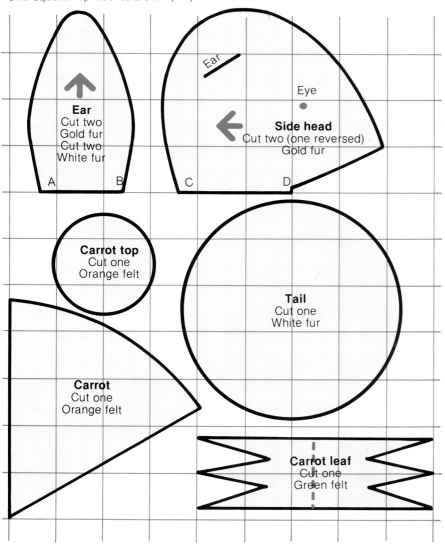

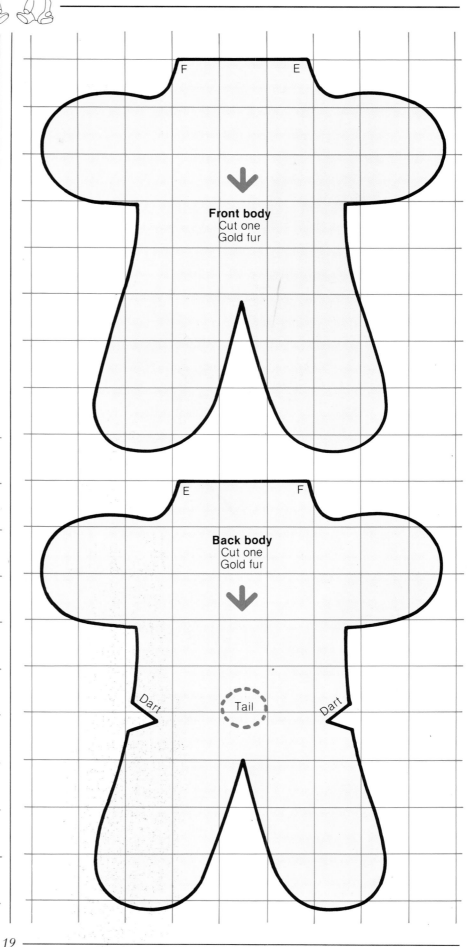

Ear
Cut two
Gold fur
Cut two
White fur

A   B

Ear

Eye

Side head
Cut two (one reversed)
Gold fur

C   D

Carrot top
Cut one
Orange felt

Tail
Cut one
White fur

Carrot
Cut one
Orange felt

Carrot leaf
Cut one
Green felt

F   E

Front body
Cut one
Gold fur

E   F

Back body
Cut one
Gold fur

Dart

Tail

Dart

With right sides together, join the two side body pieces by sewing seam C-D, making sure that you match point B, from the nose to the tip of the tail.

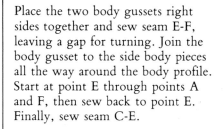

Place the two body gussets right sides together and sew seam E-F, leaving a gap for turning. Join the body gusset to the side body pieces all the way around the body profile. Start at point E through points A and F, then sew back to point E. Finally, sew seam C-E.

Pierce tiny holes for the eyes at the positions indicated. Starting at the tail tip, turn the squirrel the right way out using a long, blunt tool. Be careful to ease out the ends of the legs. Insert the safety eyes in the holes made earlier and secure on the reverse of the head with the washers.

Fill the squirrel with stuffing, placing a small amount in the tail to reach only part of the way up. Add more at the tail base and at the rear of the body. Fill the head, ensuring that the neck is firm. Then fill the legs, using only a small amount of stuffing, making sure they are not too firm.

MATERIALS

Red/brown fur fabric
Red/brown long fur fabric for tail
Small piece of white fur fabric
Scrap of brown felt for ears
1 pair 13.5mm brown safety eyes with metal washers
Black embroidery thread
Filling

On both the side body pieces, sew up the head dart. Then sew up the dart on the tail. Join the tail to the side body pieces by sewing seam A-B on both sides.

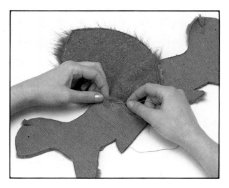

Finally, stuff the shoulders and tummy of the squirrel, shaping them gently. When satisfied with the general shape of the squirrel, close the gap underneath the body using a ladder stitch.

Cut the ears out of the brown felt. Fold one ear piece in half and oversew it at the base to the side of the head. Make sure that the ear stands upright. Repeat for other ear.

With black embroidery thread, stitch a small nose on the squirrel, referring to the instructions on page 13. If desired, the head can be tilted back and held in place with a few small stitches to give a different expression.

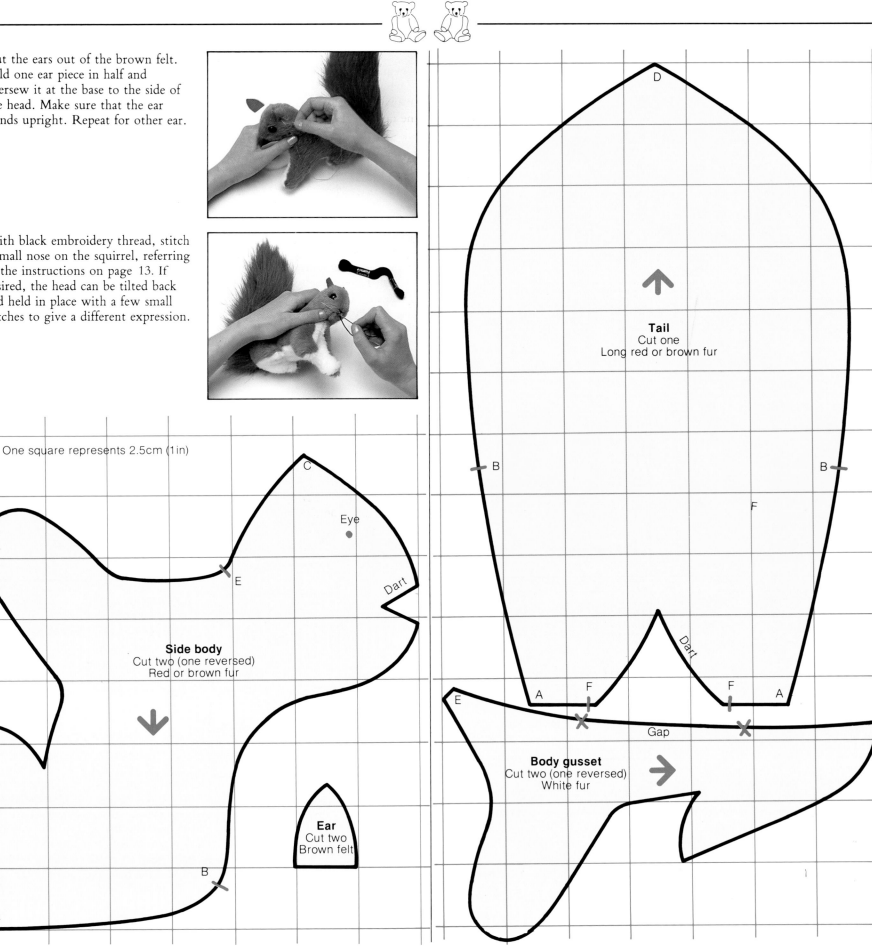

One square represents 2.5cm (1in)

Tail
Cut one
Long red or brown fur

Side body
Cut two (one reversed)
Red or brown fur

Eye

Dart

Ear
Cut two
Brown felt

Dart

Gap

Body gusset
Cut two (one reversed)
White fur

Join the two underbody pieces together by sewing seam A-B, leaving a gap where indicated for turning and filling.

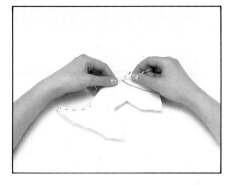

Fold the tail in half lengthwise and sew along the long edge. Insert a piece of elastic slightly longer than the tail through the tube. Oversew at the end, holding the elastic in position. Pull the elastic a little to make the tail curl, and sew into place. Cut off the excess elastic.

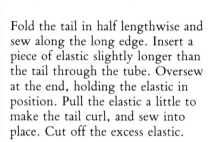

MATERIALS

20cm (8in) pink fur fabric
Scraps of pink felt
1 pair 13.5mm safety eyes with
_   metal washers_
Pink embroidery thread
Narrow elastic
Filling

On both of the side body pieces, close the darts at the rear. Join the two halves together along seam L-B, catching in the tail at the same time at the rear. Join the underbody to the side body on both sides, starting with seam A-C. Then sew seam D-E, and finally seam F-B.

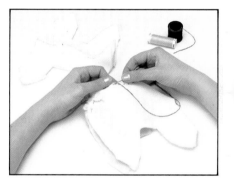

Pierce tiny holes for the eyes and slits for the ears on each side head piece. Close the darts. Sew the ear linings to the ear pieces, leaving the straight edges open. Then turn the ears and fold lengthwise, with felt innermost. With the lining facing forward, push the ears into the slits and sew them in place through all the layers of fabric.

To form the trotters, close up the end of each leg so that the two side seams meet in the middle. Then sew around the V-shaped raw edges.

Join the head gusset to the side head, sewing seam G-H. Repeat on the other side. Sew seam J-K under the chin. Open out the nose and, stretching the raw edges to fit, sew in the pink felt circle. Turn the head the right way out.

Push the head inside the body so that the right sides are together and the raw edges meet at the neck. Turn the head slightly to one side so that the seam at K is tilted to meet the point marked on the pattern. Sew around the raw edge, joining the head to the body.

Turn the pig the right way out, carefully picking out the points on the trotters. Insert safety eyes in the holes made earlier and secure with metal washers. Stuff the pig, starting at the nose. When the head is completed, start on the feet, adding a little filling at a time.

When satisfied with the general shape of the body, close the gap using a ladder stitch. To finish, embroider two pink dots on the end of the snout.

One square represents 2.5cm (1in)

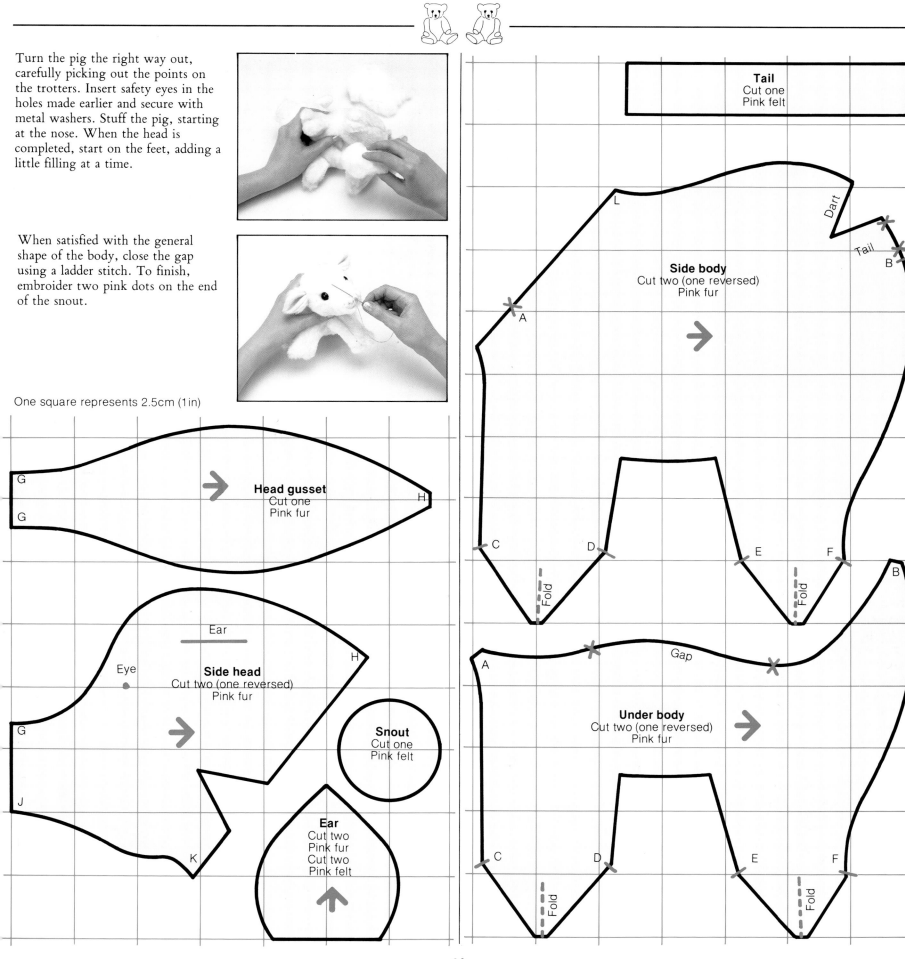

Tail
Cut one
Pink felt

Side body
Cut two (one reversed)
Pink fur

Dart

Tail

L

A

B

C

D

E

F

B

Head gusset
Cut one
Pink fur

G
G
H

Fold

Gap

Fold

A

Under body
Cut two (one reversed)
Pink fur

Ear

Side head
Cut two (one reversed)
Pink fur

Eye

H

G

J

K

Snout
Cut one
Pink felt

Ear
Cut two
Pink fur
Cut two
Pink felt

C

D

E

F

Fold

Fold

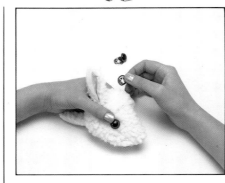

Pierce tiny holes at the eye positions and turn the head the right way out. Insert the safety eyes, securing on the reverse of the fabric with metal washers. Stuff the head firmly and close the gap with a running stitch.

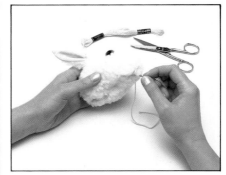

Using pink embroidery thread, embroider a nose and mouth on the lamb, referring to the instructions on page 13.

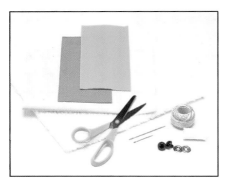

MATERIALS

25cm (10in) fleecy white fur fabric
Scraps of velvet or felt for ear lining
Scraps of green and yellow felt
1 pair 16.5mm brown safety eyes with metal washers
Pink embroidery thread
Filling

Fold the green felt grass in half one way and then the other. Sew the folded pieces of grass to the side of the head at the position of the mouth, pulling them tightly into place. Sew the yellow flower to the end of one of the blades of grass. Place the head to one side.

Sew the ears to the ear linings, leaving the straight edge open. Turn ears the right way out; fold in half lengthwise and oversew the raw edge. Insert an ear into the slit on the side of the head, with the lining facing toward nose. Sew into position, through all layers of fabric. Repeat on the other side head piece.

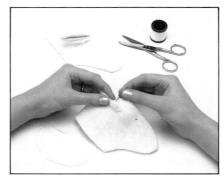

Fold the tail in half lengthwise, right sides together, and sew, leaving the straight edge open. Turn the right way out. On each side body, sew up the dart at the rear. Sew the sides together between E and F. Sew the back seam G-H, inserting the tail at the same time in a downward position at the point marked on the pattern.

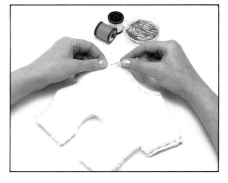

Sew up the dart on each side head piece. Take the head gusset and sew to the left hand side of the head, between A and B. Repeat on the other side, sewing from B to A, then continuing to sew the side heads together from A down to the base of the neck. Sew the seam under the chin to the base of the neck.

With right sides together, join the two inside body pieces by sewing between points C and D.

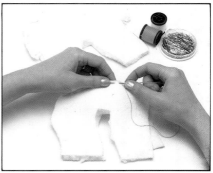

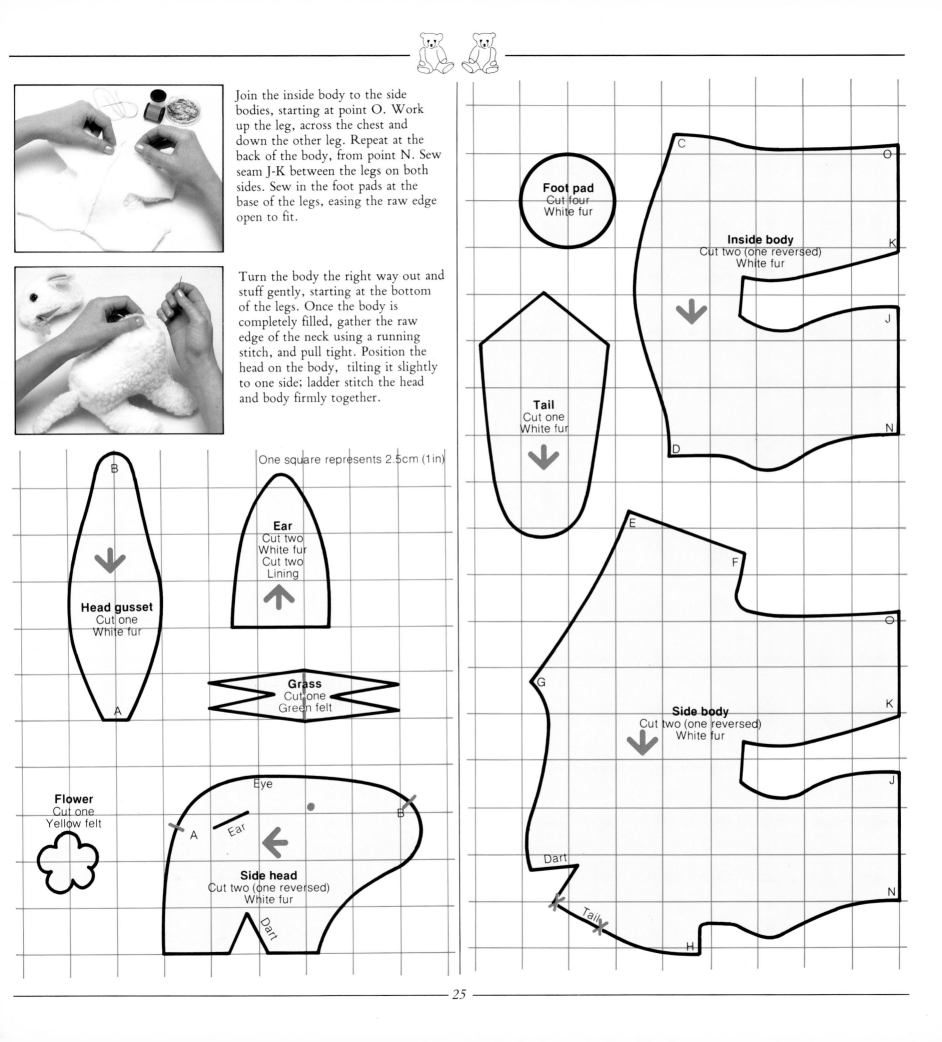

Join the inside body to the side bodies, starting at point O. Work up the leg, across the chest and down the other leg. Repeat at the back of the body, from point N. Sew seam J-K between the legs on both sides. Sew in the foot pads at the base of the legs, easing the raw edge open to fit.

Turn the body the right way out and stuff gently, starting at the bottom of the legs. Once the body is completely filled, gather the raw edge of the neck using a running stitch, and pull tight. Position the head on the body, tilting it slightly to one side; ladder stitch the head and body firmly together.

One square represents 2.5cm (1in)

Foot pad
Cut four
White fur

Inside body
Cut two (one reversed)
White fur

Tail
Cut one
White fur

Side body
Cut two (one reversed)
White fur

Head gusset
Cut one
White fur

Ear
Cut two
White fur
Cut two
Lining

Grass
Cut one
Green felt

Flower
Cut one
Yellow felt

Side head
Cut two (one reversed)
White fur

Eye

Ear

Dart

Tail

With right sides together, sew seam A-B, joining the front to the side head pieces. Repeat with the other side. Place the two halves of the front head together and sew seam C-D. Place the head on the front body and sew seam E-D-E, matching the centre seam of the head with point D.

Referring to the positions indicated on the pattern, tack the feet and wings into position on the front body.

Sew seam F-G on the back body pieces, leaving a small gap in the centre for turning. Open out the back body and sew to the back head between H, F and H.

MATERIALS

Black fur fabric
White fur fabric
Small scraps of orange felt
Small scrap of white cotton
    fabric
Small piece of fabric for tie
1 pair of 13.5mm black
    safety eyes with washers
15cm (6in) length of elastic
Filling

Place the back and front body right sides together. Sew all around, leaving the base open, and enclosing the wings in the seam at the positions indicated on the pattern. Sew the base to the body, matching point G at the tail and the centre front position. The feet should be enclosed in this seam.

Sew the wings to the linings, leaving the straight edges open. Turn wings the right way out, fold lengthwise (white inward) and oversew the top raw edge. Mark out the foot pattern twice onto a double layer of orange felt. Sew around these lines, leaving the straight edges open. Trim close to the stitches. Fill the feet with a small amount of stuffing.

Pierce tiny holes at the eye positions on the head. Turn the penguin the right side out, poking out the tail. Insert the safety eyes through the holes and secure with metal washers. Stuff the penguin, starting with the head. Ensure the base is flat to allow the toy to stand upright and, when stuffed evenly, close the gap on the back body with a ladder stitch.

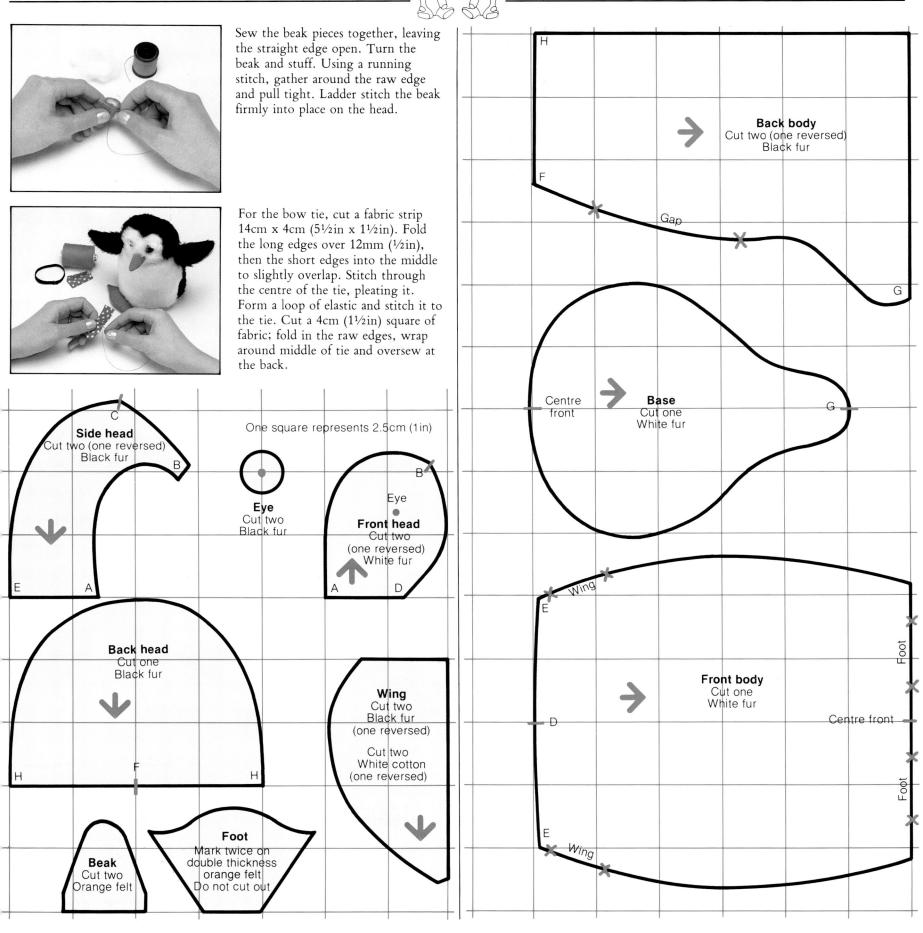

Sew the beak pieces together, leaving the straight edge open. Turn the beak and stuff. Using a running stitch, gather around the raw edge and pull tight. Ladder stitch the beak firmly into place on the head.

For the bow tie, cut a fabric strip 14cm x 4cm (5½in x 1½in). Fold the long edges over 12mm (½in), then the short edges into the middle to slightly overlap. Stitch through the centre of the tie, pleating it. Form a loop of elastic and stitch it to the tie. Cut a 4cm (1½in) square of fabric; fold in the raw edges, wrap around middle of tie and oversew at the back.

Back body
Cut two (one reversed)
Black fur

Gap

Base
Cut one
White fur

Centre front

G

H

F

Side head
Cut two (one reversed)
Black fur

C

B

E

A

One square represents 2.5cm (1in)

Eye
Cut two
Black fur

Front head
Cut two
(one reversed)
White fur

Eye

A

D

B

Back head
Cut one
Black fur

H

F

H

Wing
Cut two
Black fur
(one reversed)

Cut two
White cotton
(one reversed)

Beak
Cut two
Orange felt

Foot
Mark twice on
double thickness
orange felt
Do not cut out

Front body
Cut one
White fur

Wing

E

Foot

Foot

Centre front

D

E

Wing

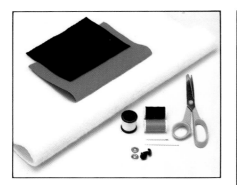

MATERIALS

*Medium length glossy white fur
    fabric
Small piece of black felt
1 large square of white felt
Small piece of orange felt
1 pair 13.5mm black safety
    eyes with metal washers
Filling*

Make the wings for the adult swans by sewing the linings to the fur fabric pieces all around, leaving a small gap for turning. Turn the wings, pushing out the curves, and close the gap using a ladder stitch. Top stitch lines across the wings according to the pattern, to give the effect of feathers.

Attach the beak to either side of the body by sewing seam A-D. Place the two side body pieces right sides together and sew seam A-B, leaving a small gap at the rear of the neck for stuffing. Then sew seam D-C at the front of the neck.

Open out the top body and sew to the base, matching points C and B. Leave a gap as shown on one side of the body only. Using orange thread, sew around the beak from the top to the bottom.

Pierce tiny holes for the eyes at the position indicated, then turn the swan the right way out through the gap at the base. Insert the safety eyes through the holes and secure on the reverse side of the head with the metal washers.

Start to fill the swan at the beak tip, using the gap at the rear of the neck for access. Once the head and neck are filled, close the neck gap. Continue to fill the body cavity and then close the gap at the base. Oversew each wing to the body sides of the adult swans in a small triangle around the wing base.

Oversew the black felt 'knob' pieces together around the curved end. Turn the right way out and fill the rounded part with a tiny amount of stuffing. Wrap the knob around the base of the adult swan's beak and oversew the ends together under the beak. Secure the knob around the head with a few small stitches.

Using black thread, sew a straight line along the swan's beak on either side. Alternatively, use a waterproof, non-toxic felt tip pen to draw the line. Embroider or draw nostrils on each side of the beak.

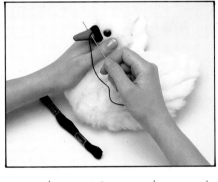

One square represents 2.5cm (1in)

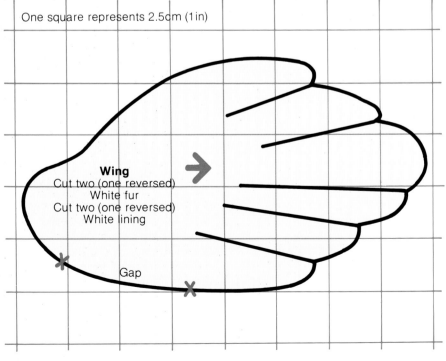

Wing
Cut two (one reversed)
White fur
Cut two (one reversed)
White lining

Gap

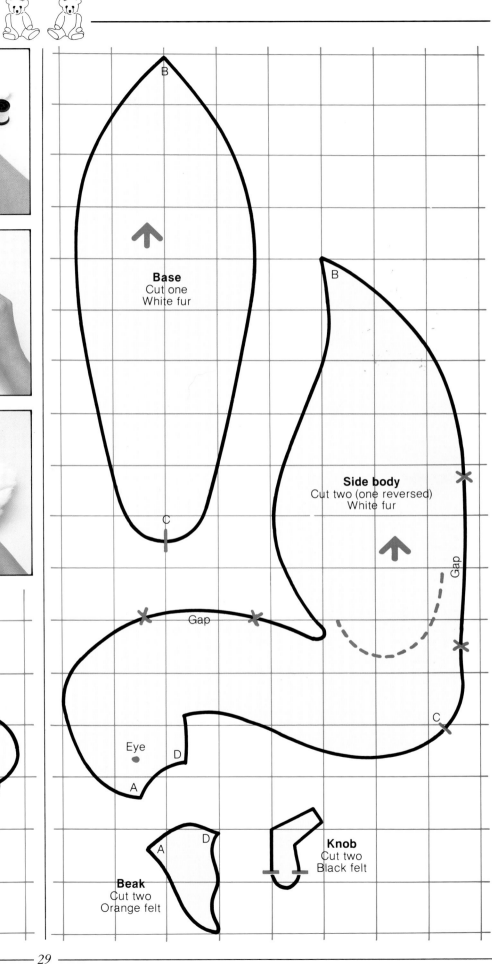

B

Base
Cut one
White fur

C

B

Side body
Cut two (one reversed)
White fur

Gap

Gap

C

Eye

D

A

D

A

Beak
Cut two
Orange felt

Knob
Cut two
Black felt

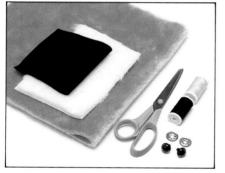

MATERIALS

Small scrap of honey-coloured fur
Small scrap of long-haired white fur
Scrap of black felt
1 pair 13.5mm brown safety eyes with washers
Filling

Place the side head pieces right sides together and sew seam A-B. Open out the head and sew the gusset to the head, starting at point A, matching points C and around to D. Repeat on the other side.

Pierce tiny holes for the eyes in the head, then turn the head the right way out. Put in the safety eyes, securing on the reverse side with metal washers. Stuff the head then, using a running stitch, gather the raw edge together tightly and finish off.

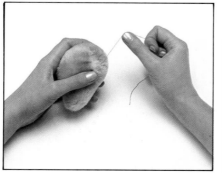

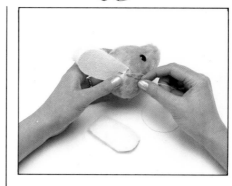

Using the white fur, carefully cut the two ears and position as shown, just beneath the gusset seam. Oversew the ears to the top of the head. Sew a couple of stitches to hold the ears in position.

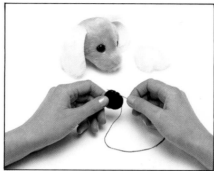

Using a running stitch, gather the raw edge of the nose. Place a little stuffing in the centre of the nose and pull the thread tight. Oversew a few times, then ladder stitch the nose into position on the puppy's head.

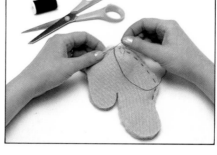

Sew the darts together on both side body pieces. Place the two body pieces right sides together and sew seam E-F.

Open out the body and place against the underbody with the right sides together. Sew the body to the underbody, matching points E and F. Cut a slit along the centre of the base.

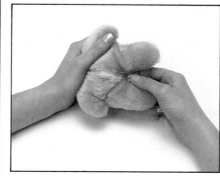

Turn and stuff the body. Close the gap with a ladder stitch. Fold the tail lengthwise and sew, leaving the straight edge open. Turn and fold the raw edges in at the end. Ladder stitch to the rear of the puppy at right angles to the back seam. Place the head on the body in a slightly tilted position and ladder stitch into position several times around.

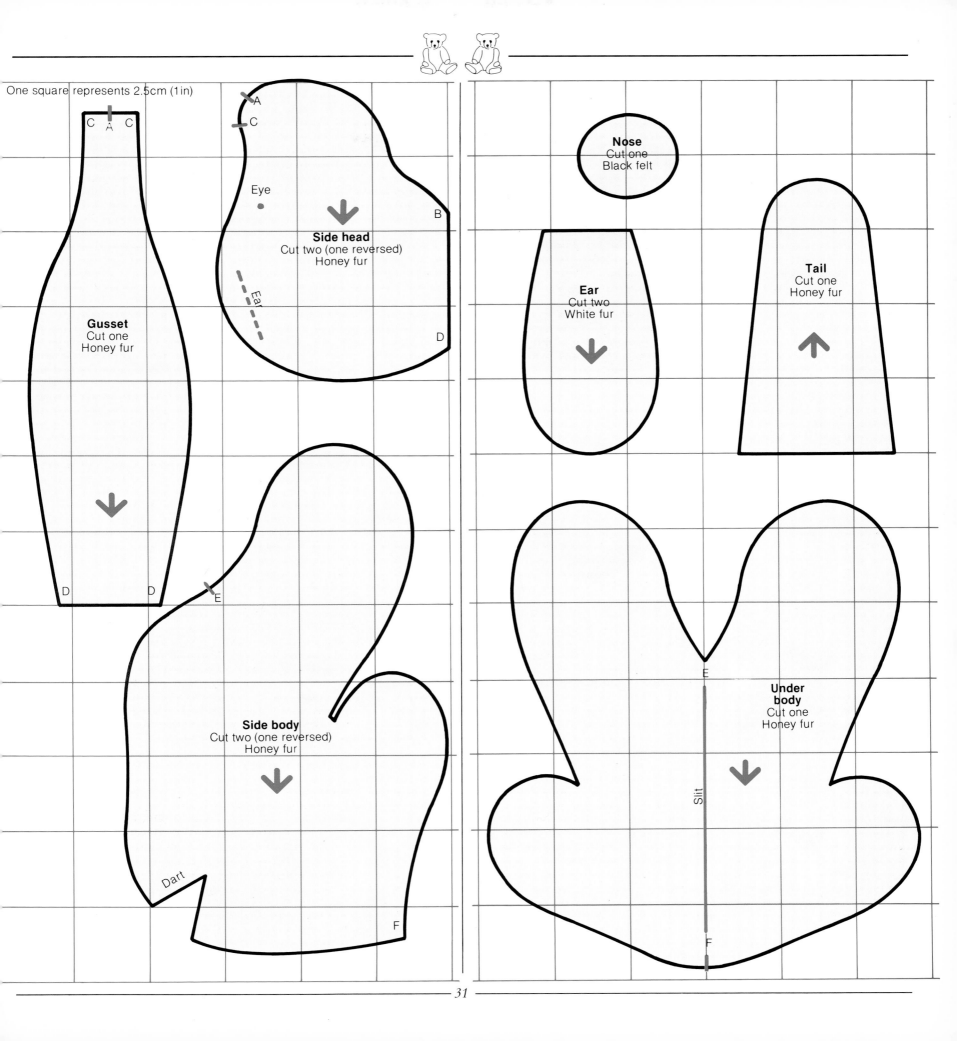

One square represents 2.5cm (1in)

Gusset
Cut one
Honey fur

C A C

D D

A
C

Eye

Side head
Cut two (one reversed)
Honey fur

B

D

Ear

E

Side body
Cut two (one reversed)
Honey fur

Dart

F

Nose
Cut one
Black felt

Ear
Cut two
White fur

Tail
Cut one
Honey fur

E

Under body
Cut one
Honey fur

Slit

F

MATERIALS

Small piece of black or white fur fabric
Scrap of pink or white felt
1 pair 13.5mm green safety eyes with washers
Filling
Pink embroidery thread

Turn the head the right way out, carefully easing out the tips of the ears. Flatten the ears and sew across the seam through all thicknesses of fabric. Insert the safety eyes, securing them with the metal washers.

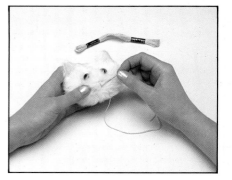

Fill the head with stuffing, easing it into a round shape. Sew a running stitch around the raw edges of the head. Pull it tight and finish off at the base. Embroider a small pink nose, referring to the instructions on page 13.

Place the two side head pieces right sides together and sew between points C and D. Then sew the two back head pieces together along seam A-B.

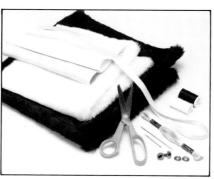

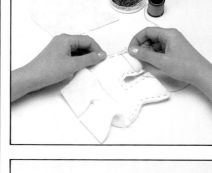

With right sides together, join the body gussets together between G and H, leaving a gap for turning. Join the gusset to the side body along seams G-K, H-J, and L-M. Repeat on the other side.

Pierce tiny holes in the fabric at the eye positions. Sew the ear lining to the side of the head on both sides between E and F. Place the back and front head pieces together and sew all around the head, leaving a small gap at the base for turning and filling.

Fold the tail in half lengthwise, wrong sides together, and sew along the edge. Trim close to the seam and turn the right way out. Give the tail a gentle pull to improve the shape. Sew the back of the body between G and H, inserting the tail into position at the same time.

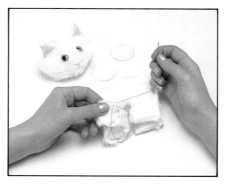

Sew the pads into the base of the feet. Turn the body the right way out and stuff gently. Close the gap with a ladder stitch. Join the head to the body firmly with a ladder stitch, working around the head twice.

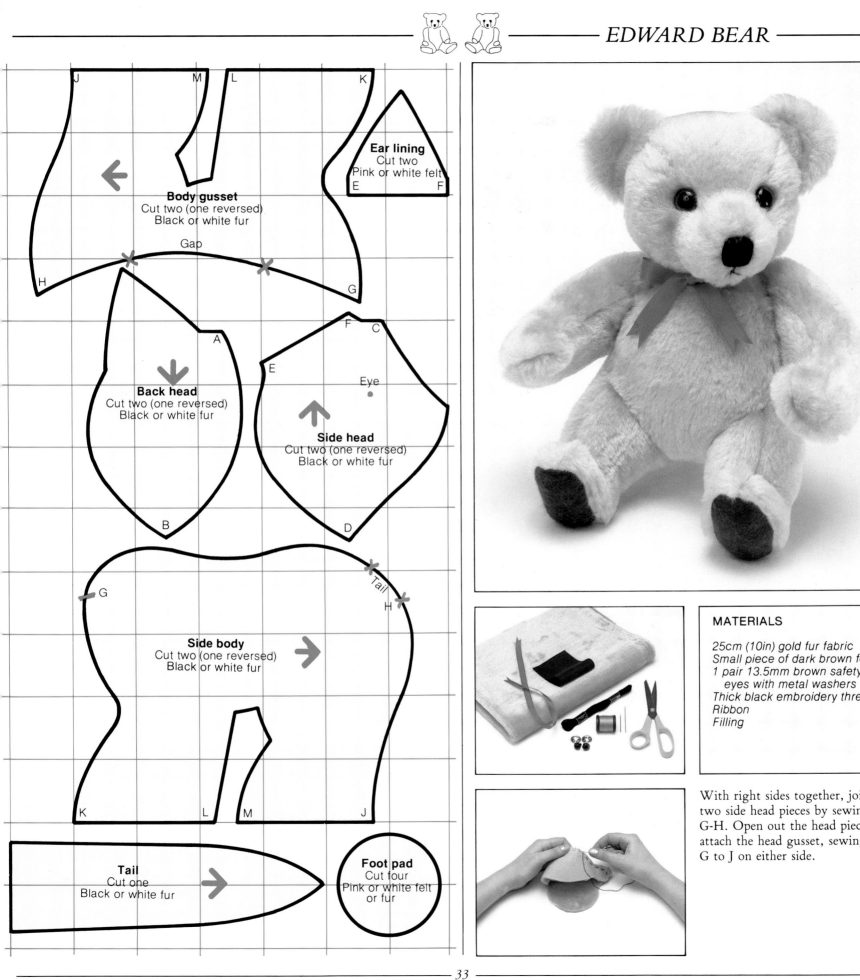

J **M** **L** **K**

Body gusset
Cut two (one reversed)
Black or white fur

Gap

H **G**

A

Back head
Cut two (one reversed)
Black or white fur

B

Ear lining
Cut two
Pink or white felt

E **F**

F **C**

E

Eye

Side head
Cut two (one reversed)
Black or white fur

D

G

Tail

H

Side body
Cut two (one reversed)
Black or white fur

K **L** **M** **J**

Tail
Cut one
Black or white fur

Foot pad
Cut four
Pink or white felt
or fur

MATERIALS

25cm (10in) gold fur fabric
Small piece of dark brown felt
1 pair 13.5mm brown safety
* eyes with metal washers*
Thick black embroidery thread
Ribbon
Filling

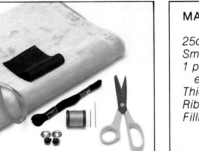

With right sides together, join the
two side head pieces by sewing seam
G-H. Open out the head pieces and
attach the head gusset, sewing from
G to J on either side.

Pierce tiny holes for the eyes at the positions indicated and turn the head the right way out. Insert the eyes through the holes and secure on the reverse with washers. Stuff the head, starting with the nose. When the head is rounded, gather the raw edge of the neck using a running stitch and fasten off securely.

Sew the ear pieces together in pairs, leaving the bottom edge open. Turn the ears the right way out. Using strong thread, oversew the ears flat onto the head and then ladder stitch them along one side of the base so that they stand in an upright position.

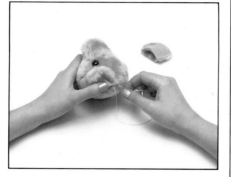

Using thick black embroidery thread, embroider the nose on the bear using long straight stitches. Embroider the mouth with the same thread, then place the head to one side.

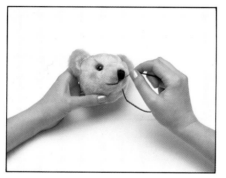

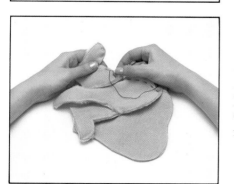

For the body, join the leg pieces to the body gusset by placing them with the right sides together and sewing from A to B on either side.

Keeping the right sides together, sew the gusset (with the attached legs) to the side piece from C to D, matching point A. Repeat for the other side. Then sew the base seams E-F, and finally sew the back seam C-F, leaving a gap for turning and filling.

Open out the raw edges of the feet. With the right sides together, place the foot pads against the raw edges of the feet and sew the pads into position. Make sure the narrow end is at the heel.

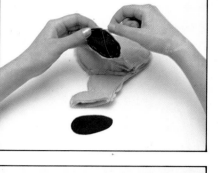

Turn the body the right way out and stuff gently, beginning with the toes. When the body is nicely rounded, close the gap with a ladder stitch. Then ladder stitch the head to the body, working around the head more than once. Finish off securely.

To make the arms, sew all the way around each pair. Cut a small slit at the inside top of each arm and turn the right way out through this slit. Stuff the arms gently, then oversew the slits. Ladder stitch the arms to the sides of the body, making sure they are attached securely. Tie a ribbon around the bear's neck, forming it into a bow.

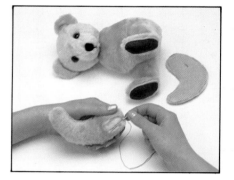

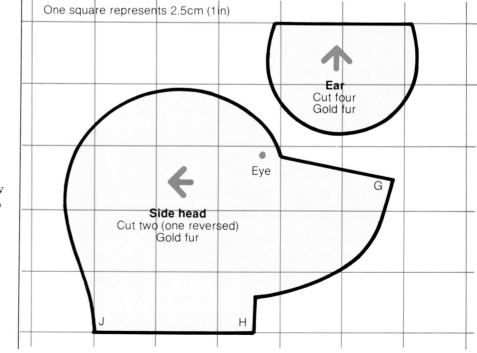

One square represents 2.5cm (1in)

Ear
Cut four
Gold fur

Eye

G

Side head
Cut two (one reversed)
Gold fur

J   H

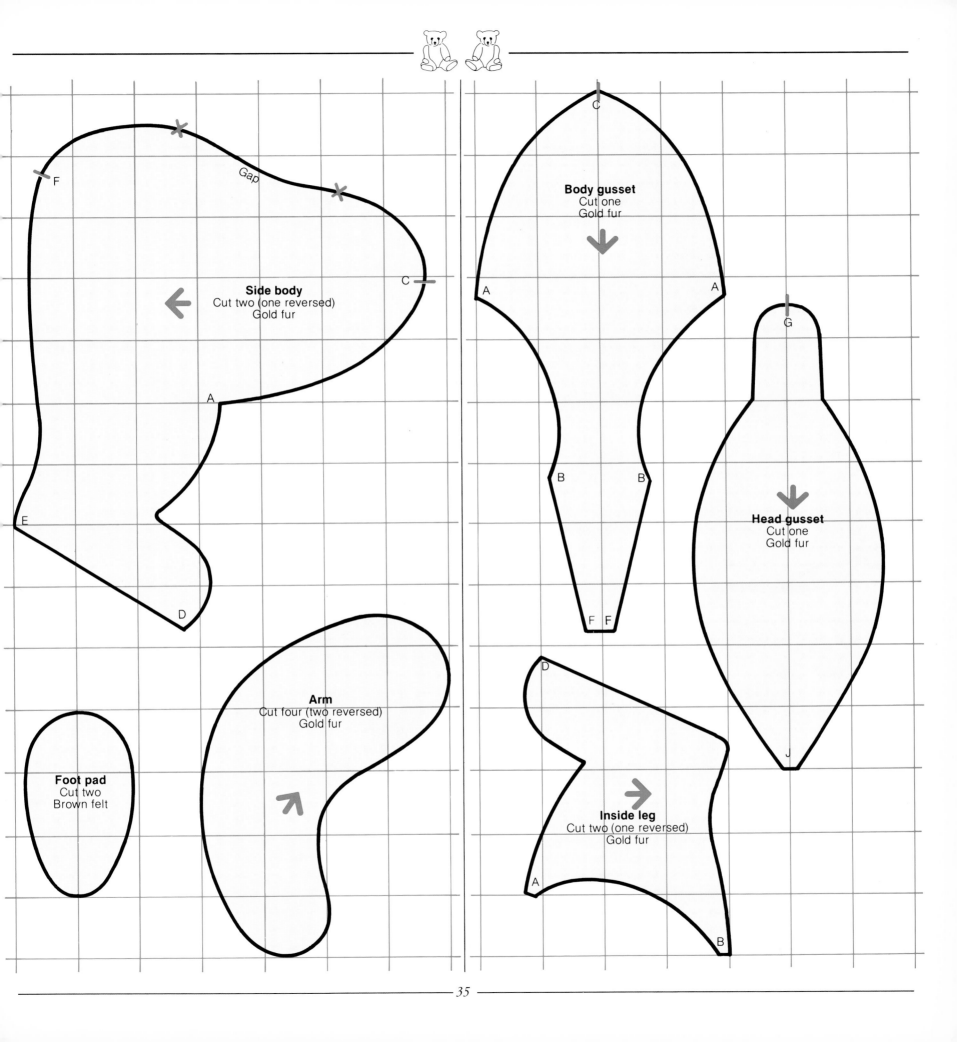

Side body
Cut two (one reversed)
Gold fur

Gap

F

C

A

E

D

Body gusset
Cut one
Gold fur

C

A

A

B

B

F F

Head gusset
Cut one
Gold fur

G

J

Foot pad
Cut two
Brown felt

Arm
Cut four (two reversed)
Gold fur

Inside leg
Cut two (one reversed)
Gold fur

D

A

B

Join the head gusset piece to the side of the head on the side body piece by sewing seam J-K. Repeat on other side. Then sew up seam J-D at the front of the head.

Sew the inside body to the side body, starting at seam D-E. Then sew seam F-G and finally seam H-B. Repeat on other side.

MATERIALS

30cm (12in) white fur fabric
1 pair 13.5mm black safety
    eyes with metal washers
1 small plastic nose
Black embroidery thread
Filling

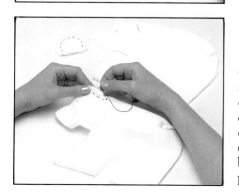

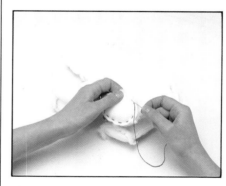

Fold the tail in half lengthwise. Sew along the curved edge, leaving the top open. Turn the tail, poking out the tip carefully. Sew seam K-B on the back of the bear, sewing in the tail at the same time where the two darts meet. Open out and stretch the bottoms of the feet and sew in the foot pads.

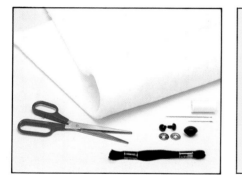

Pierce a tiny hole at the eye position and cut a slit for the ears on each side body piece, then place to one side. Join both pieces of the inside body by sewing seam A-B, leaving a gap for turning and filling. Open out the inside body. Sew the under chin piece to the inside body along seam C-A-C.

Turn the bear the right way out. Insert the safety eyes through the holes made earlier and secure on the reverse with metal washers. Poke a tiny hole at the very end of the snout and secure the plastic nose in the same way.

Sew up the darts at the rear of the side body pieces. Sew both halves of ears together, leaving the straight edge open. Turn the right way out and make a small tuck at the raw edge of the ear on both sides to curve the ear slightly inwards and oversew into place. Push the straight edge through the slit in the side body and sew the ears into position through all layers of fabric.

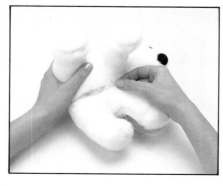

Fill the bear with stuffing, starting at the feet. Flatten the feet slightly as the filling is added. Mould the head shape by pushing more filling into the cheeks. When satisfied with the general shape of the bear, close the gap in the tummy using a ladder stitch.

With black embroidery thread, stitch through the feet four times on each paw to form claws. Using the same thread, embroider a smile on the bear's face, referring to the relevant part of the instructions on page 13. Finish off the mouth on either side with a small stitch at right angles to the main stitch.

Finally, taking a long needle and white thread, pull the eyes slightly together by passing the threaded needle from corner to corner of the opposite eyes, through the head. Fasten off securely.

One square represents 2.5cm (1in)

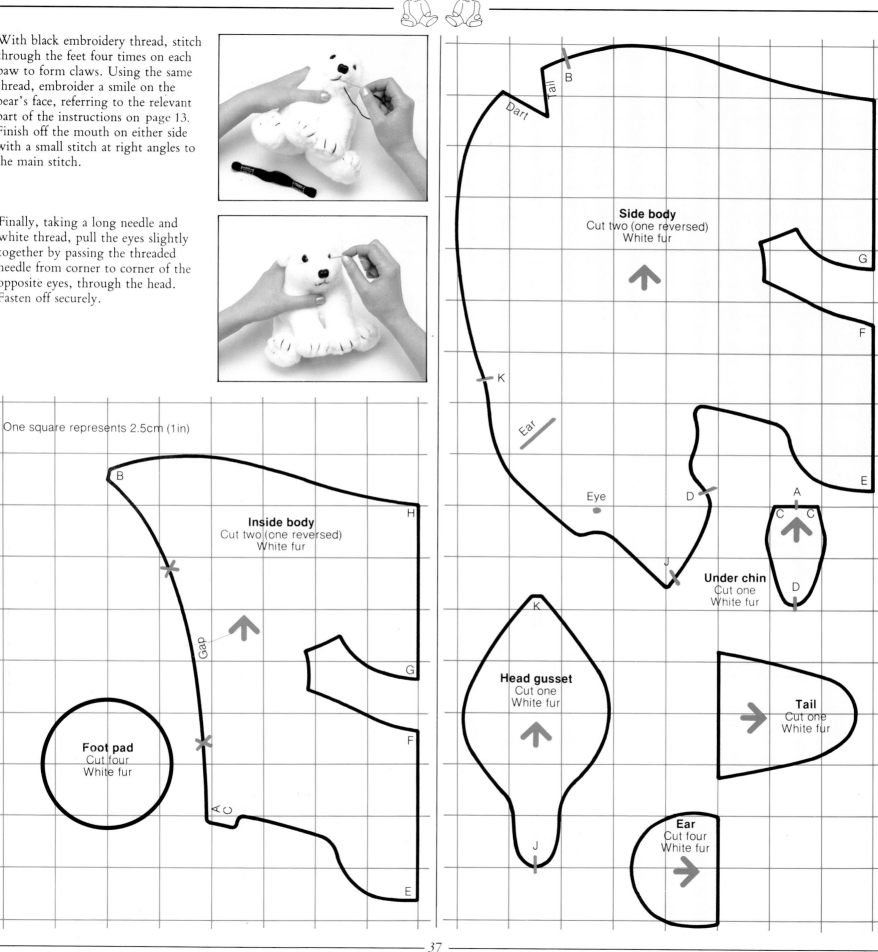

Side body
Cut two (one reversed)
White fur

Inside body
Cut two (one reversed)
White fur

Foot pad
Cut four
White fur

Under chin
Cut one
White fur

Head gusset
Cut one
White fur

Tail
Cut one
White fur

Ear
Cut four
White fur

Dart

Tail

Ear

Eye

Gap

Sew the gussets to the side body between points E and G, ensuring that points F, A/B and the notches match. Then sew seam H-J and K-L. Repeat on other side.

Open out the raw edges of the feet and stretch them gently. With right sides together, place the foot pads around the raw edges of the feet and sew them into place.

MATERIALS

30cm (12in) gold fur fabric
Scrap of long gold fur fabric
1 pair 15mm brown safety
    eyes with metal washers
Thick black embroidery thread
Filling

Take the tail tuft pieces and, with right sides together, sew along the curved edges. Trim close to the edge and turn. Fold the tail piece lengthwise and sew along the long edge. Poke the tuft into the tail and, with the raw edges level, sew across the top. Turn the tail the right way out. Sew seam E-L along the lion's back, sewing the tail into place at the same time.

On both side body pieces, close the darts at the rear and the neck. Pierce tiny holes at the eye position and cut slits for ears. Sew around each pair of ears, leaving the straight edge open. Turn the ears and make a small tuck at the base. Oversew into place. Push the raw edges into the slits made earlier and sew into position through all layers of fur.

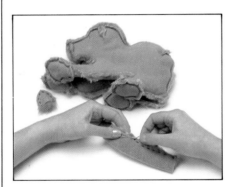

Turn the lion the right way out. Insert the eyes through the holes made earlier and secure on the reverse with metal washers. Fill the lion with stuffing, pushing it gently into the cheeks to give them a rounded shape. Close the slit on the inside body using a ladder stitch.

To join the chin piece to the head gusset, place them right sides together and sew along seam A-B. Then, also with right sides together, sew the chin piece to the under body along seam C-D.

Using a thick black thread, embroider a nose on the lion with several straight sititches, then add a mouth, referring to the instructions on page 13. Using the same thread double thickness, stitch through the feet four times on each paw to form claws.

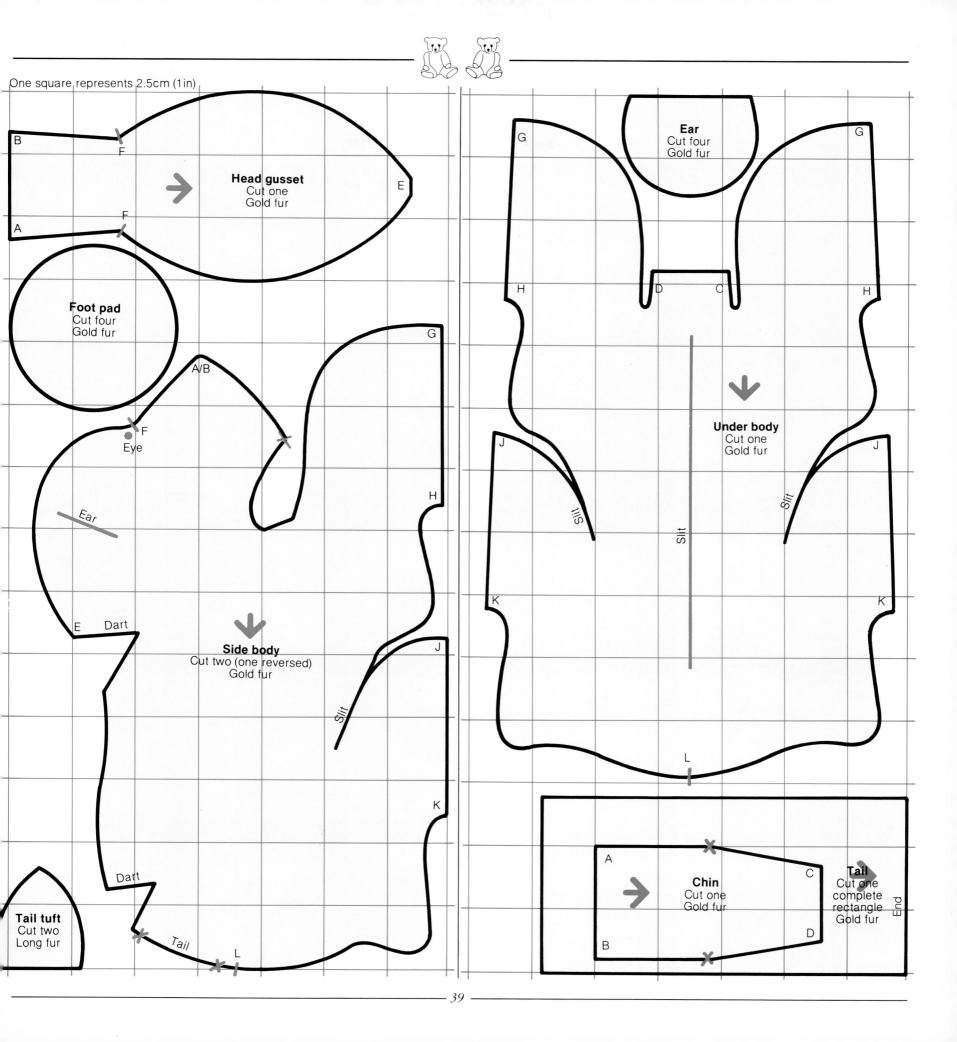

One square represents 2.5cm (1in)

Head gusset
Cut one
Gold fur

B
F
A
F
E

Foot pad
Cut four
Gold fur

A/B
F
Eye

G

Ear

H

E Dart

Side body
Cut two (one reversed)
Gold fur

J

Slit

K

Dart

Tail

L

Tail tuft
Cut two
Long fur

Ear
Cut four
Gold fur

G
G

H
D C H

Under body
Cut one
Gold fur

J
Slit

Slit

J
Slit

K
K

L

A
C
Chin
Cut one
Gold fur
B
D

Tail
Cut one
complete
rectangle
Gold fur

End

Sew the top head piece to the front head piece between A and B. Then sew the back head piece to the top head piece from C to D. Sew the front, top, and back head to the side head from point E to F. Repeat on other side. Sew the chin piece to the side head from G to H on both sides.

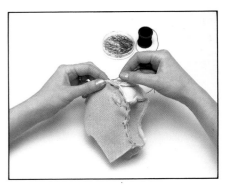

Stitch the white fur nose piece to the head, gently easing the fabric to fit. Turn the head the right way out and insert the safety eyes. Secure the eyes with the metal washers. Stuff the head, adding a little extra filling in the cheeks. Using a running stitch, gather the raw edge of the neck and fasten off securely.

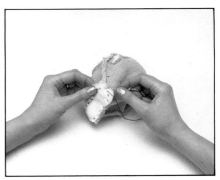

Trim a little fur away from the nose and sew the black nostrils into place. Using black embroidery thread, stitch a straight line for the mouth in a central position just under the cow's nose.

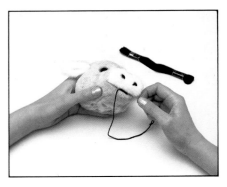

MATERIALS

30cm (12in) beige fur fabric
Small scrap of white fur fabric
Small scrap of long white fur
Small scrap of black felt
Small scrap of white felt
1 pair 18mm brown safety
  eyes with metal washers
Black embroidery thread
Filling

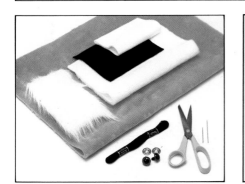

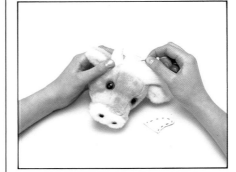

Mark out the horns onto double thickness white felt. Sew around the horn shape, leaving the straight edge open, then cut around the outline using sharp scissors. Turn the horns the right way out and stuff. Stitch around the base, pull tight and fasten off. Ladder stitch the horns into position at either side of the tuft.

Sew the ears together, leaving the straight edge open. Turn the ears the right way out, fold lengthwise with the white lining innermost and oversew fold into place. Take the side head pieces and cut slits for the ears and pierce tiny holes for the eyes. Push the raw edges of the ears through the slits and sew into position, with the lining facing forward.

With right sides together, sew the two inside gusset pieces together from J to K. Join the inside gusset to the side body by sewing seam N-O on either side.

Open out the front legs on the body piece. With the right sides together, sew the hoof pieces to the front legs along the straight edge.

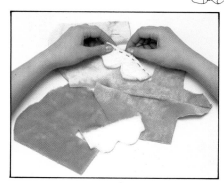

Fold the front legs over again along the seam and sew edges Q-P-T to the tip of the hoof. Then open out the back legs and attach the hooves in the same way. Fold the back legs over again and sew edges K-R-T.

Fold each of the legs so that the seam meets in the centre. Then sew all around the edges of the hooves.

Fold the tail lengthwise and sew along the long edge. Fold the tuft with the *wrong* sides together and sew, then trim close to the stitching. Push the tail end into the tail with the raw edges meeting. Sew across the top of the tail and turn right way out. Sew the back seam of the cow from L to K, catching in the tail at the same time.

Stuff the body, starting with the legs. When satisfied with the overall shape, gather the raw edge at the neck using a running stitch and fasten off securely. Place the head on the body, adjusting the position to suit. Ladder stitch the head firmly into place several times around with strong thread.

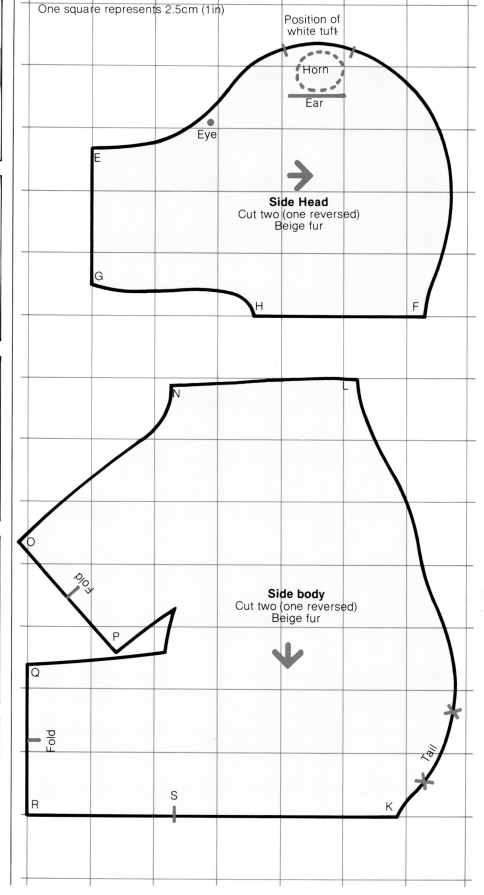

One square represents 2.5cm (1in)

Position of white tuft

Horn

Ear

Eye

E

G

H

F

Side Head
Cut two (one reversed)
Beige fur

N

L

O

Fold

P

Q

Fold

R

S

K

Tail

Side body
Cut two (one reversed)
Beige fur

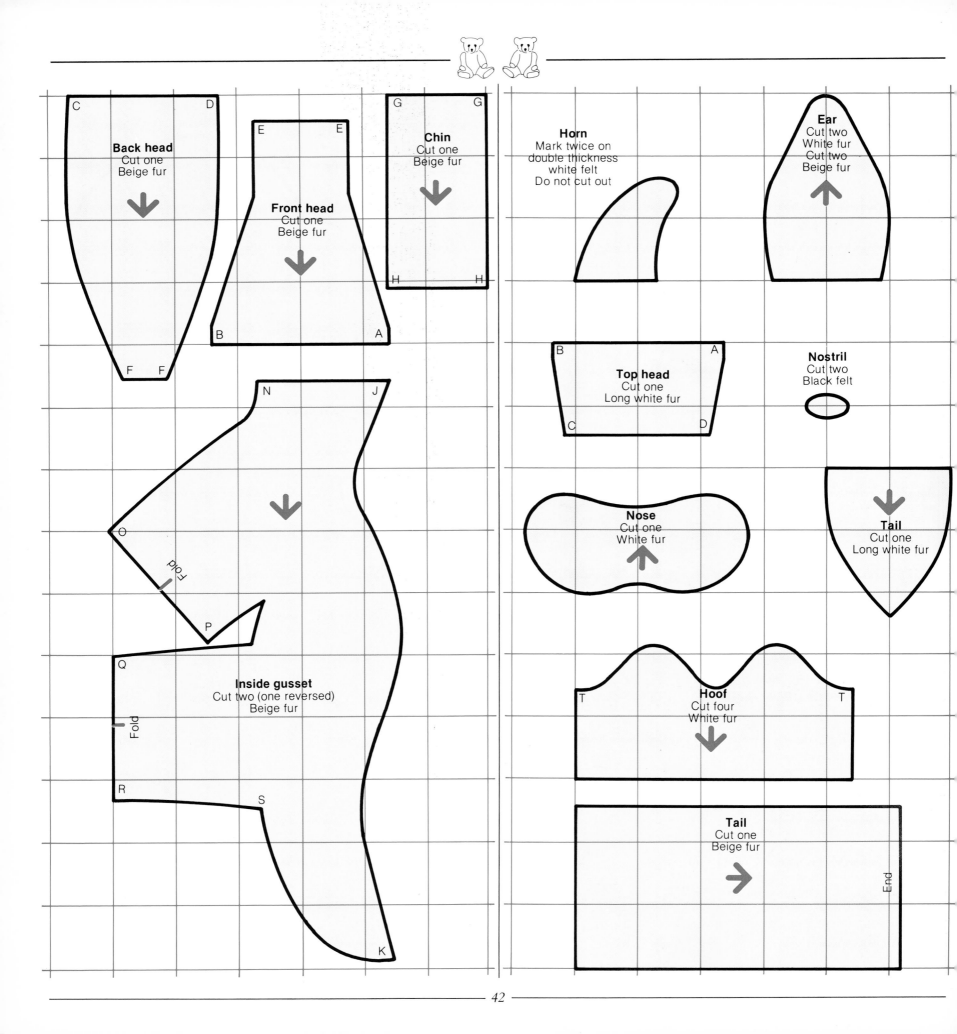

Back head
Cut one
Beige fur

C D

F F

Front head
Cut one
Beige fur

E E

B A

Chin
Cut one
Beige fur

G G

H H

Horn
Mark twice on
double thickness
white felt
Do not cut out

Ear
Cut two
White fur
Cut two
Beige fur

Top head
Cut one
Long white fur

B A

C D

Nostril
Cut two
Black felt

Nose
Cut one
White fur

Tail
Cut one
Long white fur

Inside gusset
Cut two (one reversed)
Beige fur

N J

O

Fold

P

Q

Fold

R S

K

Hoof
Cut four
White fur

T T

Tail
Cut one
Beige fur

End

With right sides together, join the face to the side head pieces, carefully matching the points all the way around. Join the two back head pieces together by sewing seam A-G.

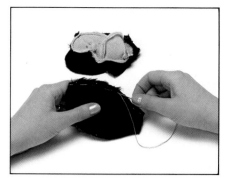

Open out the back head and place it against the completed front head with the right sides together. Sew all the way around, leaving the neck edge open.

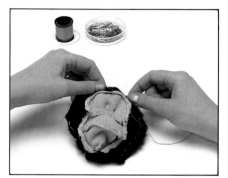

MATERIALS

Dark brown fur fabric
Beige fur fabric
Yellow felt for banana
White felt for banana
1 pair 13.5mm brown safety eyes with metal washers
Thick black embroidery thread
Filling

Pierce tiny holes for the eyes in the position indicated on the pattern. Turn the head the right way out. Insert the safety eyes through the holes and secure on the reverse with the washers.

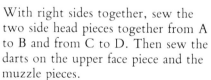

With right sides together, sew the two side head pieces together from A to B and from C to D. Then sew the darts on the upper face piece and the muzzle pieces.

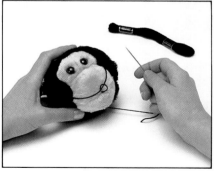

Fill the head with stuffing, easing it gently into shape. Gather the raw neck edge with a running stitch and fasten off securely. Using thick black embroidery thread and a long needle, stitch a long smile across the monkey's face with a single stitch on the seam line. Anchor the smile down with a second stitch across the centre as shown.

Join the upper face to one of the muzzle pieces together from E to E making sure the notches and the dart seams match. Then sew the two muzzle pieces together from E to E along the dart-free edges.

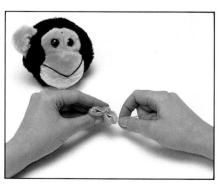

Sew the ears together in pairs, leaving the straight edge open. Turn the ears and form a pleat at the raw edge, oversewing into position as shown. Attach the ears by oversewing them flat onto the head, then lifting them upright and ladder stitching the front base of the ears down to the head to make them stand up. Place head to one side.

Sew the dart on the side body pieces. On one pair of legs and arms, mark out a circle as shown on the pattern. Lay the side body pieces right side up. Place the arms and leg pieces onto the body with the wrong side up. The legs should be pointing straight out, but the arms can be either up or down. Pin the limbs to the body in the centre of the circles and stitch carefully around the circles.

With a pair of sharp pointed scissors, cut out the centre of the circles about 5mm (¼in) from the stitching line. Push one arm right through the hole so that the wrong sides of the fabric are facing each other. Repeat with the other arm and the legs.

Take the remaining limb pieces and pair them up with each arm and leg attached to the body. Sew all the way around the arms, not leaving a gap. For the legs, sew around the curved edges, but leave the straight edge open for the foot pads.

Ease the foot pads into the bottom of the legs, making sure that the right sides are together and the narrow end is at the heel. Sew the foot pads into place, easing the fabric gently to fit if necessary.

Turn the limbs the right way out, back through the holes in the side body. Then join the two sides together all the way around, keeping the legs tucked in and leaving the neck edge J-K open. Turn the body through the neck opening.

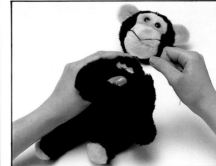

Fill the arms and legs, then the body cavity. Close the gap at the neck and ladder stitch the head to the body, adjusting the position of the head to create a cheeky pose. Fold the tail in half lengthwise. Sew along the long curved edge, leaving the top straight edge open. Turn the tail the right way out and tuck the raw edge under. Ladder stitch the tail to the body.

To make the banana, join the three white felt pieces together, leaving a small gap for turning. Turn and stuff firmly, then close the gap. Sew the three yellow outside skin pieces together halfway along the length. Turn the right way out and push the white banana down into the skin as far as it will go.

One square represents 2.5cm (1in)

Muzzle
Cut two
Beige fur

Dart

Back head
Cut two (one reversed)
Brown fur

Side head
Cut two
(one reversed)
Brown fur

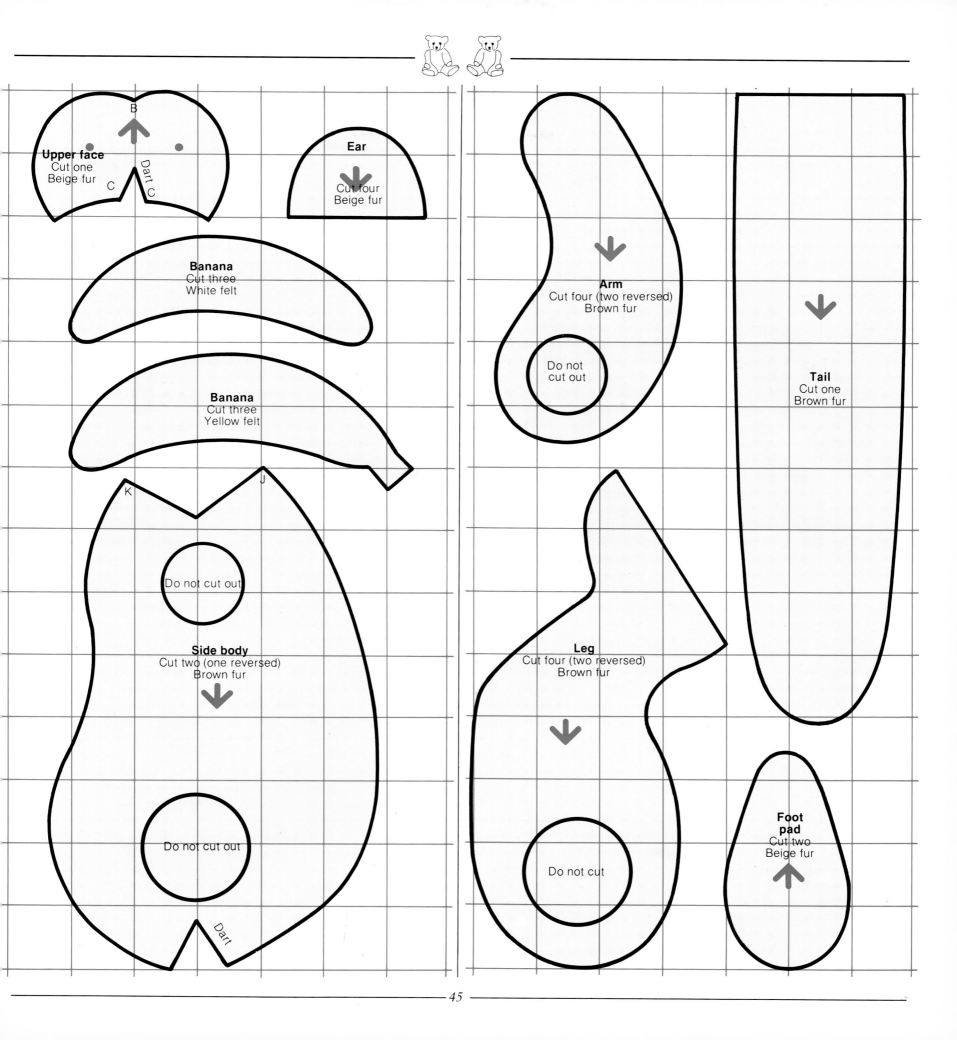

Upper face
Cut one
Beige fur

B

Dart C

C

Ear
Cut four
Beige fur

Banana
Cut three
White felt

Banana
Cut three
Yellow felt

K

J

Do not cut out

Side body
Cut two (one reversed)
Brown fur

Do not cut out

Dart

Arm
Cut four (two reversed)
Brown fur

Do not
cut out

Tail
Cut one
Brown fur

Leg
Cut four (two reversed)
Brown fur

Do not cut

**Foot
pad**
Cut two
Beige fur

Close the dart on the black upper inside body piece. Sew the black upper inside body to the white lower inside body along seam D-D. At the top neck edge, sew the upper inside body to the under chin piece along seam B-B.

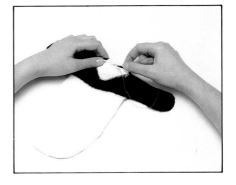

Sew the inside body to the side body between points G and F, matching points B and D, and easing the fabric to fit. Repeat on other side.

Sew the head gusset to the side head along seam E-A, making sure that point H matches. Repeat on other side. Close the seam E-G at the front of the head, then close the seam at the back of the panda from A to F.

MATERIALS

Black fur fabric
White fur fabric
Scraps of black felt
1 pair 13.5mm black safety eyes with metal washers
Black embroidery thread
Filling

Using sharp scissors, pierce tiny holes for the eyes at the position indicated. Then cut a slit down the centre of the white tummy. Turn the body the right way out through the slit, easing it out a little at a time. Be sure to poke out the ends of the arms.

To join the three side body pieces together, first place the side head and middle body pieces right sides together and sew seam A-B. Then, with right sides together, match seam C-D of lower body piece and side middle body piece and sew. Repeat for other side.

Pierce a small hole in the eye patches. Insert the safety eyes through these holes, then through the holes in the head. Secure on the reverse side of the head with the washers. Fill the panda with stuffing, starting with the arms. Take care to shape the head and the nose. Close the gap in the tummy using a ladder stitch.

Fold one hind leg lengthwise and sew around it, leaving a gap for turning as indicated. Then turn the right way out and stuff lightly. Close the gap using a ladder stitch, then firmly ladder stitch the slightly fatter end of the leg to the side of the body using strong thread. Repeat for other leg.

Place two ear pieces right sides together and sew, leaving the straight edge open. Turn the right way out and oversew the raw edge. Repeat for other ear. Place the ears flat on the head and oversew into position. Then lift the ears upright and ladder stitch the front base of the ears down to the head to make them stand up.

With a long needle and black thread, tack the eye patches down to the head at both the top and the bottom. Using long straight stitches, embroider a nose and mouth on the panda. Then, if desired, use white thread to stitch claws on each paw.

One square represents 2.5cm (1in)

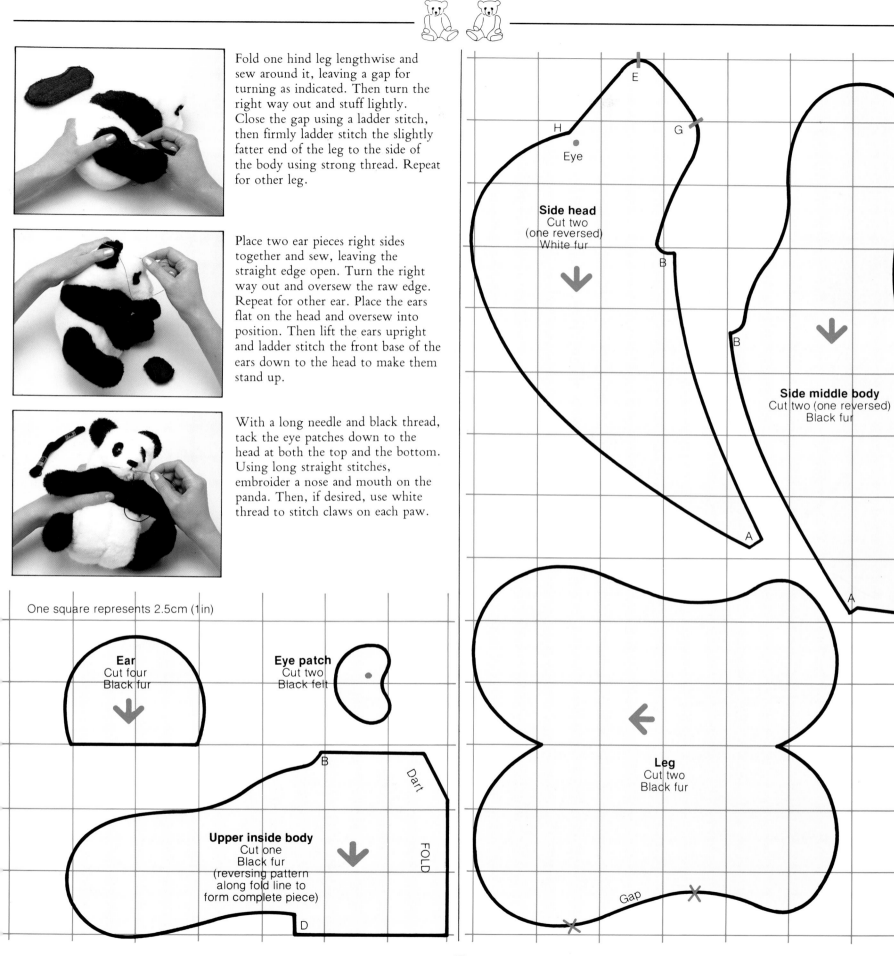

Side head
Cut two
(one reversed)
White fur

Eye

Side middle body
Cut two (one reversed)
Black fur

Ear
Cut four
Black fur

Eye patch
Cut two
Black felt

Leg
Cut two
Black fur

Gap

Upper inside body
Cut one
Black fur
(reversing pattern
along fold line to
form complete piece)

Dart

FOLD

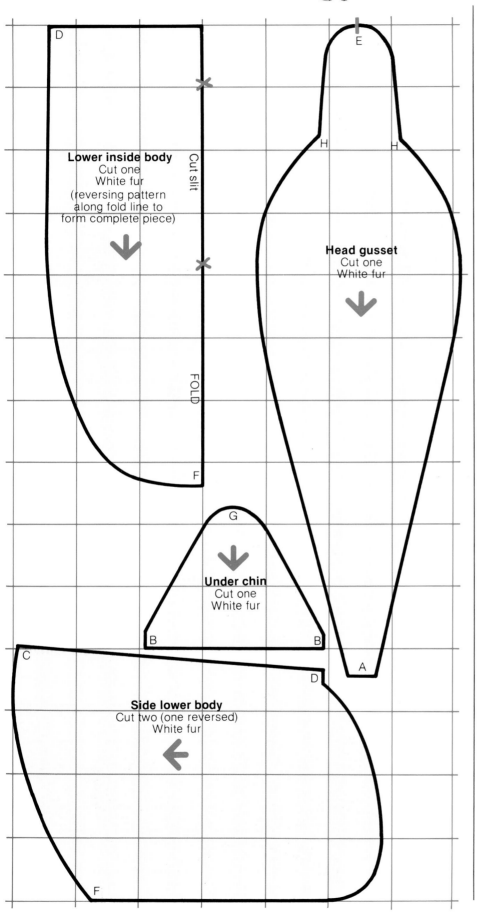

Lower inside body
Cut one
White fur
(reversing pattern along fold line to form complete piece)

Cut slit

D

X

X

FOLD

F

Head gusset
Cut one
White fur

E

H H

G

Under chin
Cut one
White fur

B B

A

C

D

Side lower body
Cut two (one reversed)
White fur

F

MATERIALS

30cm x 150cm (12in x 60in)
  grey felt, velvet or suede
  fabric
Piece of pink fabric (i.e. velvet)
  for ear lining and feet
3 pairs 12mm safety eyes
  with metal washers
Filling

Clothing

Small piece of white towelling
  for nappy (diaper)
Small pieces of white and pink
  felt for bib
Ribbon or lace for bib
Nappy (diaper) pin
Piece of red velvet
Piece of blue felt
50cm x 5cm (20in x 2in) red
  spotted material, cut on bias,
  for neckties
50cm (20in) narrow elastic

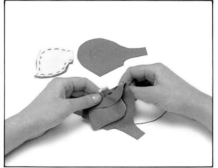

For each elephant the head should be made as follows. Cut the ear slits and pierce eye positions in the side head pieces. Sew the ears to the pink ear linings, leaving gap A-B open. Turn the ears the right way out and push the raw edge of the ears through the ear slits so that the pink lining faces forward towards the trunk. Sew across the slits.

With right sides together, sew the gusset to the side head from C to D. Repeat with the other side. Join seam E-F under the trunk. Flatten the end of the trunk so that the under trunk seam is in the centre of the top gusset. Sew across the end of the trunk.

Open out the body and match the arm piece to the body on either side between points K, J and K. Sew up the seams on both sides.

Fold the front and back body right sides together along the top seam. Sew the side seams from the tip of the arm to the foot, along M-K-L, on both sides of the body. Sew seam N-H-N between the legs.

Open out the raw edges at the end of the arms and legs and, with right sides together, sew the pink foot pads into position.

Turn the head the right way out, poking out the trunk. Insert the safety eyes through the holes and secure with metal washers. Stuff the head, starting with the trunk. Mould the head into shape, pushing stuffing into the cheeks. Using a running stitch, sew around the raw edge of the neck, pull tight and finish off securely.

To make the bodies of the adult elephants, join the two body pieces between G and H, making sure the right sides are together. Repeat with other two body pieces, leaving a gap for stuffing. This will be the front body. Open out and place the front and back body pieces right sides together. Join across the top along seam J-G-J as shown.

Turn the body the right way out and stuff firmly. Close the gap with a ladder stitch. Place the head on the body and ladder stitch into place several times; finish off securely.

For the neckties, cut the fabric in half so each piece is about 25cm (10in) long. Tie each piece around the elephants' neck. Trim to fit as necessary. For the jackets, join the shoulder seams S-T on both sides. Turn the right way out but do not hem. Place on the elephants.

For the trousers, turn up a small hem along the bottom edges R-R on both pieces. Place the two halves right sides together and sew seam P-O on both sides. Join seam R-O-R between the trouser legs. Fold over the top of the trousers twice to make an elastic casing and sew in place, leaving a small gap. Insert the elastic and pull tight, adjusting to fit waist.

For the skirt, cut out a piece of velvet 14cm x 44cm (5½in x 17½in) and fold in half, right sides together. Sew along the short edge. Turn up a small hem and sew all around. Make an elastic casing using same method as for the trousers. Insert the narrow elastic and adjust to fit the waist of the mother elephant.

One square represents 2.5cm (1in)

Adult and baby elephants

Ear
Cut two (one reversed)
Grey fabric
Cut two (one reversed)
Pink fabric

A
B

Foot pad
Cut four
Pink fabric

Head gusset
Cut one
Grey fabric

D D

C C

Ear

Eye

Side head
Cut two (one reversed)
Grey fabric

D   F   E

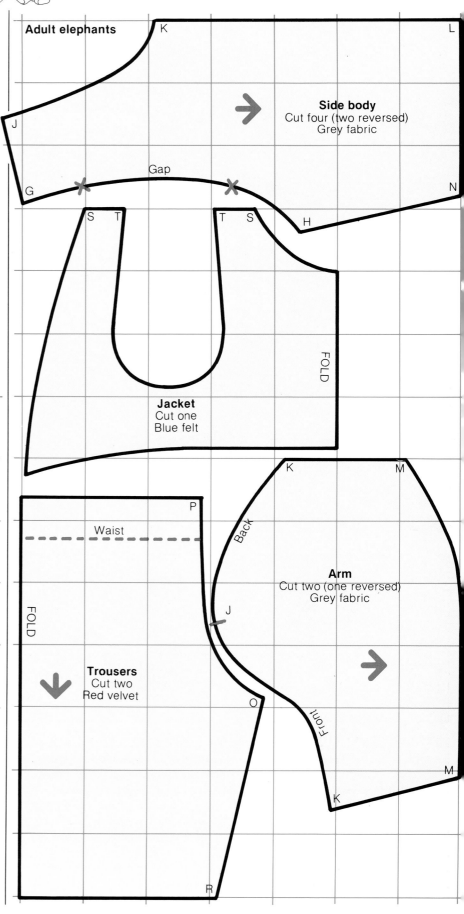

Adult elephants

K   L

Side body
Cut four (two reversed)
Grey fabric

J

Gap

G   N

S T   T S   H

FOLD

Jacket
Cut one
Blue felt

K   M

P

Waist

Back

Arm
Cut two (one reversed)
Grey fabric

FOLD

J

Trousers
Cut two
Red velvet

O

Front

M

K

R

For the baby elephant, make the head according to the instructions on pages 48–49 (using pattern pieces on page 50). For the body, use the pattern on page 50. Join the two inside body pieces from A to B. Then join the side body pieces together by sewing from A to B, leaving a small gap for turning.

Join the inside body pieces to the side bodies by sewing seams A–C on either side, easing the fabric to fit. Then sew seam D–B–D around the base. Sew the foot pads into the leg openings on the body.

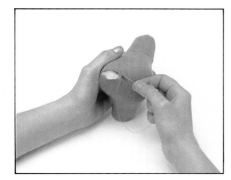

Turn the body the right way out and stuff. When satisfied with the shape, close the gap at the back using a ladder stitch.

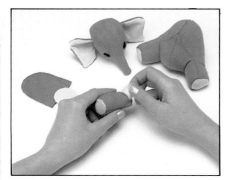

Sew around each pair of arms, leaving the bottom straight edge open. Open out the raw edges and sew in the foot pads. Snip a small slit at the top of each arm and turn the right way out. Stuff arms and oversew the gaps. Ladder stitch the head to the body and add arms on either side.

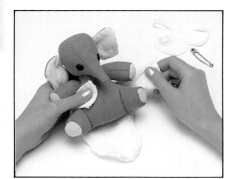

Turn in the raw edge all around the nappy (diaper) towelling and sew. Put on the baby elephant and secure with a pin. Sew a piece of ribbon or lace to the top edge of the bib and add a felt flower for decoration.

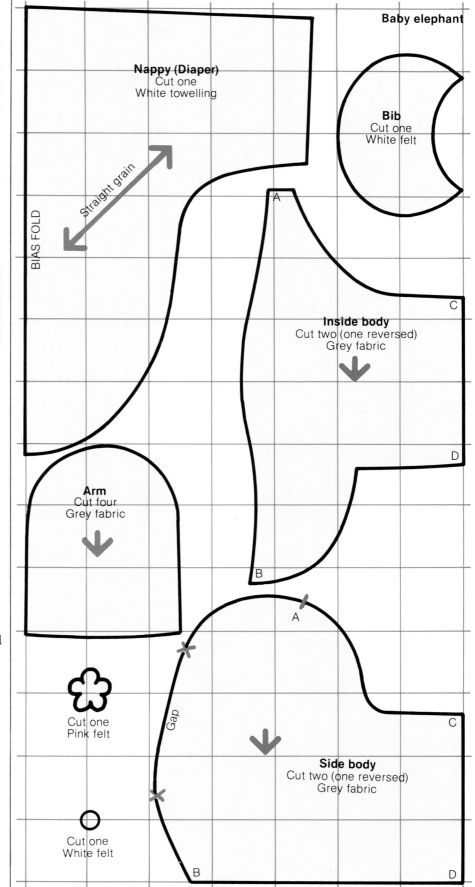

Baby elephant

Nappy (Diaper)
Cut one
White towelling

Bib
Cut one
White felt

BIAS FOLD

Straight grain

A

C

Inside body
Cut two (one reversed)
Grey fabric

D

Arm
Cut four
Grey fabric

B

A

Cut one
Pink felt

Gap

Cut one
White felt

Side body
Cut two (one reversed)
Grey fabric

C

B

D

Stitch doll leg seams C–A–C curving lower edges. Trim fabric around curves. Turn body through to right side out.

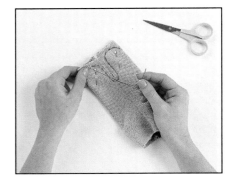

Fill legs with stuffing and stitch across top of them at a slight angle to allow them to bend. Fill body.

MATERIALS: *For one doll – 1 man's towelling sock; small doll's vinyl face; 36cm × 7mm (14in × ¼in) wide satin ribbon; 20cm (8in) narrow broderie anglaise edging or lace; 3 daisy motifs; 70cm (28in) fine yellow or brown yarn; matching sewing threads; filling*

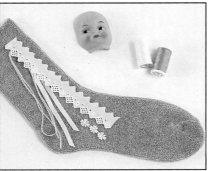

Turn sock to wrong side out and cut along all solid lines as shown on diagram. Discard ribbing.

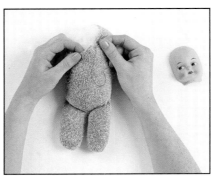

Sew a line of long running stitches close to open edge, pull up stitches until opening is slightly smaller than doll's face and securely fasten thread.

Oversew all cut edges to prevent fraying. Open out body section to bring A–A and fold doll's legs along centre lines B–C–D.

Oversew face to cover opening, adding extra filling behind it as you do so. Sew running stitches around the body below the head, pull up thread until gathers pull in body to form a neck, then secure it.

For the hair, wind yarn around two fingers to form loops and sew these to fabric above centre of face.

With wrong sides facing and raw edges even, fold brim section along its centre, matching F–F and G–G. Oversew raw edges together adding a little filling as you work to make brim into a soft 'ring doughnut' roll.

Fit brim around face with seam to the back and sew to body. Cut ribbon into two lengths, sew one end of each through brim at sides of neck and tie in a bow. Take several stitches through bow to prevent it coming undone.

Sew broiderie anglaise or lace around neck with the joins at the back. Sew three daisy trimmings down centre front of body.

Fold arms along centres H–K, matching J–J. Stitch seam, curving it as shown on broken line and leaving open J–K. Trim fabric around curves. Turn arms through to right side out and fill lightly with stuffing.

To form the hands, secure threads and wind them around arms 2.5cm (1in) from closed ends. Turn in open edges and sew arms to body.

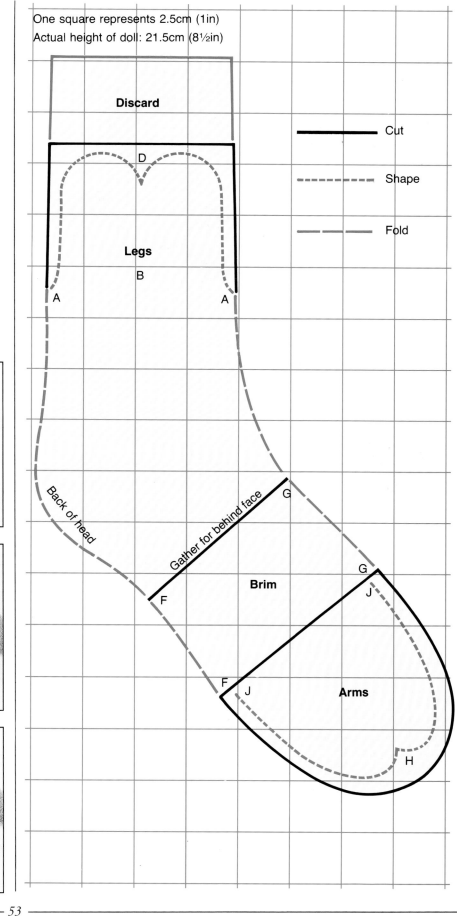

One square represents 2.5cm (1in)
Actual height of doll: 21.5cm (8½in)

Discard

Legs

Cut

Shape

Fold

Back of head

Gather for behind face

Brim

Arms

Place raw edges of legs to right side of one of the body pieces F–C. Baste then stitch legs to body. Fold an arm along centre line A–G. Lightly mark curve of hand onto fabric. Stitch seam H–K leaving open A–H. Trim fabric close to seam. Turn arm to right side out and press. Lightly fill with stuffing and oversew open edges.

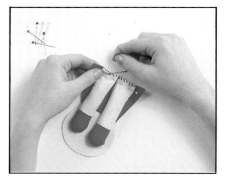

Stitch a narrow hem at sleeve wrist J–J. Stitch sleeve seam H–J. Turn sleeve to right side out and press. Sew a line of running stitches along upper edge between dots to gather the edge. Fit sleeve onto arm, pull up gathers to fit and oversew raw edges of sleeve to raw edges of arm. Make second arm and sleeve.

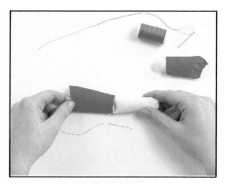

Place arms onto right side of body with raw edges even, matching A–H. **Note:** The arms will cross the body in centre front while this is done and when body side seams are stitched. Baste raw edges of arms and body together.

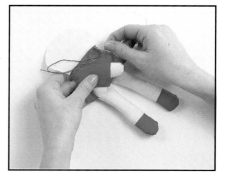

MATERIALS: *Small amount of each fabric – pink calico, blue felt, check fabric, red fabric; lightweight interfacing; scrap of black felt; brown double knitting yarn; narrow elastic and bodkin; matching sewing threads; scrap of red embroidery thread; red crayon; filling; thin card*

Cut out all pieces. Press interfacing to one cap peak before cutting out. Cut two straps from check fabric 4cm × 12cm (1½in × 4¾in). Seam allowance is ½cm (⅜in) – this also applies to Teresa Twin. Stitch a head to a body at neck A–A. Repeat for second pair.

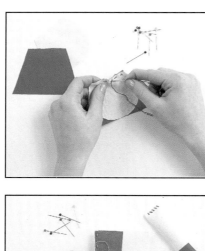

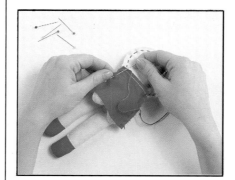

With right sides together stitch bodies together at side seams, including arms and around head L–H–A–A–H–L but leaving open lower straight edges. Turn body through to right side and press. Fill with stuffing. Turn ends of legs to inside of body, turn under opposite raw edge and sew across lower straight edge L–L to cover top of legs and enclose body stuffing.

Stitch foot to leg B–D–B. Fold leg and foot along centre line C–D–E. Lightly mark foot curve onto fabric. Stitch leg seam F–B and around curve of foot B–E. Trim fabric close to seam. Turn leg through to right side and press. Fill lightly with stuffing and oversew open edges to enclose stuffing. Make second leg.

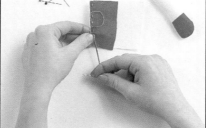

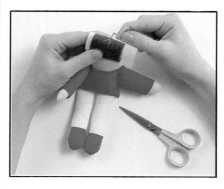

For the fringe, cut a piece of card 7cm × 3cm (2¾in × 1¼in). Wind 20 strands of brown knitting yarn around shorter width. Hold one long edge of card to centre front of head seam with yarn to front of head and oversew fold of each strand to fabric. Slide card from loops and sew strands to head in front of seam line to hold flat.

For back hair, cut card 10cm × 6cm (4in × 2½in). Wind yarn around shorter width until card is covered, push strands together until they fit head covering head seam to above ear positions. Sew upper fold of each strand to head seam. Remove card.

Cut 30 strands of yarn each 20cm (8in) long. Hold all strands together at their centre and sew to head at a centre parting with yarn covering join of fringe and back hair. Smooth hair over head and sew strands to cover side seams and across back head at natural hair line. Cut loops and trim yarn.

Cut two small black felt circles (paper punch size) for eyes. Take a stitch through head from back to front and through eye, then through eye again and head. Pull thread and secure. For mouth embroider two small straight stitches into a V shape using two strands of red embroidery thread. With same thread make a tiny stitch for nose. Mark cheeks and eyebrows with red crayon.

Stitch trouser pieces together at one centre (front) seam only M–N and press open. Stitch narrow hems at legs P–P.

Fold and stitch a double hem at waist to form casing for elastic. Thread through elastic sewing it at one end to fabric. Pull up to fit waist and sew other end to secure. Trim excess elastic. Stitch remaining centre seam M–N. Stitch inner leg seams P–N–P. Turn trousers to right side out and fit onto doll. With wrong sides facing, fold and press straps along length in centre.

Turn in raw edges of straps to meet centre fold and top stitch together. Top stitch opposite edge. Place straps across doll's shoulders crossing them at back. Tuck strap ends inside trousers and sew to waist gathers. Cut two small circles of blue felt as buttons (use a shirt button as a template) and sew to ends of straps at front.

Press to wrong side a single hem 1cm (⅜in) around edge of cap Q–T–Q. Press a further 1cm (⅜in) single hem to wrong side around edge. Pleat or gather second fold to lie flat. Stitch very close to folded edge and to outer edge to form a channel. Thread through elastic and sew one end to fabric. Gather fabric to 18cm (7in), secure and trim excess elastic.

Stitch curved edges of peaks together R–S–S–R. Trim fabric close to stitches. Turn peak to right side out and press. Baste open edges together. With right sides facing stitch peak to gathered cap matching T's. By hand oversew raw edges of peak and cap together. Stitch cap seam Q–W–Q. Cut blue felt scarf 25cm × 1.5cm (10in × ⅝in). Cut a fringe at short ends.

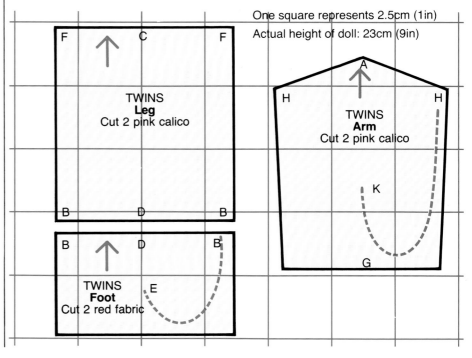

One square represents 2.5cm (1in)
Actual height of doll: 23cm (9in)

TWINS
Leg
Cut 2 pink calico

TWINS
Foot
Cut 2 red fabric

TWINS
Arm
Cut 2 pink calico

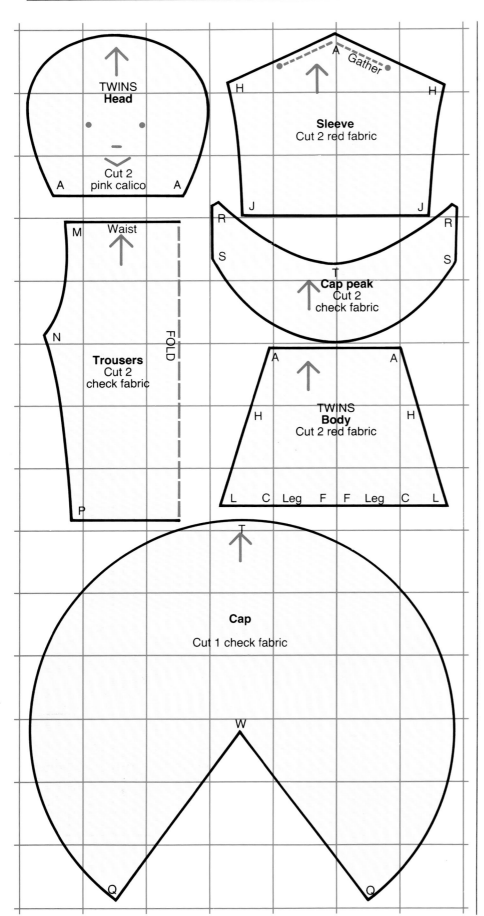

TWINS
Head

TWINS
Cut 2
pink calico

A · · A

Sleeve
Cut 2 red fabric

A

Gather

H · · H

J J

Trousers
Cut 2
check fabric

M Waist

N

FOLD

P

R R

S S

T

Cap peak
Cut 2
check fabric

A A

H H

TWINS
Body
Cut 2 red fabric

L C Leg F F Leg C L

Cap
Cut 1 check fabric

T

W

Q Q

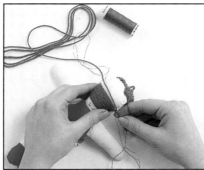

MATERIALS: *Small amounts of each fabric– pink calico; red fabric; spotted fabric; 130cm (51in) narrow lace; 1m (1yd) very narrow satin ribbon; scrap of black felt; brown double knitting yarn; narrow elastic and bodkin; scrap of stranded red embroidery thread; red crayon; filling; thin card*

Cut out skirt 10cm × 42cm (4in x 16½in) and two straps 4cm × 10cm (1½in × 4in). Follow steps 1–6 of Tom Twin. Sew lace around neck and lower edge of body. Follow Tom Twin step 7; loops remain uncut. For back hair, secure yarn 1cm (⅜in) above neck seam just in front of side seam with one needle. Take yarn across back of head and secure with second needle.

Continue to take strands of yarn across back of head keeping them very close together and sewing at each seam with separate needle and thread. Cover whole back head to top seam. Sew the centre back of hair to head to form a parting, pulling up lower strands to make a natural hair line.

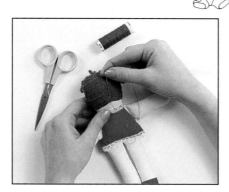

Stitch curved edge of bonnet brims Y–V–V–Y together leaving open straight edges Y–Z–Y. Trim fabric close to stitches and turn brim to right side out. Press and baste open edges together. Turn under and stitch a narrow hem at straight edge of bonnet back Y–Y. Stitch brim to bonnet back Y–Z–Y. Stitch lace inside of brim and lower edge of back. Sew ribbons to sides at Y.

For the plaits cut 21 strands of yarn each 43cm (17in) long. Sew centre of each strand to centre of head from front to back for 1cm (⅜in) each side of head seam to cover fringe stitches. Gather each bunch of hair to front of face and sew at lower edge of back hair. Plait hair and tie with red thread. Trim plaits.

Follow step 8–10 of Tom Twin. Stitch a narrow hem at one long edge of skirt. Stitch lace to wrong side to show below. Stitch ribbon to right side above hem. Stitch a double hem at opposite long edge to form a casing. Thread through elastic using bodkin and sew at one end to fabric. Pull up to fit waist, sew to fabric and trim elastic. Stitch short edges of skirt together.

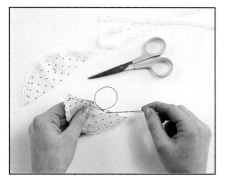

Press under a single hem to wrong side of curved edge of a shoulder frill X–X. Stitch lace to wrong side over hem edge, to show beyond fabric. Sew a line of long running stitches along straight edge, pull up stitches to gather frill to 4cm (1½in) and secure thread. Make second frill.

With wrong sides facing fold and press a strap piece along centre length. Turn in raw edges to centre fold and press. Insert and baste gathered edge of a frill into a folded strap at centre of length. Top stitch together open edges of strap with frill in-between. Make second strap and frill. Place straps on doll, crossing them at back. Tuck ends into skirt waist and sew.

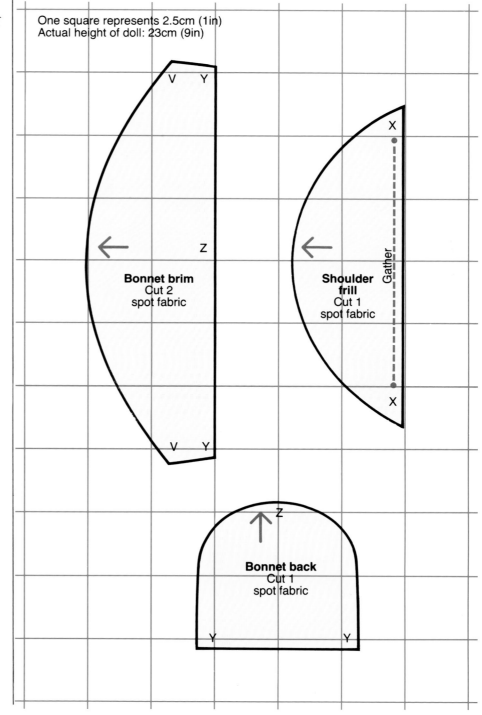

One square represents 2.5cm (1in)
Actual height of doll: 23cm (9in)

Bonnet brim
Cut 2
spot fabric

Shoulder frill
Cut 1
spot fabric

Gather

Bonnet back
Cut 1
spot fabric

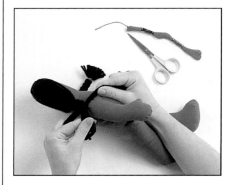

For front hair cut 40 strands of yarn 55cm (22in) long. Turn under ends of black tape and sew centre of each strand to centre of tape. Lightly mark centre front of head on forehead 2.5cm (1in) below seam. Sew tape to head with one end at front centre mark and the other end covering back hair. Bring hair to front of doll and sew to head over seam at lower edge of back hair.

Plait hair and tie ends with red thread. Trim ends of hair. Lightly mark position for features onto face. Cut two black felt circles for eyes, sew a white thread highlight in centre of each and sew to head. Embroider mouth with two straight red stitches. Mark eyebrows, nose and inner corners of eyes with pen.

With right sides facing match trouser pieces together in pairs. Place **uncut** felt fringe, with one long edge even with trouser side edges, between dots. Stitch seam J–K including fringe. Stitch second fringe and side seam. Stitch trouser pieces together at centre front seam only M–N. Press seam open and side seams towards back. Stitch both edges of braid to right side of ankles L–K–L.

Turn under and stitch single hem at waist to form a casing. Thread through elastic until one end is level with felt and stitch through elastic and casing to secure. Pull up elastic to fit doll, stitch other end of elastic to secure and trim excess. Stitch centre back seam M–N and inside leg seams L–N–L. Turn trousers to right side out and snip leg and side fringes.

Stitch jacket sleeves to jacket back P–Q. Stitch sleeves to fronts P–Q. Press seams open. On right side stitch braid to sleeves R–R. Stitch fronts to back at side seams Q–S and underarm seams Q–R. On right side stitch braid to lower edges of jacket. Fold under and stitch a single hem at centre fronts X–W.

MATERIALS: 40cm × 80cm (16in × 31in) brown calico: 61cm × 61cm (24in × 24in) fawn felt; 14cm × 24cm (5½in × 9in) yellow felt; scrap of black felt; 140cm (55in) decorative braid; black double knitting yarn; 6cm (2¼in) narrow black tape; narrow elastic and bodkin; 3 small press fasteners; matching sewing threads; red braid for neck band; red embroidery thread; 3 feathers; black crayon

Follow steps 1–5 of Cowboy to make body. For back hair, thread two needles with black sewing threads. With first needle secure end of yarn to just in front of head side seam 1.5cm (⅝in) above back neck seam. Take yarn across back head to opposite seam and sew with second needle. Cover back head to top seam. Sew parting down centre back pulling up lower strands.

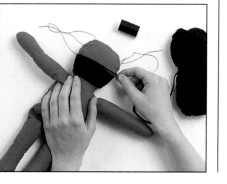

Stitch collar to wrong side of jacket neck matching dots at centre back and at X's in the front. Turn collar over raw edges to right side out. Cut fringes at collar, wrists and lower edges of jacket. Fit jacket onto doll, overlap fronts and sew a press fastener at the neck, centre and lower edges, to close them.

Cut a braid band to fit around head and oversew ends. Cut feathers, if too long, and tuck them into band at back and sew feathers and band to head.

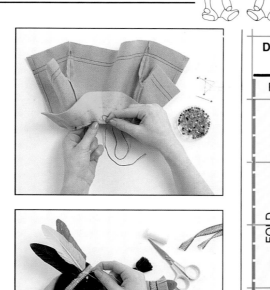

One square represents 2.5cm (1in)

Actual height of doll: 33cm (13in)

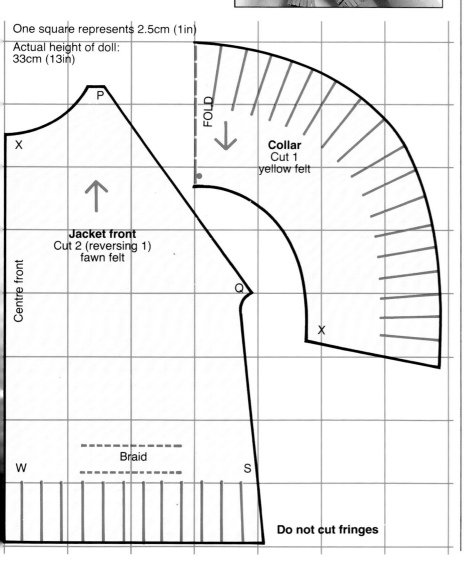

Do not cut fringes

Jacket front
Cut 2 (reversing 1)
fawn felt

Centre front

Collar
Cut 1
yellow felt

FOLD

Braid

W

X

P

Q

S

Do not cut fringes

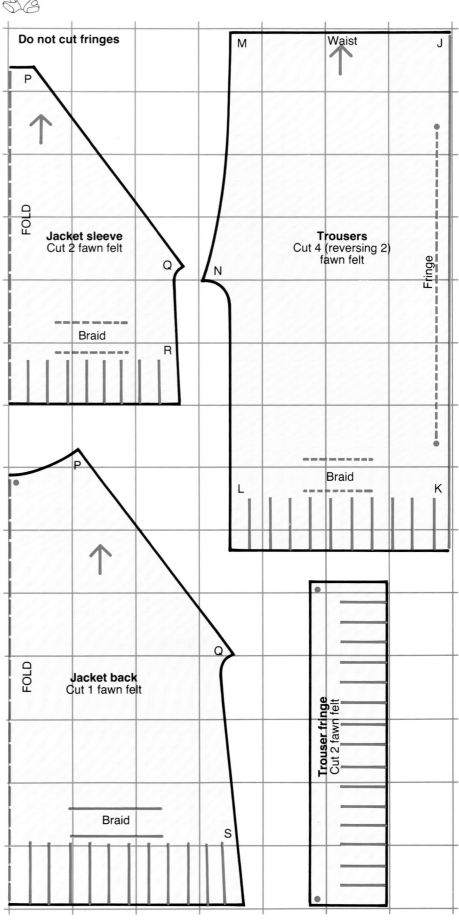

Do not cut fringes

M

Waist

J

P

FOLD

Jacket sleeve
Cut 2 fawn felt

Q

N

Braid

R

Trousers
Cut 4 (reversing 2)
fawn felt

Fringe

Braid

L

K

P

FOLD

Jacket back
Cut 1 fawn felt

Q

Braid

S

Trouser fringe
Cut 2 fawn felt

Follow steps 1–5 of Cowboy instructions to make body. Follow steps 1–3 of Little Bear's instructions to make hair and face. Do not plait hair but sew it in front of head side seams.

Stitch trouser pieces together at centre front seam only M–N. Turn under and stitch a single hem at waist to form a casing. Thread through elastic until one end is level with felt and stitch through elastic and casing to secure. Pull up elastic to fit doll, stitch other end of elastic through casing and trim excess. Stitch centre back seam M–N. Stitch inside leg seams L–N–L.

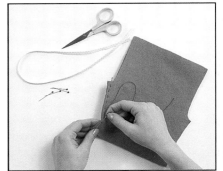

Stitch decorative braid to centre front of dress R–W. Stitch braid to centre of sleeves turning under lower ends to neaten. Stitch sleeves to dress front P–Q and to backs P–Q.

Stitch fronts to the back at side seams Q–S and the underarm seams Q–Y. On right side stitch braid to lower edges of dress just above the ends of the side seams W–S–S–W, covering the end of centre front braid.

With right sides together stitch centre backs together X–W. Stitch narrow hems to wrong side T–X. Turn under and stitch a narrow hem at neck. On right side place collar around neck, fold one long edge to inside and hand stitch over hem. Sew press fasteners to close centre back. Cut fringes. Thread beads and sew around neck. See page 59 for head band and feather details.

MATERIALS: 40cm × 80cm (16in × 13in) brown calico; 26cm × 90cm (10in × 36in) orange felt; scrap of black felt; 110cm (43in) decorative braid; black double knitting wool; matching sewing threads; red embroidery thread; narrow elastic and bodkin; two small press fasteners; one feather; beads (optional)

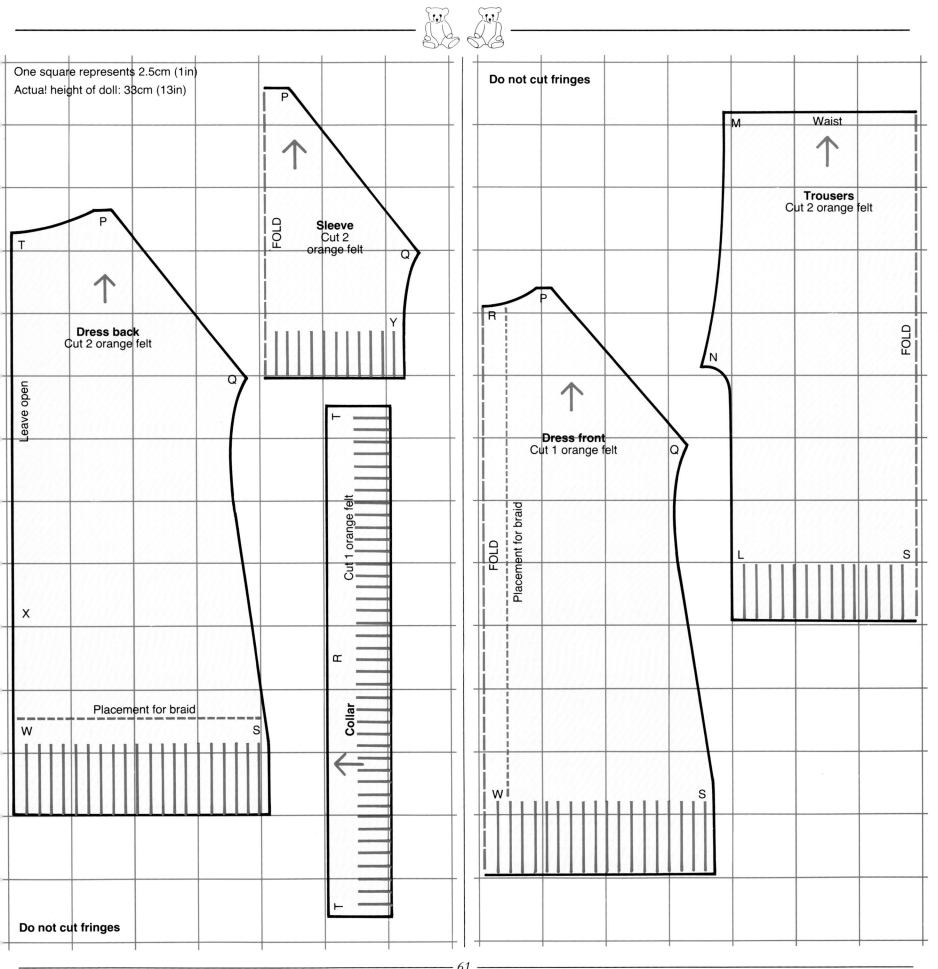

One square represents 2.5cm (1in)

Actual height of doll: 33cm (13in)

Do not cut fringes

P

FOLD

Sleeve
Cut 2
orange felt

Q

Y

M Waist

Trousers
Cut 2 orange felt

FOLD

T P

Leave open

Dress back
Cut 2 orange felt

Q

R P

Dress front
Cut 1 orange felt

Q

N

T

Cut 1 orange felt

R

Collar

FOLD

Placement for braid

L S

X

W Placement for braid S

Placement for braid

W S

W S

T

Do not cut fringes

Lightly mark position for features on face. Cut two black felt eyes, sew a small white thread highlight on each eye and glue eyes to face. Embroider mouth with two straight red stitches. Mark eyebrows with black crayon and nose and cheeks with red crayon.

With right sides facing match both trouser pieces. Stitch one centre seam only J–K. Turn under and stitch a narrow double hem at lower edge of legs L–L. Stitch braid over leg hem stitches. Turn under a double hem at waist. Thread elastic through casing, stitching at one end. Pull up to fit waist and secure. Stitch second centre seam J–K and inside leg seams L–K–L.

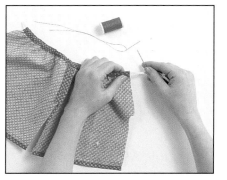

Stitch a narrow double hem at sleeve wrist edge P–P. Stitch braid over hem stitches. Stitch sleeves to jacket fronts and to jacket back M–N. Open out bias binding and place right side to wrong side of jacket front, with raw edges even. Stitch binding along its fold line to jacket fronts and back Q–M–M–Q. Turn binding over raw edges to right side. Top stitch close to binding edge.

MATERIALS: 40cm × 80cm (16in × 31 in) cream calico; printed fabric and matching bias binding; green felt; scrap of black felt; 120cm (47in) narrow straight decorative binding; 80cm (31½in) ric-rac (or novelty) braid; 20cm (8in) dolls' black mohair; matching sewing threads; narrow elastic and bodkin; three small press fasteners; thin card; black and red crayon; filling; craft glue

Stitch fronts to back at side seams N–R and underarm seams N–P. Turn under and stitch a narrow double hem at lower edge of jacket Q–R–R–Q. Cut braid slightly longer than this lower edge, turn under ends and on right side stitch braid over seam stitches. Fit jacket onto doll overlapping the fronts. Sew press fasteners in given positions.

Follow steps 1–5 of Cowboy instructions to make body using cream calico. Spread mohair into a single layer to form a fringe and to cover head. Spread glue onto head and allow to dry slightly. Place hair onto head with one end making a low fringe. Pull hair over head seams at sides. When the glue is dry sew hair to head. Trim hair to a fringe and at shoulders.

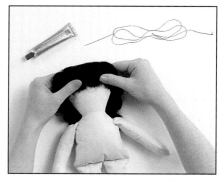

Fold upper edge of shoe to wrong side, and stitch a narrow single hem S–T–S. Fold shoes T–V and stitch front seam S–X. Stitch shoe sole to shoe matching X and V. Turn shoe to right side out and fit onto doll. Make second shoe.

From card cut one hat shape. Spread glue on one side of card and press to an oversize piece of felt. Make sure that felt is smooth and note chin strap placement positions. Trim felt to edge of card. Glue felt to second face of card and trim to size. Glue or sew ric-rac braid around upper edge of hat.

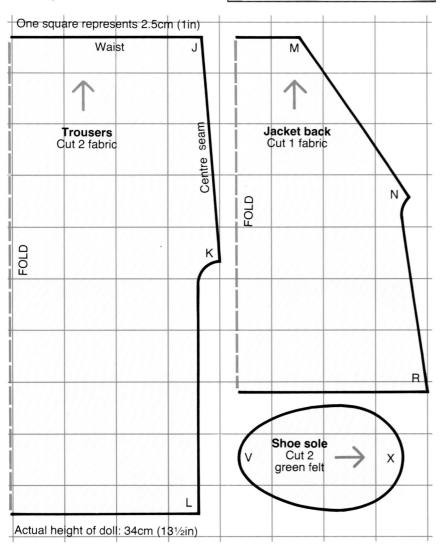

Cut 28cm (11in) of ric-rac for chin strap and sew to underside of hat on placement marks. Match edges Y–Y and oversew seam X–Y. Turn hat to right side out, with seam ridge on underside. Press if necessary and fit onto doll. The hat can be sewn to head. **Note:** If making this doll for a small child, use black knitting yarn to make hair (mohair is not washable).

One square represents 2.5cm (1in)

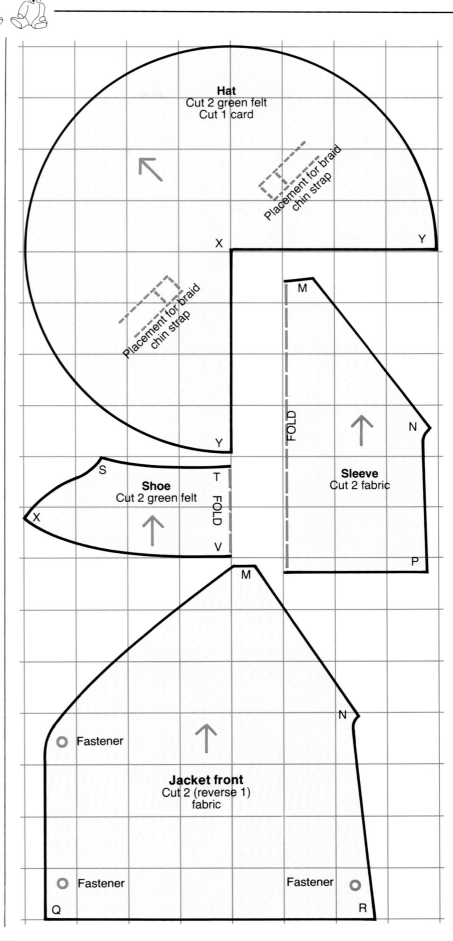

Hat
Cut 2 green felt
Cut 1 card

Placement for braid chin strap

Placement for braid chin strap

X   Y

Y

Sleeve
Cut 2 fabric

M

FOLD

N

P

Shoe
Cut 2 green felt

S   T

X

FOLD

V

Waist   J

Trousers
Cut 2 fabric

Centre seam

FOLD

K

FOLD

L

M

Jacket back
Cut 1 fabric

FOLD

N

R

Shoe sole
Cut 2
green felt

V   X

M

Jacket front
Cut 2 (reverse 1)
fabric

○ Fastener

N

○ Fastener   Fastener ○

Q   R

Actual height of doll: 34cm (13½in)

Using red embroidery thread, make two small stitches in a 'V' shape for the mouth. Cut two circles out of black felt for the eyes and sew into position on the face with a few small stitches.

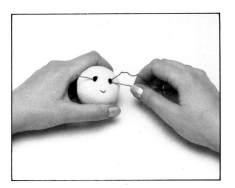

Sew the two body pieces together, leaving the bottom straight edge open. Turn the body the right way out and fill with stuffing. Turning the raw edges in, close the base of the body. Place the body to one side.

Join the short edges of the leg pieces to each shoe across the top. Fold the leg and shoe in half lengthwise and sew from the top of the leg to the bottom of the shoe, leaving the base open. Open out the base of the shoes and carefully sew in the shoe soles.

MATERIALS

Striped jersey fabric
Small pieces of pink stockinette
Black felt for shoes and eyes
Blue denim fabric for trousers
64cm (26in) curly mohair for hair
Red ribbon
Red embroidery thread
Elastic
Filling

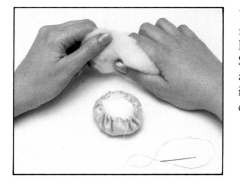

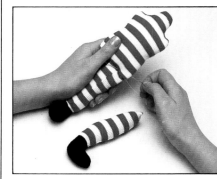

Turn the legs the right way out and stuff, ensuring that a good firm shape is maintained. Turn in the raw edges at the top of each leg. Keeping the seam at the centre, close the gap with a ladder stitch. Then oversew the tops of the legs to the base of the body using strong thread.

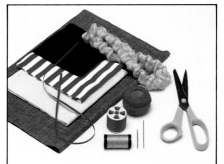

Using double layer fabric, sew a running stitch all the way around the head circle and begin to pull tight. Stuff the centre of the head as you are pulling the thread until the head is full and firm. Oversew and finish off firmly.

Fold the sleeve pieces in half lengthwise and sew from the bottom of the raw edge all the way around the top, rounding off the corners. Turn up a small hem and then place to one side. Fold the arm pieces in half lengthwise and sew around them, leaving the top straight edge open. Turn the arms the right way out and fill softly with stuffing.

Place the arm against the wrong side of the completed sleeve so the top edges are level. Oversew through all thicknesses, then pull the sleeves over the arms. Hold the completed arms against the body sides and sew into place at shoulder level. Place the head against the neck of the body, adjust the position and then ladder stitch firmly into place.

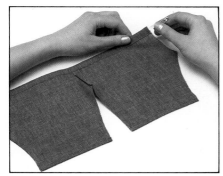

Take two lengths of mohair about 32cm (13in) long. Place one centrally across the top of the head. Starting at the centre forehead, back stitch the mohair firmly to the head. Add the second length of mohair at the back of the head and sew into place. Gather the hair at either side of the head and sew firmly onto the neck. Plait or braid the hair and add ribbons.

For the trousers, place the two pieces right sides together and sew seam A-B on one side only. Open out the two sides with the wrong side facing up. Turn up a small double hem on each leg. Turn down a double hem at the top edge to make a casing. Thread a piece of elastic through the casing so that it protrudes slightly on either side.

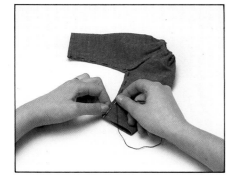

On one side, sew through the casing and elastic to hold in place. Pull the free end of elastic to gather the waist slightly and secure at the edge with a few stitches. Fold the trousers in half again and, with right sides together, sew the back seam A-B. Fold again so that the seams A-B meet in the middle. Sew seam C-B-C, then turn the trousers the right way out.

Fold the straps in half lengthwise. Fold the raw edges inside and sew along this edge. Sew the straps into position at the front and back of the trousers. Place the trousers on the doll, then turn up the bottoms of the legs twice.

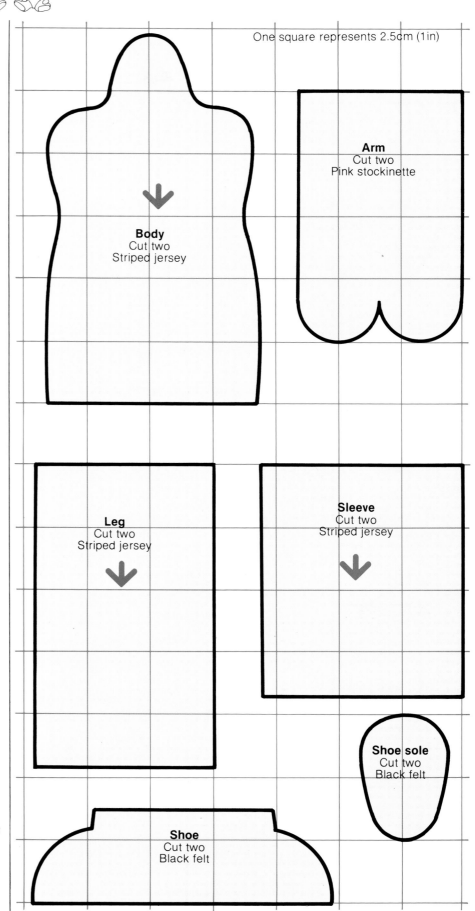

One square represents 2.5cm (1in)

Body
Cut two
Striped jersey

Arm
Cut two
Pink stockinette

Leg
Cut two
Striped jersey

Sleeve
Cut two
Striped jersey

Shoe sole
Cut two
Black felt

Shoe
Cut two
Black felt

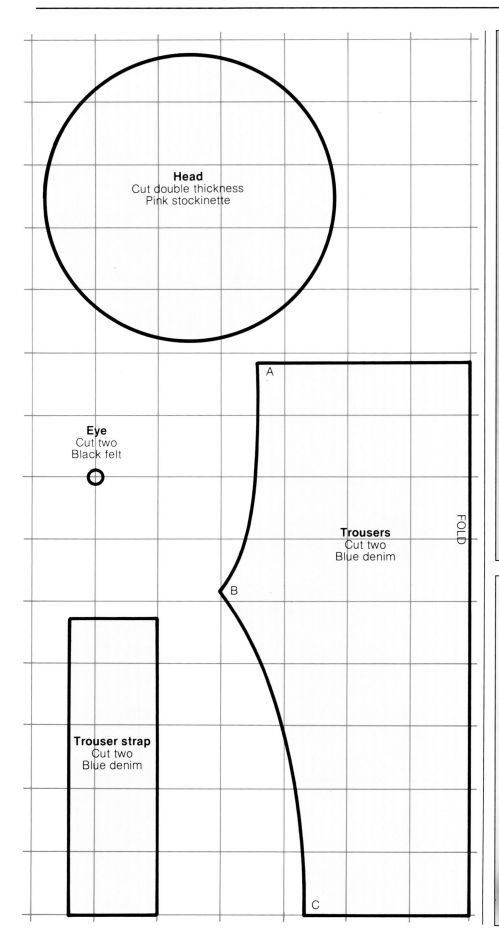

Head
Cut double thickness
Pink stockinette

Eye
Cut two
Black felt

A

Trousers
Cut two
Blue denim

FOLD

B

Trouser strap
Cut two
Blue denim

C

MATERIALS: *Body – 40cm × 90cm (16in × 36in) pink calico; 18cm × 18cm (7in × 7in) lightweight stretch; interfacing; 18cm ×18cm (7in × 7in) tracing paper; 30cm × 6cm (12in × 2in) wide lace for socks; 23cm × 23cm (9in × 9in) blue felt; 50g (1½oz) ball brown 4-ply knitting yarn; 16cm (6in) brown narrow tape; blue, black, white, brown and pink stranded embroidery threads; pink and light brown crayons; 5cm × 7cm (2in × 2¾in) stiff card; filling. Dress and pants – 50cm × 90cm (20in × 36in) fine print fabric; 220cm (87in) decorative pre-gathered lace; 140cm × 7mm (55in × ¼in) wide pink satin; ribbon; 100cm × 2.5cm (39in × 1in) wide pink satin ribbon; very narrow elastic and bodkin; 3 small press fasteners; 5 small buttons. Petticoat – 20cm × 74cm (8in × 29in) white fabric; narrow white bias binding; 120cm (47in) pre-gathered white lace; 2 small press fasteners; sewing threads to match all fabrics and yarn*

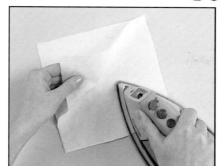

Cut 15cm (6in) of 6cm (2in) wide lace for each sock. Place wrong side of lace to right side of leg and baste lace to fabric around raw edges. Stitch upper edge of lace across legs on broken lines. Trim lace to curved edges of front legs H–G–E.

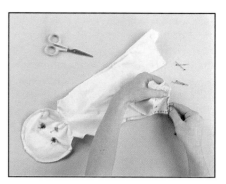

Cut out all pattern pieces. Arrows indicate straight of fabric. Before cutting front head press interfacing to wrong side of calico with a warm iron. Also cut from print fabric, dress skirt 21cm × 70cm (8in × 28in) and from white fabric, petticoat skirt 19cm × 60cm (7in × 24in).

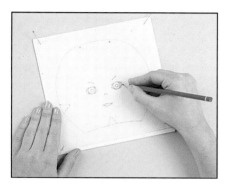

Stitch shoes to legs matching H–G–E–J–H. Stitch the short edges of the shoes together H–L. Stitch shoe soles into shoes K–Z. Stitch inside leg seams H–C–H.

Trace front head features and place tracing onto front head fabric. To mark features onto fabric, prick through paper with a sharp pencil point and lightly draw the outlines or use dressmakers' carbon.

Turn body through to right side, easing out legs and head. Press fabric if necessary. Fill head with stuffing, moulding it into cheeks and chin. Complete filling body and legs leaving a gap in stuffing at top of legs to allow them to bend.

Embroider features with two strands of embroidery thread. Use satin stitch for blue eye and black centre. Brown stem stitches outline eyes and form eyebrows. Two tiny white straight stitches make a highlight in eye centres and two longer white stitches in a V-shape mark outer eyes.

Ladder stitch open edges together to enclose filling. Machine stitch around shoe straps close to edges. Sew straps around upper edges of shoes with ends to side seam of body. Sew button to overlapped ends.

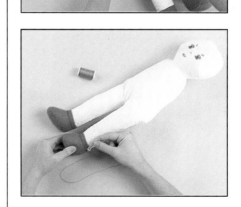

Work the mouth and nose in pink stem stitches. Lightly rub pink crayon onto fabric to colour cheeks and above nose. Colour inside mouth pink. Mark brown crayon dots for freckles. Cut out front head, stitch darts and clip open. Stitch back heads together A–U–B.

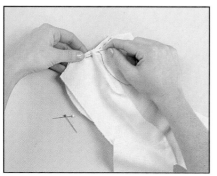

Stitch darts in inner arms, remembering to reverse one arm. Stitch arms together in pairs leaving open P–Q–N. Turn through to right side easing seam around hand. Fill arm lightly with stuffing.

Stitch back bodies together B–C, leaving open between dots. Stitch back head to back body D–B–D. Stitch front head to front body D–D. Stitch front head and body to back head and body, around side seams and head, E–F–D–A–D–F–E leaving open lower edges of legs and inside leg seams H–C–H.

Fold upper arm at Q and inner arm at Q bringing together P–N, turn in raw edges and oversew together. To mark fingers and thumb, stab stitch through fabric and filling on broken lines, taking needle vertically through arm.

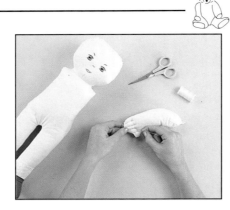

Firmly sew arms, with thumbs to front, to body side seams between dots.

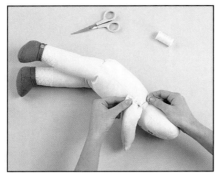

For the hair fringe, cut a piece of stiff card 5cm × 7.5cm (2in × 3in). Wind 22 strands of yarn around longer measurement. Hold short edge of card to centre seam of head with yarn to front. Sew folds of loops to fabric before sliding them off card.

Cut remaining yarn into strands 74cm (29in) long. Turn under the ends of brown tape to neaten. Stitch centre of strands to tape to form a centre parting. Place one end of tape onto front head at M and other end to the back head seam at U.

Sew tape to head. Gather yarn into two bunches at front of head and sew with brown yarn to sides of head at triangles. Trim hair.

Stitch narrow hems at leg edges of pants S–S. Stitch decorative lace to right side of legs over hem stitches. Cut 15cm (6in) elastic for each leg. On wrong side place one end of elastic to edge of pant piece at placement line. Stitch through elastic stretching it as it is stitched.

Stitch both pant pieces together at one centre seam only O–R. Press a 13mm (½in) double hem to wrong side at upper edge. Stitch both edges of hem to form a channel for the elastic.

Thread through elastic, sew one end to secure and pull up to fit doll's waist. Sew other end to fabric and cut off excess. Stitch remaining centre seam O–R and inside leg seam S–R–S.

To trim dress front bodice, cut 8cm (3in) of decorative lace and 8cm (3in) of 2.5cm (1in) wide ribbon. Stitch ribbon across lower edge of panel with the lace above it.

Cut and baste decorative lace around panel, folding the corners and covering raw edges of the first ribbon and lace. Stitch in place.

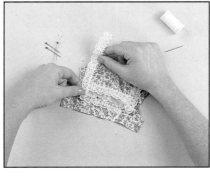

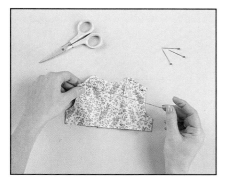

Stitch front bodice to back bodices at shoulders V–X. Stitch narrow hems to wrong side at centre backs. With wrong sides facing press dress neck binding along centre length, fold in raw edges to centre and press.

Stitch narrow 6cm (2in) long hems at waist ends of both short sides of skirt for centre back opening. Sew a line of long running stitches close to raw edge of long side to gather it, pull up skirt to fit lower edge of bodice.

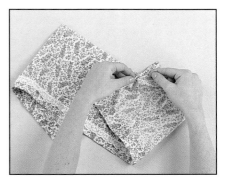

With right sides facing and raw edges even, place binding around neck edge. Stitch along fold nearest to edge. Fold binding to wrong side, turn in ends to neaten and hem binding to previous stitches.

With right sides facing and gathers evenly spaced, stitch skirt to bodice. Neaten seam and press to bodice. Lap right over left at centre back and sew on press fasteners. Sew buttons on right half of bodice on top.

Hem lower edge of sleeves T–T. Stitch decorative lace to right side over hem stitches and 13cm (5in) elastic to wrong side on broken lines in the same way as for the pants.

Stitch petticoat bodice front to backs at shoulders. Hem centre backs. Bind neck and arm holes with bias binding. Stitch a narrow hem at lower edge of skirt.

Sew a line of long running stitches to gather the top of sleeves between dots. Pull up gathers to fit and stitch sleeves into bodice arm holes W–X–W. Stitch under arm and bodice seams T–W–Y.

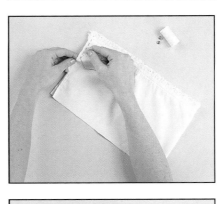

Stitch one length of gathered lace to hem edge and a second length to right side above hem. Complete skirt and bodice in the same way as the dress, omitting sleeves and using two press fasteners to close bodice back.

Press 4cm (1⅝in) to wrong side of one long edge of skirt, turn under 1cm (⅜in) and stitch hem. On right side stitch a band of 7mm (¼in) ribbon just below hem stitches with decorative lace above it.

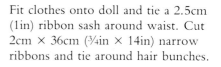

Fit clothes onto doll and tie a 2.5cm (1in) ribbon sash around waist. Cut 2cm × 36cm (¾in × 14in) narrow ribbons and tie around hair bunches.

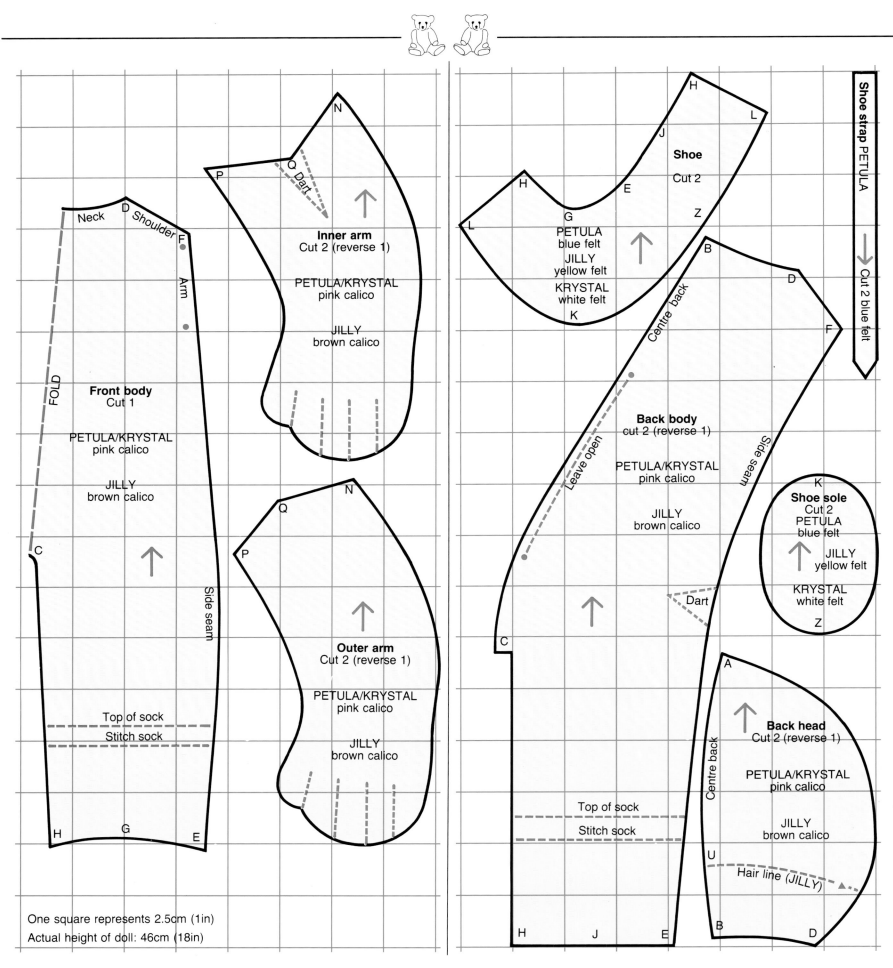

Shoe strap PETULA
↓ Cut 2 blue felt

Inner arm
Cut 2 (reverse 1)

PETULA/KRYSTAL
pink calico

JILLY
brown calico

Shoe
Cut 2

PETULA
blue felt

JILLY
yellow felt

KRYSTAL
white felt

Centre back

Leave open

Side seam

Back body
cut 2 (reverse 1)

PETULA/KRYSTAL
pink calico

JILLY
brown calico

Dart

Shoe sole
Cut 2
PETULA
blue felt

JILLY
yellow felt

KRYSTAL
white felt

Neck   Shoulder
Arm

Front body
Cut 1

PETULA/KRYSTAL
pink calico

JILLY
brown calico

FOLD

Side seam

Top of sock

Stitch sock

Q Dart

Outer arm
Cut 2 (reverse 1)

PETULA/KRYSTAL
pink calico

JILLY
brown calico

Top of sock

Stitch sock

Centre back

Back head
Cut 2 (reverse 1)

PETULA/KRYSTAL
pink calico

JILLY
brown calico

Hair line (JILLY)

One square represents 2.5cm (1in)

Actual height of doll: 46cm (18in)

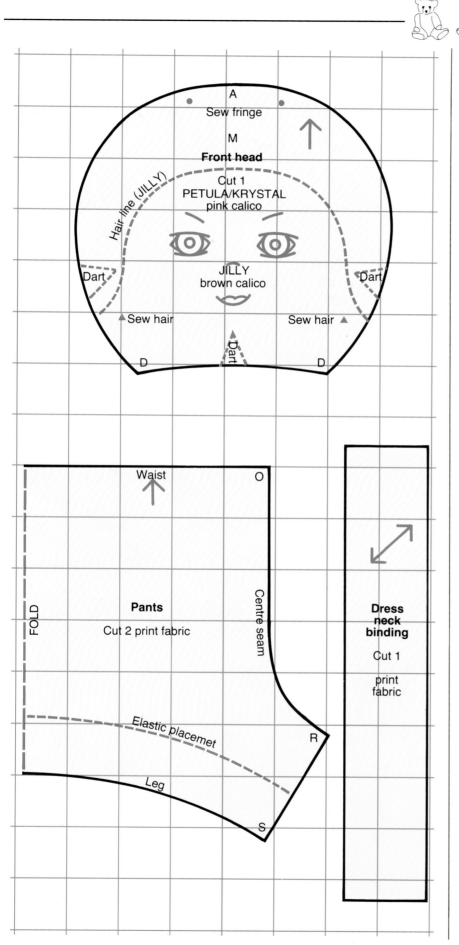

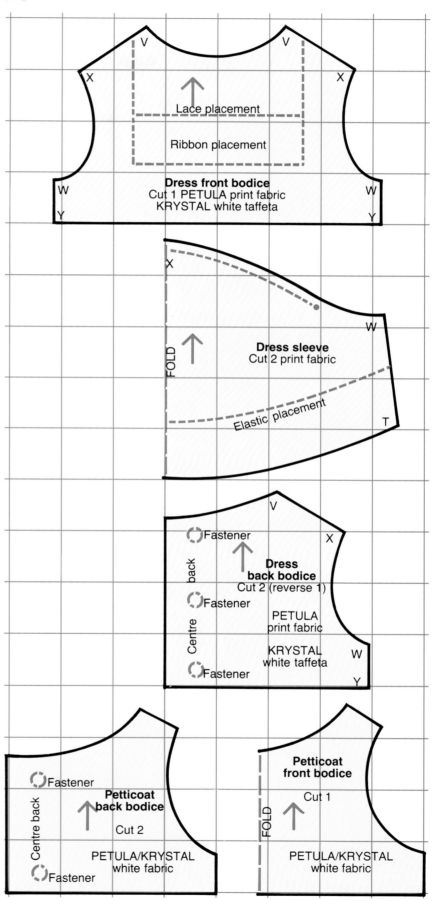

Front head

Cut 1
PETULA/KRYSTAL
pink calico

A

Sew fringe

M

Hair line (JILLY)

Dart

JILLY
brown calico

Dart

Dart

Sew hair

Sew hair

D

D

Waist

O

FOLD

Pants

Cut 2 print fabric

Centre seam

Elastic placemet

R

Leg

S

Dress neck binding

Cut 1

print fabric

V

V

X

X

Lace placement

Ribbon placement

W

W

Y

Y

Dress front bodice
Cut 1 PETULA print fabric
KRYSTAL white taffeta

X

W

FOLD

Dress sleeve
Cut 2 print fabric

Elastic placement

T

V

Fastener

X

Centre back

Fastener

Dress back bodice
Cut 2 (reverse 1)

PETULA
print fabric

KRYSTAL
white taffeta

W

Y

Fastener

Fastener

Petticoat back bodice

Centre back

Cut 2

PETULA/KRYSTAL
white fabric

Fastener

Petticoat front bodice

Cut 1

FOLD

PETULA/KRYSTAL
white fabric

71

Cut out all pieces. **Note:** Omit shoe strap – this is for Petula only.

Follow steps 2–12 of the Petula instructions using light brown stranded thread in place of blue thread for the eyes and omitting lace socks. Sew white cord around shoe sole with joins at shoe seam. Sew cord bows to front of shoes.

Cut yarn into 75cm (30in) lengths. Make a light pencil mark around head on hair placement line. Keep 20 strands for curls. Place strands to head with centre of each on hair line. One end of yarn will cover face as you sew.

MATERIALS: *Body – 40cm × 90cm (16in × 36in) brown calico; 18cm × 18cm (7in × 7in) lightweight interfacing; 18cm × 18cm (7in × 7in) tracing paper; 23cm × 23cm (9in × 9in) yellow felt; 80cm (31in) white cord braid; 50g (1½oz) ball brown 4-ply knitting yarn; 50cm (20in) narrow striped ribbon; light brown, dark brown, black, white and red stranded embroidery threads; red crayon; filling. Track suit – 40cm × 100cm (16in × 39in) blue fleecy fabric; 100cm × 7mm (39in × ¼in) wide white ribbon; 100cm (39in) narrow yellow cord braid; narrow elastic and bodkin; 13cm (5in) white nylon press and fix fastening (Velcro); small motif. Vest – 18cm × 40cm (7in × 16in) yellow stretch fabric; 60cm × 2.5cm (24in × 1in) wide blue bias binding; 3 small press fasteners; sewing threads to match all fabrics and the yarn*

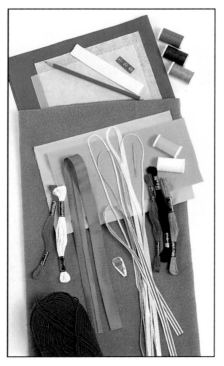

Continue sewing strands around back of head on placement line, leaving no gaps. Hold doll upside-down, smooth and gather strands into a pony tail hair style and tie close to head with yarn. Wind each of the 20 strands around two fingers to form loops.

Sew centre of loops around front hair line. Trim pony tail and tie with striped ribbon.

Cut 2 × 32cm (13in) lengths of white ribbon and place on fold lines of trousers. Stitch both edges of ribbon. Cut and stitch yellow braid to centre of ribbon. Stitch trouser pieces together at one centre seam only, O–R. Machine, using zig-zag or overlock stitch, raw edges at waist O–O and leg edges S–S to prevent fraying.

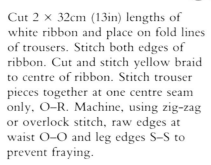

Sew long running stitches around sleeve head between dots.

Fold and stitch 1.5cm (⅝in) single hem to wrong side at waist and ankles to form channels for elastic.

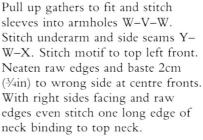

Pull up gathers to fit and stitch sleeves into armholes W–V–W. Stitch underarm and side seams Y–W–X. Stitch motif to top left front. Neaten raw edges and baste 2cm (¾in) to wrong side at centre fronts. With right sides facing and raw edges even stitch one long edge of neck binding to top neck.

Thread elastic and sew one end of each to fabric at ends of channels. Pull up elastic to fit waist and ankles, sew other end of each to secure and cut off excess.

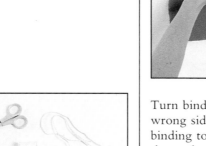

Turn binding over raw edges to wrong side. Turn in edges of binding to neaten, and slip stitch short edges together and long edge over previous stitches.

Stitch remaining centre seam O–R, including elastic. Stitch inside leg seams S–R–S. Turn trousers through to right side.

Stitch a channel at waist as for trousers. Thread through elastic and pull up to fit doll over the trousers. Machine stitch ends of elastic through fabric to secure.

Stitch track suit top fronts to top back at shoulders T–V. Stitch ribbon and braid to the centre of sleeves on fold line as for trousers. At wrist stitch a channel and thread elastic to fit as for waist and ankles.

Cut the press and fix fastening in half along its length and discard one half of each piece. On left front of track suit top stitch soft piece of fastening to outside of fabric, from below neck band to lower edge. Stitch corresponding fastening to inside of right front.

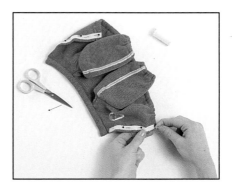

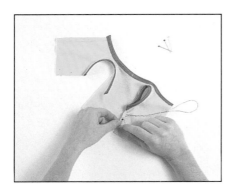

Stitch vest front to vest backs at shoulders. Stitch narrow hems to wrong side at centre backs. Bind neck and arm hole edges. Stitch side seams and a hem to wrong side at lower edge.

Sew three press fasteners, one at neck, one in centre and one at lower edge to close back. Fit cloths onto doll.

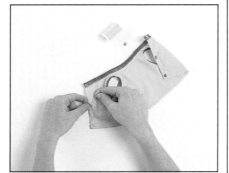

One square represents 2.5cm (1in)

Vest front
Cut 2
Yellow stretch fabric

Centre back

⭕ Fastener
⭕ Fastner

Vest back
Cut 1
yellow stretch fabric

FOLD

Actual height of doll: 46cm (18in)

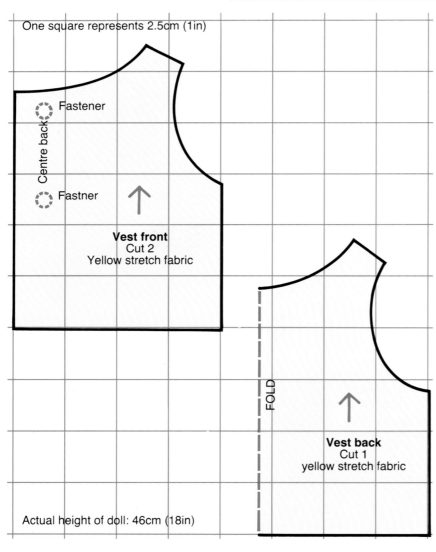

Waist   O

Centre seam

Track suit trousers
Cut 2
blue fleecy fabric

FOLD

R

S

Track suit neck band
Cut 1
blue fleecy fabric

W   Y

Track suit sleeve
Cut 2
blue fleecy fabric

FOLD

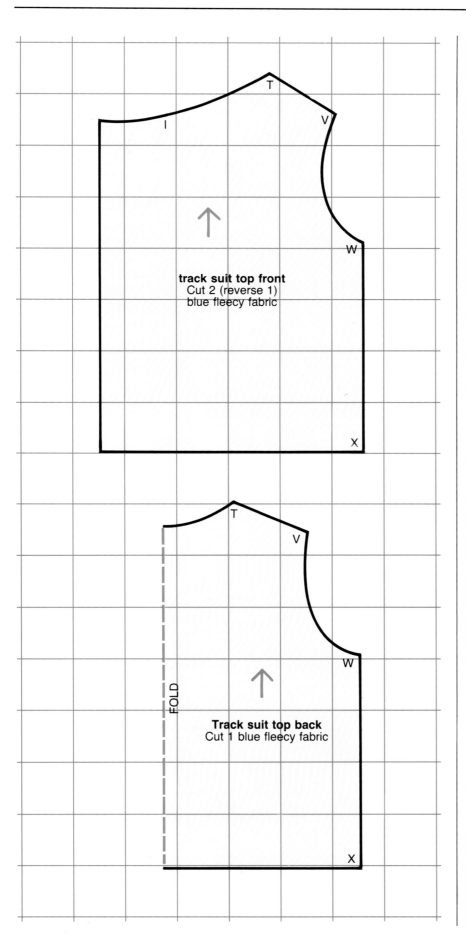

track suit top front
Cut 2 (reverse 1)
blue fleecy fabric

I

T

V

W

X

T

V

W

FOLD

Track suit top back
Cut 1 blue fleecy fabric

X

MATERIALS: 40cm × 80cm (16in × 31 in) pink calico; 20cm × 80cm (8in × 31in) red and white gingham fabric; 26cm × 42cm (10in × 17in) blue denim fabric; 20cm × 60cm (8in × 24in) fawn felt; 12cm × 32cm (5in × 13in) dark brown felt; 16cm × 40cm (6in × 16in) red felt; scrap of blue felt; 8cm × 25cm (3in × 10in) golden brown fur fabric (pile to stroke down shorter length); three small press fasteners; narrow elastic; bonding web; filling; matching and orange sewing threads; red crayon; red embroidery thread; 1m (1yd) piping cord

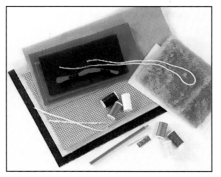

Cut out all parts. See step 12 before cutting hat brim. Stitch dart at neck on both bodies A–A. With right sides together stitch bodies leaving open lower edge B–B. Turn body through to right side and press. Fill head and neck firmly with stuffing, moulding to a good even shape. Fill body more softly. Turn under lower edges and sew together to enclose filling.

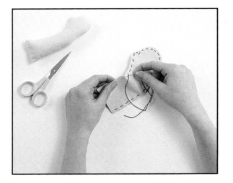

Stitch arms together in pairs leaving open C–D. Trim seam and snip fabric to dot at thumb, turn arm through to the right side and press. Fill softly with stuffing, turn in open edges and sew together.

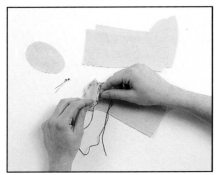

Stitch legs E–F and G–H and trim seams at foot. Baste foot soles to legs F–H and stitch in place. Turn legs to right side out and press. Fill feet firmly and the legs more softly with stuffing. Turn in raw edges and sew together.

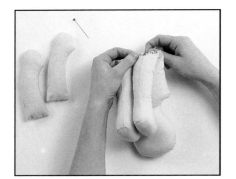

With feet facing forward pin straight edges of legs to lower edge of body and oversew in place.

Position and pin straight edges of arms onto shoulders with thumbs upwards and oversew firmly to body.

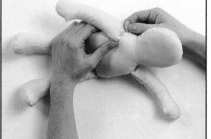

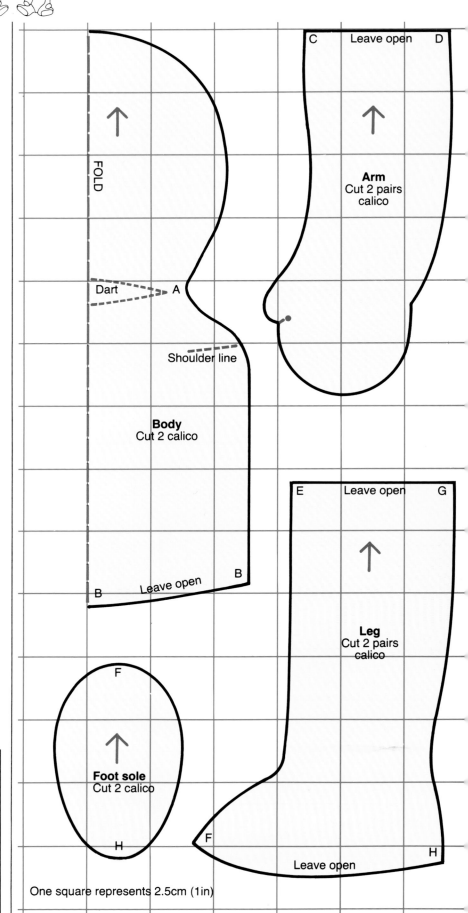

FOLD

Dart — A

Shoulder line

Body
Cut 2 calico

B — Leave open — B

C — Leave open — D

Arm
Cut 2 pairs calico

E — Leave open — G

Leg
Cut 2 pairs calico

F

H

Foot sole
Cut 2 calico

F

Leave open — H

One square represents 2.5cm (1in)

To make hair, with right sides facing oversew the two shorter edges together. Stroke fur towards one long edge, turn under this edge and slip stitch to wrong side. Sew running stitches along opposite edge to gather it. Pull up stitches as tightly as possible and secure thread. Turn hair to right side out and pull onto head bringing to a low hair line in front. Sew to head.

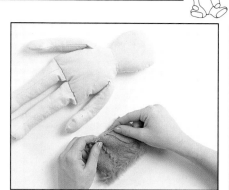

Lightly mark position for features onto face. From brown felt cut two circles for eyes and sew in place. Mark nose with red crayon. Embroider mouth with three straight red stitches.

Stitch shirt sleeves to shirt front and to shirt backs J–K. Turn under and stitch a narrow double hem at sleeve wrist edges L–L and at centre front edges M–N. Stitch underarm seams L–K and shirt fronts to back at side seams K–P. Stitch a double hem at lower edge N–P–P–N. Turn under neck edge M–J–J–M and stitch. Sew press fasteners to close centre fronts. Fit shirt onto doll.

With orange thread stitch two lines of machine stitches 6mm (¼in) apart on side fold of each jeans' piece. For pockets cut two pieces of denim 5cm x 5cm (2in × 2in). Press under edges and top stitch one edge in orange. With matching thread stitch centre front seam Q–R on one side only. Lay jeans right side upwards, position pockets and stitch three edges. Stitch felt patch to one knee.

Turn to wrong side a narrow double hem at lower legs S–S and stitch. Turn down and stitch a double hem at waist to form a casing. Thread through elastic and stitch it firmly at one end. Pull up elastic to fit doll's waist and stitch elastic to secure it.

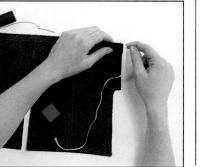

Stitch remaining seam Q–R and inside leg seams S–R–S. Fit jeans onto doll turning up lower legs.

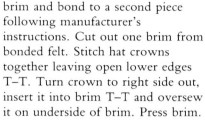

Cut an oversize piece of felt for hat brim and bond to a second piece following manufacturer's instructions. Cut out one brim from bonded felt. Stitch hat crowns together leaving open lower edges T–T. Turn crown to right side out, insert it into brim T–T and oversew it on underside of brim. Press brim.

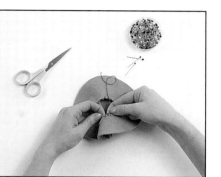

Cut a strip of dark brown felt 1.5cm x 23cm (⅝in × 9in) and sew around outside of crown as a hat band. Add filling to hat crown and place hat onto head with crown seams to sides and the crown covering centre of hair. Sew hat to head.

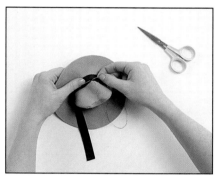

Stitch front seam of boots W–F. Turn seam to inside. With wrong sides facing baste boot sole to boot F–H–F and top stitch. Fit boots onto cowboy. Cut the scarf from blue felt and tie around the neck.

Stitch waistcoat fronts to back at shoulders V–X. Press seams. Machine a row of stitches just inside armhole edges Y–X–Y, through single felt. Stitch side seams Y–Z. Make a line of machine stitches just inside edges of fronts and back. Fold one end of cord into a small loop to fit hand, the other into a larger loop. Bind ends of cord with thread to secure. Sew lasso to hands.

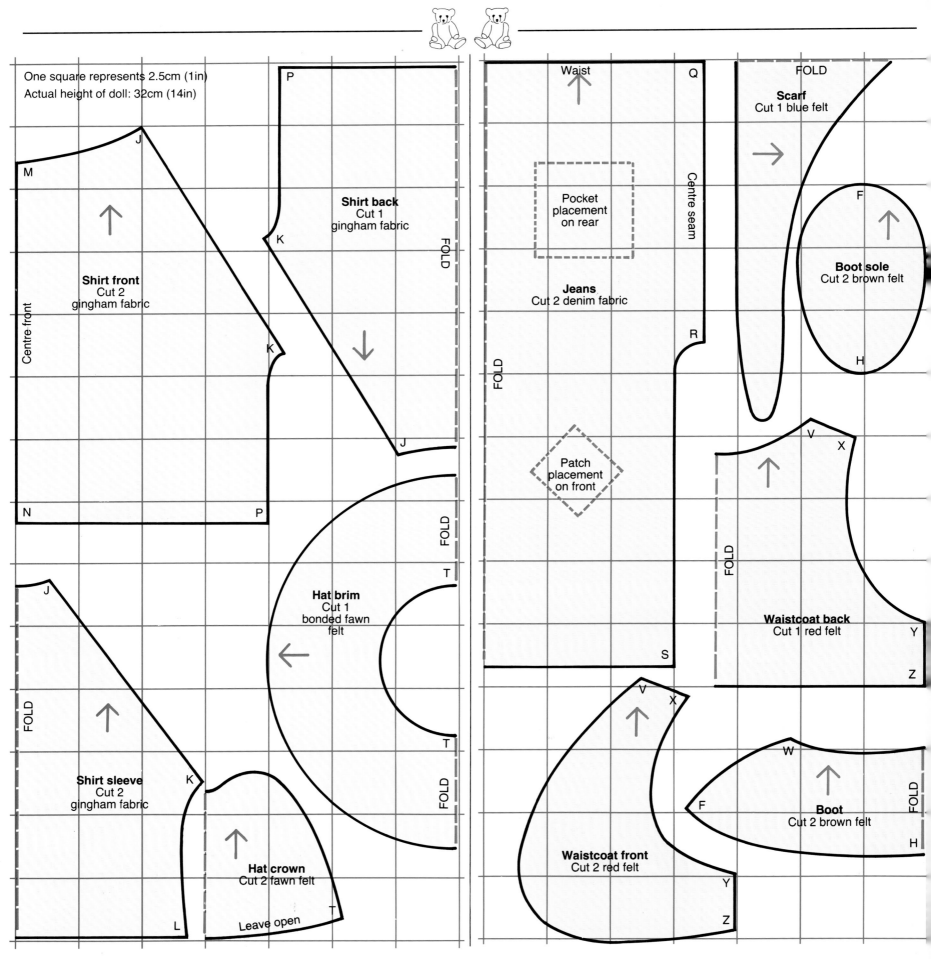

One square represents 2.5cm (1in)
Actual height of doll: 32cm (14in)

Shirt front
Cut 2
gingham fabric

Centre front

M

J

Shirt back
Cut 1
gingham fabric

P

K

K

J

FOLD

N P

Shirt sleeve
Cut 2
gingham fabric

FOLD

J

K

L

Hat crown
Cut 2 fawn felt

Leave open

T

Hat brim
Cut 1
bonded fawn
felt

T

FOLD

FOLD

FOLD

Waist

Q

Pocket
placement
on rear

Centre seam

Jeans
Cut 2 denim fabric

FOLD

R

Patch
placement
on front

S

FOLD

Scarf
Cut 1 blue felt

F

Boot sole
Cut 2 brown felt

H

V X

Waistcoat back
Cut 1 red felt

FOLD

Y

Z

V X

FOLD

W

Boot
Cut 2 brown felt

F

FOLD

H

Waistcoat front
Cut 2 red felt

Y

Z

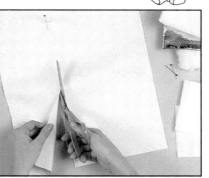

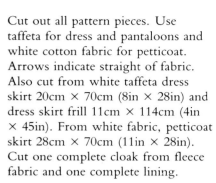

Cut out all pattern pieces. Use taffeta for dress and pantaloons and white cotton fabric for petticoat. Arrows indicate straight of fabric. Also cut from white taffeta dress skirt 20cm × 70cm (8in × 28in) and dress skirt frill 11cm × 114cm (4in × 45in). From white fabric, petticoat skirt 28cm × 70cm (11in × 28in). Cut one complete cloak from fleece fabric and one complete lining.

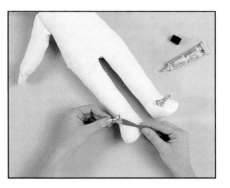

Follow steps 2–12 of the Petula instructions using pale blue stranded thread for the eye. Tie small silver ribbon bows and sew to front of shoes.

The hair is made in same way as Petula but do not tie it into two bunches. To hold hair to head use a needle and yarn to make a stitch at one side seam of head on triangle, take yarn across all hair and make a second stitch on centre back seam at U. Pull yarn to bring hair close to head. Repeat for remaining hair.

MATERIALS: Body – 40cm × 90cm (16in × 36in) pink calico; 18cm × 18cm (7in × 7in) lightweight stretch interfacing; 18cm × 18cm (7in × 7in) tracing paper; 23cm × 23cm (9in × 9in) white felt; 60cm × 1cm (24in × ³⁄₈in) wide silver ribbon; 50g (1½oz) ball cream 4-ply knitting yarn; 16cm (6in) cream tape; pale blue, black, white, light brown and pale pink stranded embroidery silks; pale pink crayon; 95cm (37in) small pearl type beads; 5cm × 7cm (2in × 2¾in) stiff card; clear drying craft glue; filling. Dress and pantaloons – 70cm × 114cm (28in × 45in) white taffeta fabric; 220cm (87in) narrow lace; 260cm (102in) silver braid; 150cm × 24mm (59in × ⅞in) wide white ribbon; very narrow elastic and bodkin; 3 small press fasteners; 3 small buttons. Petticoat – 30cm × 90cm (12in × 36in) white cotton fabric; 140cm (55in) narrow lace; narrow white bias binding; 2 small press fasteners. Cloak – 20cm × 100cm (8in × 39in) white fleece fabric; 20cm × 100cm (8in × 39in) silver lining fabric; 6cm × 140cm (2in × 55in) short pile white fur fabric (cut across width of fabric); 100cm × 13mm (39in × ½in) white ribbon; sewing threads to match all fabrics and yarn

Make several stitches across hair. Cut three lengths of pearl beads each 25cm (10in) long, hold ends together and tie with thread. Twist strands and sew ends to head under front hair line. Secure beads around head with stitches taken through head.

Follow Petula steps 16–18 noting that pantaloons for Krystal have long legs and lace is straight. Follow Petula steps 21 and 22. Stitch lace around neck with silver braid above it.

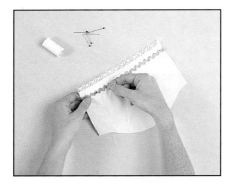

To form a channel for wrist elastic, fold a 2cm (¾in) hem to wrong side of sleeve T–T. Turn under raw edge and stitch hem. On right side stitch one length of lace to edge of sleeve and a second length on hem stitches, taking care not to block channel. Stitch silver braid across sleeve above lace.

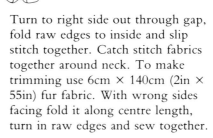

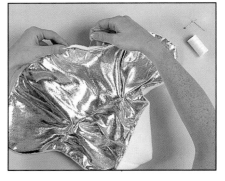

Turn to right side out through gap, fold raw edges to inside and slip stitch together. Catch stitch fabrics together around neck. To make trimming use 6cm × 140cm (2in × 55in) fur fabric. With wrong sides facing fold it along centre length, turn in raw edges and sew together.

Thread elastic and sew one end to fabric, pull up to fit wrist and secure other end. Trim excess elastic. Sew a line of long running stitches to gather top of sleeves between dots. Pull up gathers to fit and stitch sleeves into arm holes W–X–W. Stitch underarm and bodice seams T–W–Y.

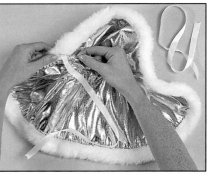

Beginning at lower centre back, sew fur trimming to fleece around cloak and hood, keeping fur edges to fabric. To join ends of trimming, open them out and sew both pieces together across width, refold and sew in place. Cut 1cm (⅜in) wide ribbon into two pieces and sew at M on neck seams. Fit clothes onto doll and tie 2.5cm (1in) ribbon sash around waist.

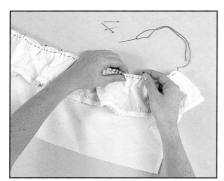

Stitch a narrow hem to one long edge of skirt frill. On right side stitch straight edge of lace over hem stitches, and silver braid above lace. Sew long running stitches to gather opposite long edge of frill. Pull up stitches and with right sides together and raw edges even sew frill to one long edge of skirt.

Press seam to skirt and sew silver braid to right side over seam. Refer to Petula steps 26 and 27. Sew end of remaining 20cm (8in) pearl beads to each end of neck band. Follow Petula steps 28 and 29 noting that petticoat skirt is longer and only one length of straight lace is stitched to right side of hem.

Using white fleece stitch cloak fronts to cloak back AA–BB. Stitch darts at hood neck. Stitch hood seam CC–DD. Stitch hood to cloak neck M–M matching dots at centre back. Make up lining in same way. With right sides facing stitch cloak and hood to lining around all edges leaving a gap open at lower back between triangles.

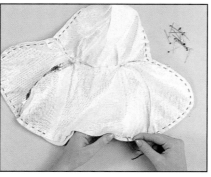

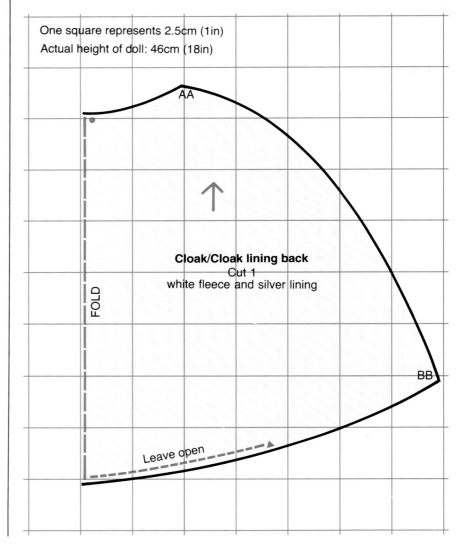

One square represents 2.5cm (1in)
Actual height of doll: 46cm (18in)

AA

FOLD

Cloak/Cloak lining back
Cut 1
white fleece and silver lining

BB

Leave open

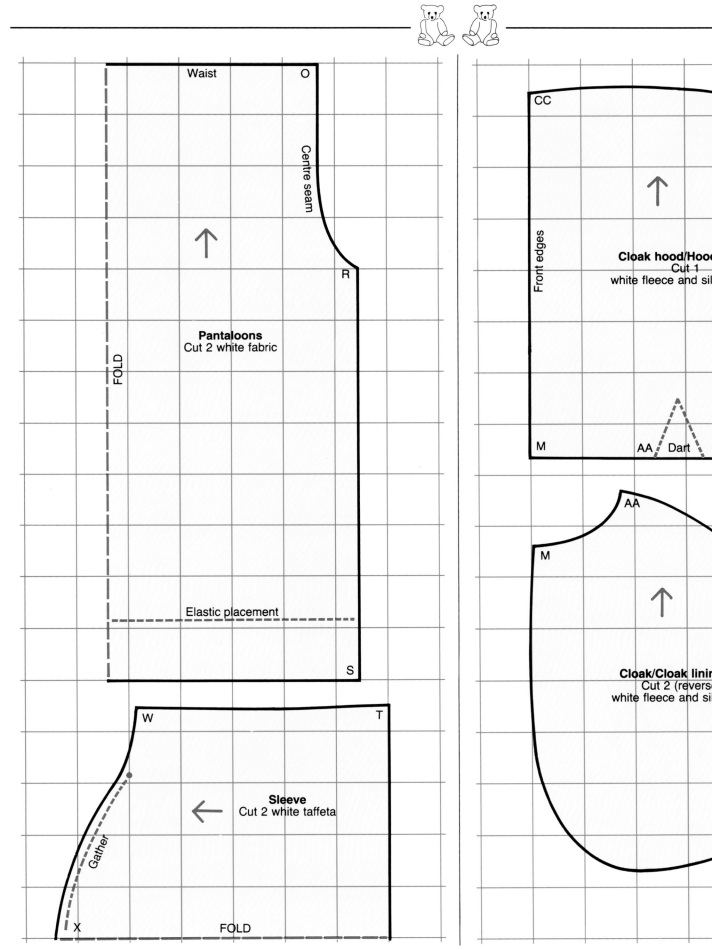

Pantaloons
Cut 2 white fabric

Waist O

Centre seam

R

FOLD

Elastic placement

S

Sleeve
Cut 2 white taffeta

W   T

Gather

X   FOLD

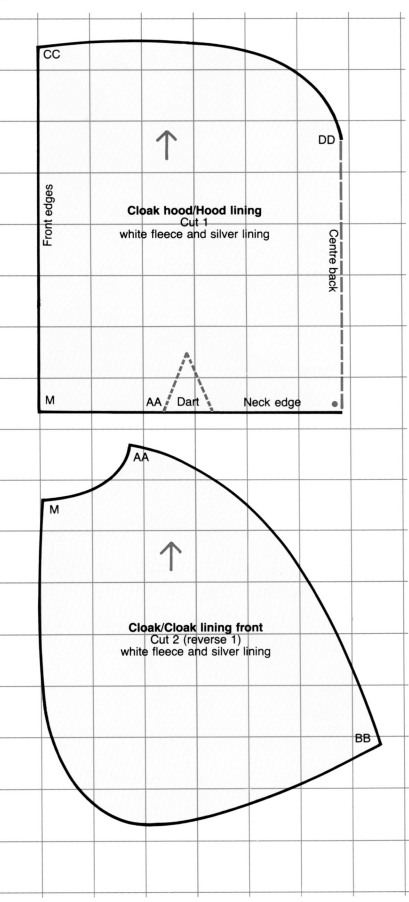

CC

Front edges

Cloak hood/Hood lining
Cut 1
white fleece and silver lining

DD

Centre back

M   AA   Dart   Neck edge

AA

M

Cloak/Cloak lining front
Cut 2 (reverse 1)
white fleece and silver lining

BB

MATERIALS: 30cm × 68cm (12in × 27in) double thickness pink stockinette; 40cm × 114cm (16in × 45in) green spotted fabric; 40cm × 96cm (16in × 38in) blue spotted fabric; 20cm × 90cm (8in × 36in) yellow fabric; 30cm × 30cm (12in × 12in) red felt; scraps of white, blue and black felts; 70cm (28in) red ric-rac braid; red and black stranded embroidery threads; black soft embroidery thread; matching sewing threads; narrow elastic and bodkin; double knitting yarn; filling; clear drying craft glue

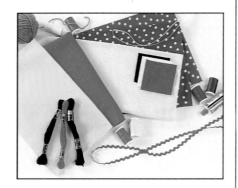

Cut all pieces from patterns. From stockinette cut two legs 20cm × 11cm (8in × 4in) and two arms 17cm × 9cm (7in × 3½in), with most stretch across shorter measurements. From yellow fabric cut one ruff 70cm × 16cm (28in × 6in) and one circle of 6cm (2⅜in) diameter.

On right side of body stockinette mark a light pencil line to indicate neck gathers. Stitch together edges A–B, to form a tube. Turn body to right side out. Sew a line of long running stitches on pencil line but do not pull up stitches.

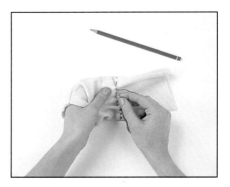

Fill head with stuffing until it has a circumference of 23cm (9in). To give a good shape to head, mould filling into a ball in your hands before placing in head. Sew a line of running stitches to gather top of head. Pull up stitches until stockinette is tightly bunched, oversew across gathers and secure thread. Add a little filling to neck.

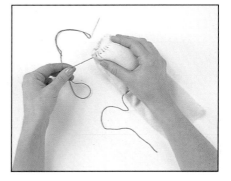

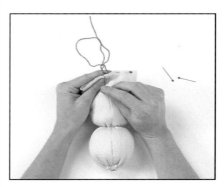

Pull up running stitches until the neck measures 10cm (4in) in circumference, take several stitches through neck and fasten thread. Fill body. Fold lower edge of body matching B and C; the seam will be at centre back of doll. Turn in raw edges and oversew together.

Fold a leg along length. Stitch long edge and one short edge. Turn leg to right side out and fill lightly with stuffing. Sew long running stitches around open edge. Pull up stitches to tightly gather fabric and fasten thread.

Flatten leg in centre of length and by hand make a line of stab stitches across leg through the fabric and filling to make leg bend. Make second leg.

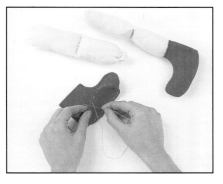

Stitch boots together in pairs D–E and F–G. Stitch boot soles into boots E–G. Turn boots to right side out and fill with stuffing. Insert gathered end of leg into boot and sew top of boot to leg. Check that the second boot and leg are made to the same length as first one.

Glue the white outer eyes in place with the blue inner eyes and black eye centres on top of them. With a pencil lightly mark curved mouth and embroider with two strands of red embroidery thread. Glue red cheek circles at the ends of mouth.

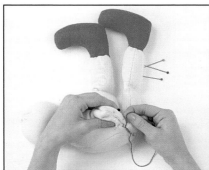

Place legs to lower edge of body with fronts facing and leg seams meeting at body centre C. Firmly oversew legs to body.

Sew features in place with stitches taken from back of head, under hat edge through head and felt features. Then take needle back through felt part and head and fasten thread at back head. A small straight black stitch at centre top of blue inner eye will add to clown's expression. Stitch back hat hem to head.

Stitch a 2.5cm (1in) hem to wrong side of hat H–H. Fold hat matching H and H and stitch seam J–H. Turn to right side out. Sew running stitches around edge of yellow fabric circle. Add filling to centre of circle and pull up stitches, shape it into a ball and secure thread.

Stitch hems to wrong side at suit legs K–K. Stitch blue suit piece to green suit piece at centre front L–M and at centre back L–M. Stitch inside leg seams K–M–K. Turn suit to right side out and fit onto doll. Turn under neck edge and sew a line of running stitches around folded edge to gather it.

Sew bobble to front of hat point. Fill hat lightly with stuffing and fit onto head with lower back seam edge almost at centre back neck gathers. Stitch hat hem to head at front.

Pull up stitches and sew gathers to doll's neck, checking that suit centre seams at L are central to body. Sew running stitches on broken lines to gather lower edge of each leg. Sew gathers to top of boots. Work a black cross stitch in centre of each red felt button using black soft embroidery thread. Sew 'buttons' to suit front centre seam.

For the hair, wind 10 strands of yarn around two fingers and sew them together at one place. Cut yarn ends close to these stitches. Make twelve bunches of yarn and sew six to each side of face at hat hem.

Make up stockinette arms as for legs. Stitch hands together in pairs leaving open straight edges N–P. Turn to right side out. On broken lines top stitch finger markings. Place a little filling into palm of hands. Insert gathered ends of arms into hands N–P and sew in place.

Stitch a 1cm (⅜in) hem at one edge of a sleeve N–N. Stitch edges of sleeve together Q–N and turn sleeve to right side out. Turn seam allowance on remaining edge Q–Q to wrong side and sew a line of long running stitches around this folded edge to gather it.

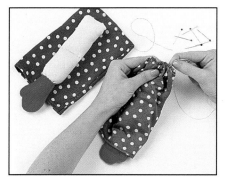

Fit arm into sleeve with gathers to the shoulder. Pull up running stitches gathering sleeve to fit upper edge of arm. Arrange sleeve gathers evenly around arm, with sleeve seam to the side of arm. Sew gathers to arm covering all the pink stockinette.

Sew running stitches on broken lines to gather sleeve at wrist, pull up stitches and sew gathers to hand. Make second sleeve. Join arms to body, with thumbs to the front, just below suit neck gathers Q–Q. Firmly oversew tops of arms through suit to body.

With right sides facing fold ruff along centre length. Stitch together long edges. Turn ruff through to right side out. Press with seam to one edge. Top stitch 1cm (⅜in) from this edge to form a channel. Stitch ric-rac braid to right side of folded edge. Thread elastic through channel and sew one end to secure it.

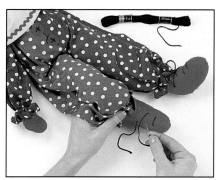

Pull up gathers to fit clown's neck and sew elastic with thread to fasten. Trim excess. Stitch short ends of ruff together. Fit ruff onto doll with seam at centre back. With black soft embroidery thread and a long needle, thread 'laces' through boots. Knot threads and tie in a firm bow to prevent them being pulled out.

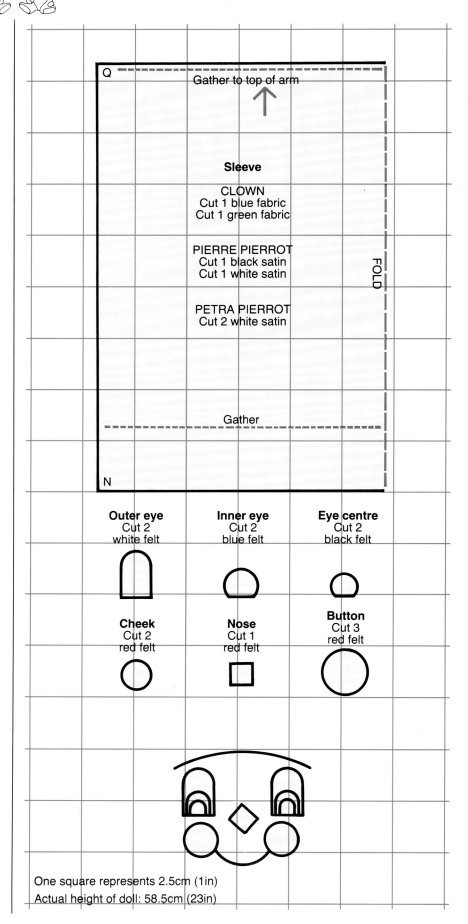

Q
Gather to top of arm

Sleeve

CLOWN
Cut 1 blue fabric
Cut 1 green fabric

PIERRE PIERROT
Cut 1 black satin
Cut 1 white satin

PETRA PIERROT
Cut 2 white satin

FOLD

Gather

N

Outer eye Cut 2 white felt	**Inner eye** Cut 2 blue felt	**Eye centre** Cut 2 black felt
Cheek Cut 2 red felt	**Nose** Cut 1 red felt	**Button** Cut 3 red felt

One square represents 2.5cm (1in)
Actual height of doll: 58.5cm (23in)

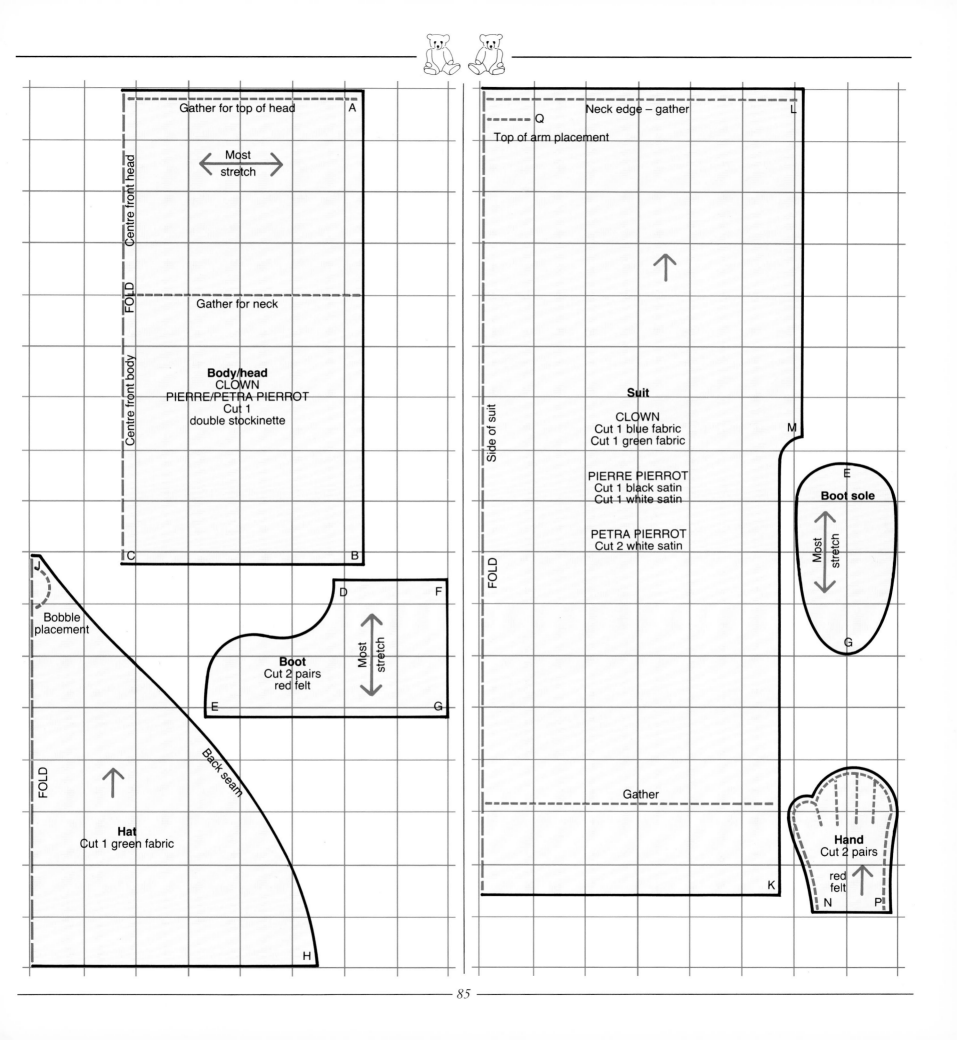

Gather for top of head   A

← Most stretch →

Centre front head

FOLD

Gather for neck

Centre front body

Body/head
CLOWN
PIERRE/PETRA PIERROT
Cut 1
double stockinette

C   B

J

Bobble placement

D   F

Boot
Cut 2 pairs
red felt

Most stretch

E   G

Back seam

FOLD

Hat
Cut 1 green fabric

H

Neck edge – gather   L

Q

Top of arm placement

↑

Side of suit

Suit

CLOWN
Cut 1 blue fabric
Cut 1 green fabric

PIERRE PIERROT
Cut 1 black satin
Cut 1 white satin

PETRA PIERROT
Cut 2 white satin

M

E

Boot sole

Most stretch

G

FOLD

Gather

K

Hand
Cut 2 pairs

red felt

N   P

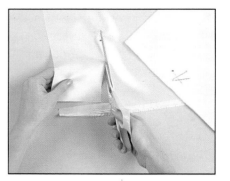

Cut out all pieces from patterns. From white satin also cut ruff 10cm × 60cm (4in × 24in). From stockinette cut two legs 20cm × 11cm (8in × 4in) and two arms 17cm × 9cm (7in × 3½in) with most stretch across shorter measurements. Follow steps 2–8 of Clown instructions to make body. Note that the boots are a different shape.

Stitch front hat to centre hat J–H, matching dots. Stitch dart in back hat. Stitch centre hat to back hat K–L, matching triangles. Turn hat to right side out, place a little filling in centre of hat and fit onto head. Sew edge of hat to head.

Place eyes, cheeks and mouth on face. Mark position of nose and eyebrows. This can be done with pins, then a light pencil line. When satisfied with the expression, glue or sew felt features to fabric.

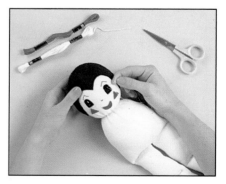

Using two strands of embroidery thread work two straight red stitches for each eyebrow and two tiny stitches for nose. With two strands of white thread stitch highlights onto eyes.

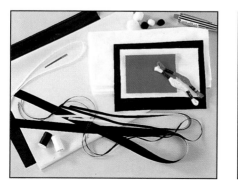

MATERIALS: 30cm × 68cm (12in × 27in) double thickness white stockinette; 50cm × 60cm (20in × 24in) black satin (polyester), 70cm × 90cm (28in × 36in) white satin; 30cm × 40cm (12in × 16in) black felt, 16cm × 16cm (6in × 6in) white felt, scrap of red felt; 60cm × 3mm (24in × ⅛in), 24cm × 7mm (9in × ¼in), 70cm × 25mm (28in × 1in) black satin ribbon; 24cm × 7mm (9in × ¼in) white satin ribbon; 2 × 30mm (1¼in) white pom poms, 2 × 18mm (¾in) black pom poms, 1 × 18mm (¾in) white pom pom; red and white stranded embroidery threads; matching sewing threads; narrow elastic and bodkin; filling; clear drying glue

Follow step 14 from Clown instructions, stitching black satin suit piece to white satin suit piece. Pull up running stitches around folded neck edge, checking that suit centre seams at L are central to body. Sew running stitches on broken lines to gather lower edge of legs. Sew gathers to top of boots.

Make up white stockinette arms and white felt hands – see step 16 in Clown's instructions for full details.

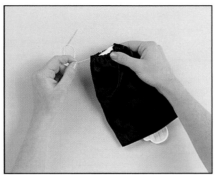

Follow steps 17–19 of Clown's instructions to make up sleeves – one in black and the other in white satin – and attach arms to body.
Note: Black-sleeved arm is attached to white side of suit, white-sleeved to black half of suit.

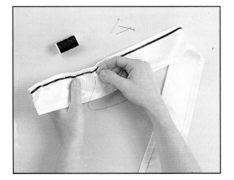

Stitch 1cm (⅜in) hem at one long edge of the ruff. Stitch a 13mm (½in) hem at the opposite long edge to form a channel for the elastic. On right side stitch 3mm (⅛in) black ribbon over first hem stitches.

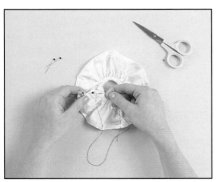

Thread elastic through ruff channel, stitching one end to fabric to secure it. Pull up fabric to fit doll's neck. Stitch two short edges of ruff together. Trim excess elastic and neaten seam. Fit ruff onto doll.

Tie a 2.5cm (1in) black ribbon around neck with bow at front. Sew a band of contrast 7mm (¼in) ribbon around each wrist and ankle with the joins at the backs. Sew two black and one white 18mm (¾in) pom pom evenly spaced to suit centre front seam. Sew one 30mm (1¼in) white pom pom to each boot.

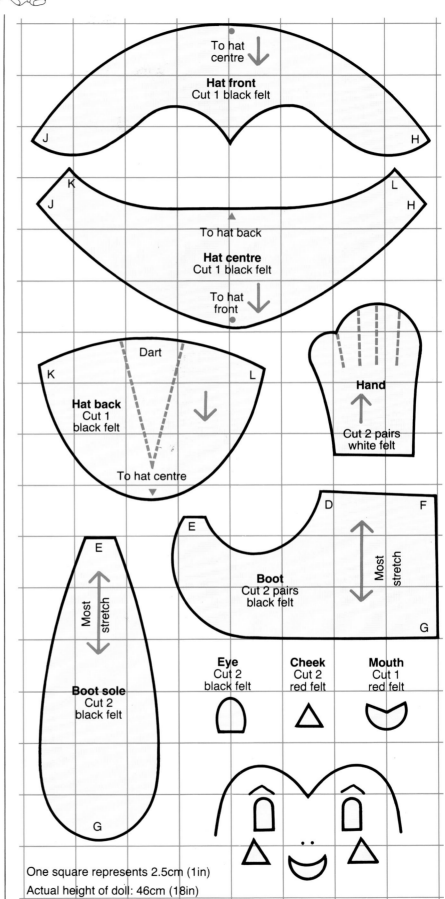

Hat front
Cut 1 black felt

J H

K L

J H

To hat back

Hat centre
Cut 1 black felt

To hat front

Dart

K L

Hat back
Cut 1
black felt

To hat centre

Hand
Cut 2 pairs
white felt

D F

E

E

Boot
Cut 2 pairs
black felt

Most stretch

G

Boot sole
Cut 2
black felt

Most stretch

E

G

Eye
Cut 2
black felt

Cheek
Cut 2
red felt

Mouth
Cut 1
red felt

One square represents 2.5cm (1in)
Actual height of doll: 46cm (18in)

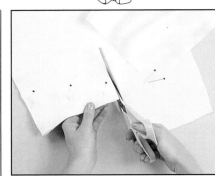

Cut all pieces from patterns. From satin also cut the skirt 28cm × 76cm (11in × 30in) and ruff 7cm × 40cm (3in × 16in). From stockinette cut legs and arms as for the Clown doll.

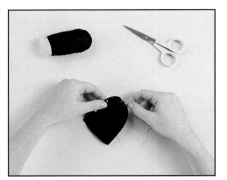

Follow steps 2–8 of Clown instructions. Note that the shoes are a different shape. Stitch shoes together in pairs leaving open straight edge X–Y. Turn shoes to right side out and fill with stuffing. Insert gathered end of leg into shoe and sew shoe to leg. Check that second shoe and leg are made to the same length as first one.

Stitch front hat to centre hat R–S, matching dots. Stitch dart in back hat and stitch centre hat to back hat W–T, matching triangles.

Turn hat to right side out, place a little filling in centre of hat and fit onto head. Sew edge of hat to head.

Follow steps 3 and 4 of Pierre Pierrot instructions for features but use the girl's patterns.

MATERIALS: 30cm × 68cm (12in × 27in) double thickness white stockinette; 80cm × 100cm (31in × 39in) white satin; 26cm × 26cm (10in × 10in) black felt; 16cm × 14cm (6in × 5½in) white felt; Scrap of red felt; 270cm × 3mm (106in × ⅛in) black satin ribbon; 100cm × 2.5cm (39in × 1in) black satin ribbon; 120cm (47in) black ric-rac braid; 4 × 30mm (1¼in) white pom poms; 1 × 18mm (¾in) black pom pom; narrow elastic and bodkin; red and white embroidery threads; filling; clear drying craft glue

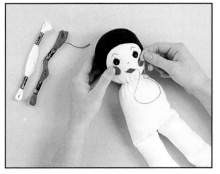

Follow steps 14–19 of Clown instructions with these alterations: use white satin for both suit pieces and sleeves. After stitching hem at sleeve wrist N–N, stitch 3mm (⅛in) black ribbon to right side of sleeve over hem stitches.

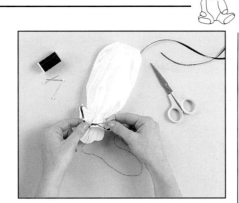

Stitch a 15mm (⅝in) hem to wrong side at one long edge of skirt. On right side stitch a band of 3mm (⅛in) ribbon over hem stitches with a band of ric-rac braid above it. To form a channel for waist elastic, stitch a 13mm (½in) double hem at opposite long edge.

Thread through elastic and sew one end to fabric to secure it. Pull up elastic to fit doll's waist. Stitch short edges of skirt together including elastic. Fit skirt onto doll. Arrange suit to make an evenly gathered bodice and sew skirt waist to suit and body.

Tie a 2.5cm (1in) ribbon sash around waist to cover top of skirt. Catch stitch lower edge of sash to skirt and take a few stitches through bow to secure it.

Sew a 30mm (1¼in) white pom pom to the front of each shoe. Cut two 30cm (12in) lengths of 3mm (⅛in) wide black ribbon and tie around suit legs, to cover ankle gathers with bows at front. Sew remaining pom poms, two white and one black, to hat.

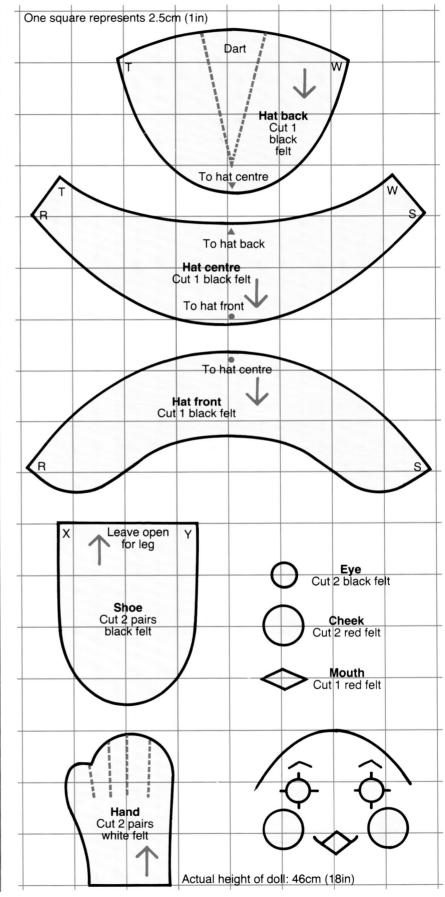

One square represents 2.5cm (1in)

Dart

T W

Hat back
Cut 1
black
felt

To hat centre

T W
R S

To hat back

Hat centre
Cut 1 black felt

To hat front

To hat centre

Hat front
Cut 1 black felt

R S

X Leave open for leg Y

Shoe
Cut 2 pairs
black felt

Eye
Cut 2 black felt

Cheek
Cut 2 red felt

Mouth
Cut 1 red felt

Hand
Cut 2 pairs
white felt

Actual height of doll: 46cm (18in)

Pierce tiny holes in the eye positions and turn the head the right way out. Insert the safety eyes in the holes and secure on the reverse with metal washers. Stuff the head, shaping it into a round fat ball. Using a running stitch, gather the raw edge at the base and finish off securely.

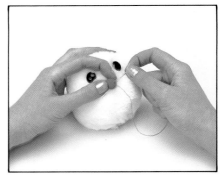

Fold the nose piece in half and sew along the straight edge. Turn the right way out and stuff firmly. Gather the raw edge of the nose and finish off. Place this end on head at a central position between the eyes and ladder stitch firmly into place. Using black embroidery thread, stitch a 'V'-shaped mouth below the eyes. Then ladder stitch the head to the body.

Place each pair of arms right sides together and sew all around, leaving the top straight edges open. Turn the arms the right way out and stuff them, adding far less filling to the top halves. Turn the raw edges in and oversew the arms into position on either side of the neck. Secure the hands to the body with a couple of stitches.

MATERIALS

Short pile white fur fabric
Black, red and green felt
Scrap of orange felt for nose
1 pair 13.5mm black safety
  eyes with metal washers
Black embroidery thread
Filling

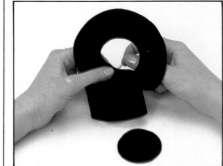

Sew the two hat brim pieces together around both the outer and inner edges. Fold the main body of the hat in half and sew around the short edge. Place the completed cylinder on top of the hat brim in a central position and oversew the two pieces together around the inner circle. Oversew the hat top into position and put some filling inside the hat.

Make up the snowman body using the same method as for Santa's body (see pages 92/93). Use white fur for the body and black felt for the feet. Stuff the body well, making it fat and rounded; place to one side. Sew dart on each of the head pieces. Then place the two halves right sides together and sew around the head, leaving the bottom straight edge open.

Put the hat on the head in a lopsided position and stitch down. Wrap a red felt strip 19cm x 2cm (7½in x ¾in) around the base of the hat. Overlap ends and sew into place. Sew holly leaves onto the hat and buttons onto the body. Cut a red or green felt strip 5cm x 40cm (2in x 16in). Fringe the ends and tie scarf around the snowman's neck.

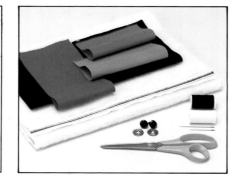

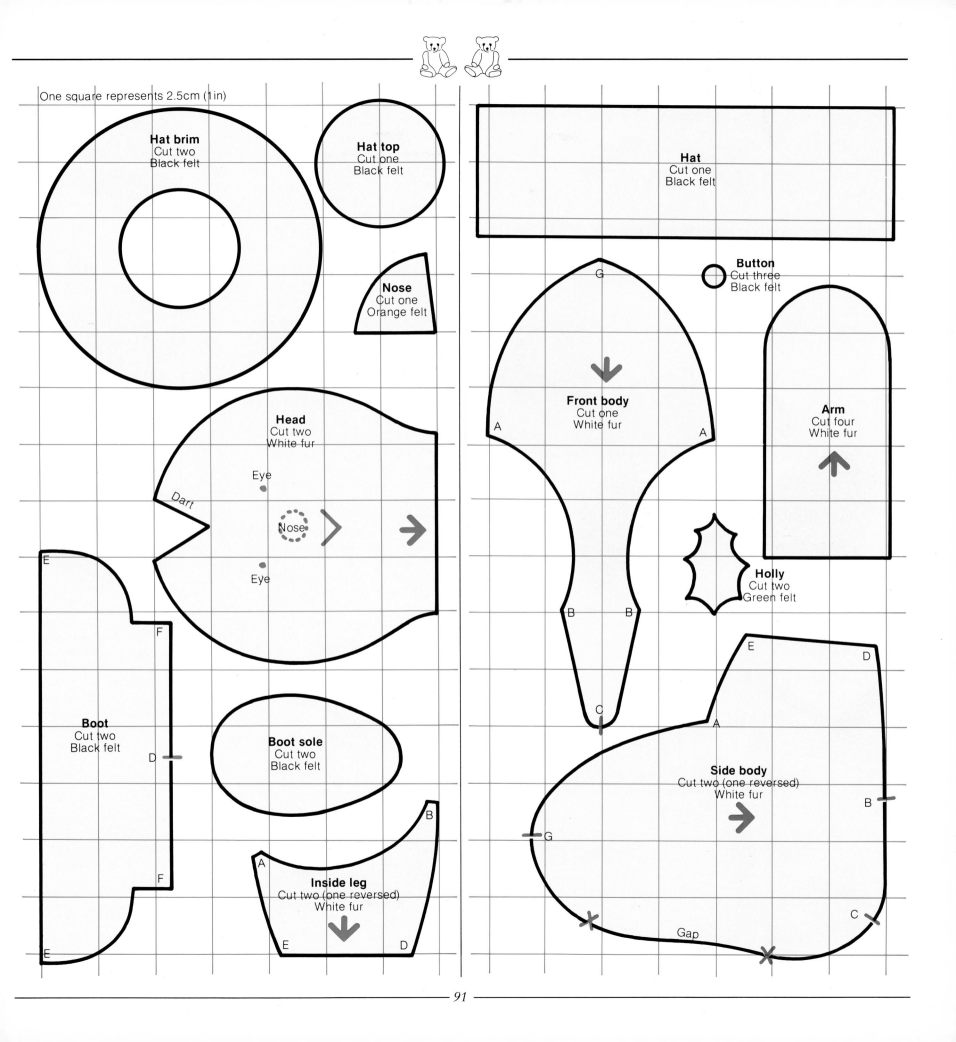

One square represents 2.5cm (1 in)

Hat brim
Cut two
Black felt

Hat top
Cut one
Black felt

Hat
Cut one
Black felt

Button
Cut three
Black felt

Nose
Cut one
Orange felt

Front body
Cut one
White fur

Arm
Cut four
White fur

Head
Cut two
White fur

Eye

Dart

Nose

Eye

Holly
Cut two
Green felt

Boot
Cut two
Black felt

Boot sole
Cut two
Black felt

Side body
Cut two (one reversed)
White fur

Inside leg
Cut two (one reversed)
White fur

Gap

Open out the leg seams and sew the boot to the leg along E-D-E. Then fold the boot with right sides facing and sew the front to the side body along seam G-E on both sides, ensuring that point A matches. Sew seam E-F in black thread.

Close the back seam from G to C, leaving a gap for turning. Sew the boot soles into place. Turn the body the right way out and stuff firmly. Ladder stitch the back opening closed and place the body to one side.

For the jacket, join the two halves together by sewing seam L-M-L. Sew the sleeves to the jacket along J-K-J, easing to fit. Sew a strip of white fur fabric 14cm x 4cm (5½in x 1½in) to the edge of the sleeves, keeping the right sides together. Fold the strip over the raw edge of the sleeve and sew down on the reverse side.

MATERIALS

Red velvet or felt
Black felt
Pink or flesh coloured felt
Very long white fur fabric
Short white fur fabric, for
* pom pom*
Ribbon
Filling

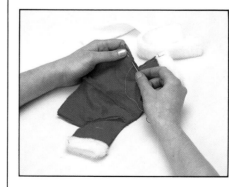

Fold the sleeves in half and sew up the side seam O-J-N on both sides. At the base of the jacket, sew a strip of white fur fabric 42cm x 4cm (16½in x 1½in). Fold the strip back over the raw edge of the jacket and sew into place on the reverse side.

For the body, sew the inside legs to the front body from A to B on either side. With right sides together, join the front body with attached legs to the side body from point D to C, matching point B. Repeat for the other side.

For the hood, turn up a narrow double hem on each short side. Sew a strip of white fur fabric 23cm x 4cm (9¼in x 1½in) to the front edge in the same way as for the jacket. Fold the hood in half and, with right sides together, sew seam P-Q.

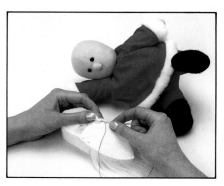

Turn the hood the right way out and add a short piece of ribbon to each front corner of the hood. Fold down the point of the hood. Sew a running stitch around the edge of the pom pom and gather. Stuff gently, then pull the thread to gather tightly. Attach the pom pom to the side of the hood.

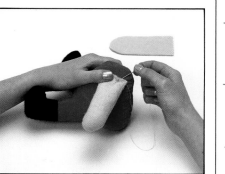

Place the pairs of arms right sides together and sew all around, leaving the top straight edges open. Turn and stuff the arms, then oversew arms to the body sides. Place the jacket on the body.

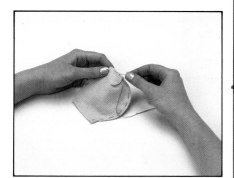

To make the head, sew up the darts on both head pieces. Place the two halves together with right sides facing and sew around the head, leaving the bottom straight edge open.

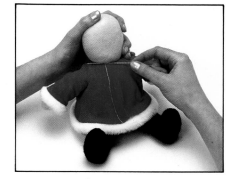

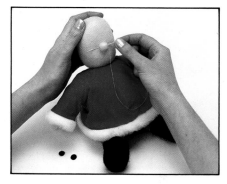

Turn the head the right way out. Place some filling into the head, stuffing it firmly. Gather the bottom edge of the head with a running stitch, then ladder stitch the head to the body.

Using a running stitch, gather the edge of the nose. Place a small amount of filling in the centre, then fasten off securely. Stitch the nose to the centre of the face. Cut two eye circles out of black felt and sew them into position above the nose.

Fold the side flaps of the long white hair piece down and sew seam R-S on either side. Sew the beard to the front of the hair piece from T to U on both sides. Turn the right way out and pull onto Santa's head so that the top of the beard just touches the nose. Stitch into place. Put the hood on Santa's head and tie into place under the beard.

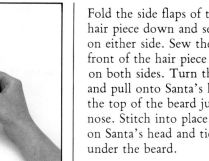

One square represents 2.5cm (1in)

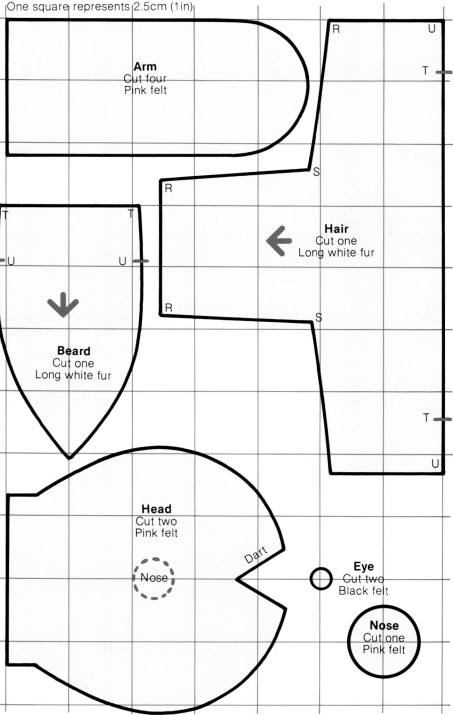

Arm
Cut four
Pink felt

Hair
Cut one
Long white fur

Beard
Cut one
Long white fur

Head
Cut two
Pink felt

Nose

Dart

Eye
Cut two
Black felt

Nose
Cut one
Pink felt

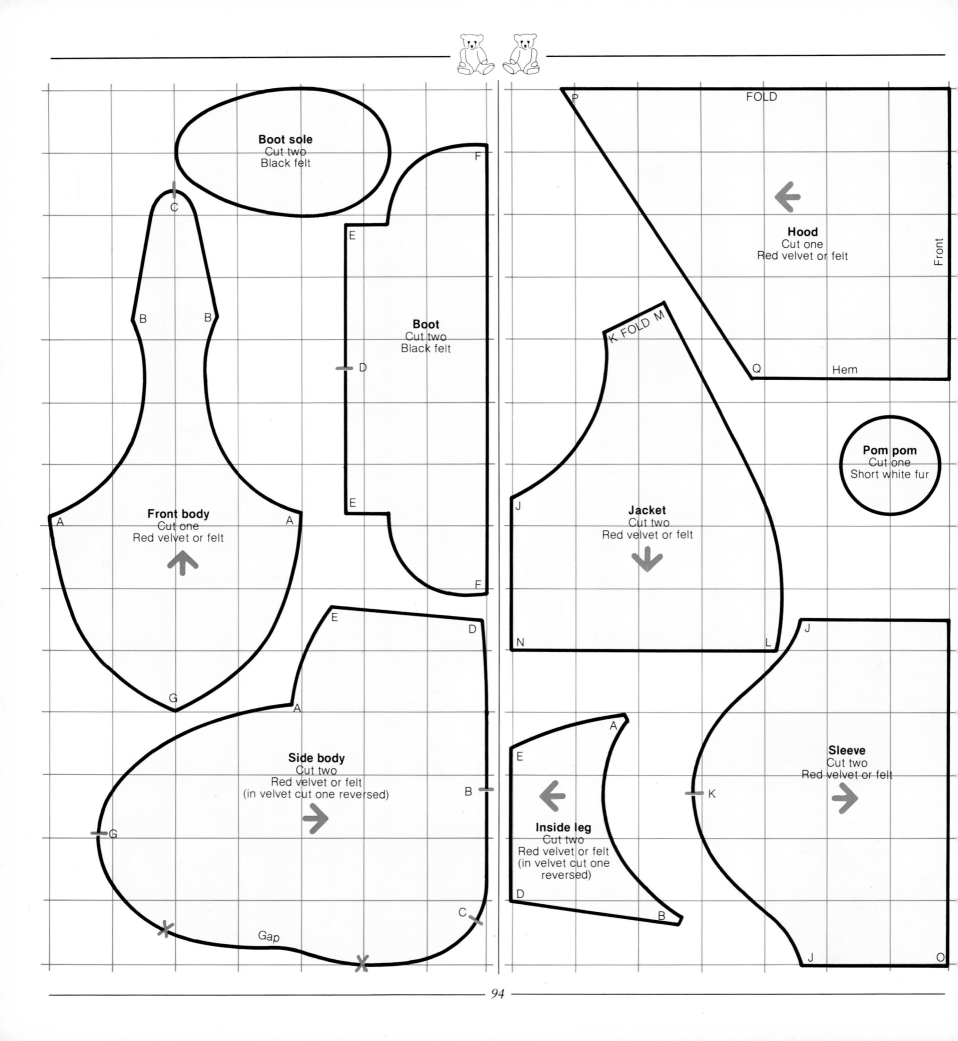

Boot sole
Cut two
Black felt

Boot
Cut two
Black felt

F

E

D

E

F

C

B   B

A   A

Front body
Cut one
Red velvet or felt

G

E   D

A

Side body
Cut two
Red velvet or felt
(in velvet cut one reversed)

B

G

Gap

C

P   FOLD

Hood
Cut one
Red velvet or felt

Front

K FOLD M

Q   Hem

J

Jacket
Cut two
Red velvet or felt

Pom pom
Cut one
Short white fur

N   L   J

A

E

Inside leg
Cut two
Red velvet or felt
(in velvet cut one
reversed)

D   B

K

Sleeve
Cut two
Red velvet or felt

J   O

INDEX

UFO
ENCOUNTERS

SIGHTINGS, VISITATIONS, AND INVESTIGATIONS

Contributing Writer: Jerome Clark

Consultant: Marcello Truzzi

PUBLICATIONS INTERNATIONAL, LTD.

JEROME CLARK is editor of *International UFO Reporter* and columnist for *Fate* magazine, which he edited for more than a decade. He is author of the three-volume series, *UFO Encyclopedia,* and coauthor of *New Age Encyclopedia.* Mr. Clark is also vice president of the Center for UFO Studies.

MARCELLO TRUZZI is an internationally recognized scholar and consultant to many organizations, including the Center for UFO Studies and *Strange* magazine. He has appeared on *Nightline, Donahue, The Oprah Winfrey Show, Current Affair,* and *Geraldo.* Mr. Truzzi is a professor of sociology at Eastern Michigan University and the founder of the Center for Scientific Anomalies Research.

CONTENTS

INTRODUCTION: REACH BEYOND THE CLOUDS

Barney Hill (above) and his wife, Betty, recounted under hypnosis that they were abducted by extraterrestrials on the evening of September 19, 1961. While in the spacecraft, they each experienced separate medical examinations.

Flying saucers, better known as unidentified flying objects or UFOs: Some people believe in their existence without question. The skepticism of others knows no bounds, and in fact the skeptics find much to ridicule in the world of ufology.

But the world is full of strange and eerie phenomena. To paraphrase Dr. J. Allen Hynek: Is ridicule the best approach to the phenomenon of UFOs? The scientific community has a duty and responsibility to give serious scientific examination to reports of UFO sightings. The first step toward an understanding of UFOs is to study the stories and photographs of those who have had some sort of contact with these phenomena.

UFO Encounters presents the stories and case histories of individuals who claim to have seen or come in contact with UFOs. Some stories are patently false, while others are told by reputable people with supporting evidence. The many photographs presented were taken by people who saw UFOs. Again, some are obviously hoaxes, but other pictures continue to defy conventional explanation, even decades after the photograph was taken.

The first chapter, "In the Beginning," gives a quick overview of UFO history before Kenneth Arnold's sighting in 1947. The second chapter, "UFOs: The Official Story," presents the official position of the United States government, which attempts to explain all UFO reports in terms of conventional phenomena. Chapter 3, "The Dimensions of a Phenomenon," explores

In October of 1981, Hannah McRoberts took a photograph of a mountain on Vancouver Island, British Columbia, Canada. Neither she nor her companions noticed the UFO at the time.

the many ways UFOs have made their presence known on Earth: nocturnal lights, daylight discs, radar/visual detection, and close encounters of the first, second, and third kind. Of course, UFOs provide fertile ground for hoaxes and scams of all sorts, and the fourth chapter, "Into the Wild Blue," details the fringe elements of ufology. Finally, the last chapter, "The Ultimate Secret," looks into the slow, painstaking unraveling of the most significant episode in ufology, the Roswell incident.

Many possible explanations are offered for UFOs: natural phenomena, psychic visions, and, of course, visits by extraterrestrial beings. The idea of other life forms somewhere in the universe stirs up enormous controversy. But such respected astronomers as Carl Sagan and Clyde Tombaugh believe there are thousands of habitable planets in the galaxy, any number of which could support an advanced civilization.

So, turn these pages with an open mind and come explore the phenomenon of UFOs.

IN THE BEGINNING

Although strange aerial phenomena had been sighted for decades, it was Kenneth Arnold's report of "flying saucers" over Mount Rainier, Washington, on June 24, 1947, that brought unidentified flying objects into popular consciousness.

The date was June 24, 1947, a Tuesday; the time, just before three o'clock in the afternoon. Kenneth Arnold, a private pilot and fire-control-equipment salesman from Boise, Idaho, was flying over the Cascade Mountains searching for the remains of a lost C-46 for which a $5,000 reward had been offered.

Arnold never found the missing aircraft, but what he did see put his name in newspapers all over the world. He had just made a 180-degree turn over Mineral, Washington, when a bright flash of light startled him. During the next 30 seconds, Arnold frantically searched the sky for its source—he was afraid he was about to collide with another airplane. Then he saw another flash to his left, toward the north. When he looked in that direction, Arnold spotted nine objects, the lead one at a higher elevation than the rest, streaking south over Mount Baker toward Mount Rainier. Watching their progress from one peak to the next, he calculated their speed at 1,700 miles per hour. Even when he arbitrarily knocked 500 miles off that estimate, Arnold was still dealing with an impossible speed figure.

The objects, darting in and out of the smaller peaks, periodically flipped on their sides in unison. As they did so, the sunlight reflected off their lateral surfaces—thus explaining the flashes that had first caught his attention. Arnold wrote later, "They were flying diagonally in an echelon formation with a larger gap in their echelon between the first four and the last five." The

The cover of the first issue of Fate *depicted a highly sensationalized version of Kenneth Arnold's encounter.*

lead object looked like a dark crescent; the other eight were flat and disc-shaped. Arnold estimated that the chain they comprised was five miles long. After two and a half minutes, they disappeared, heading south over Mount Adams. The age of unidentified flying objects (UFOs) had begun.

"FLYING SAUCERS"

The next day Arnold told his story to two reporters for Pendleton's *East Oregonian.* One of the reporters, Bill Bequette, put the story on the Associated Press wires. Within days, as similar sightings erupted around the country, an anony-

mous headline writer coined the phrase "flying saucers." But that name was not entirely original. On January 25, 1878, a Texas newspaper, the Denison *Daily News,* remarked on a local event that had taken place three days earlier. On the morning of January 22, farmer John Martin noted the swift passage, through the southern sky, of something like a "large saucer." The newspaper said, "Mr. Martin is a gentleman of undoubted veracity and this strange occurrence, if it was not a balloon, deserves the attention of our scientists."

There were as many as 18 other sightings of strange flying objects in the Pacific Northwest that same June 24. For example, that morning prospector Fred M. Johnson had spotted five or six "round, metallic-looking discs" about 30 feet in diameter and 1,000 feet above him. He focused a telescope on one and saw that it had tails or fins (unlike those Arnold would observe a few hours later). For the duration of the sighting—close to a minute—Johnson's compass needle spun wildly, stopping only after the discs headed off to the southeast.

Actually, sightings of silvery discs had been going on since at least April 1947, when a U.S. Weather Bureau meteorologist and his staff had tracked a large, flat-bottomed ellipsoid as it shot from east to west over the skies of Richmond, Virginia. Sightings of similar objects took place the next month in Oklahoma, Colorado, Tennessee, Georgia, and New Jersey. These incidents went unnoted in the local press until after Kenneth Arnold's sighting opened the way to publication of such stories.

By the late 1940s Air Force investigators had taken to calling such things "unidentified flying objects." This was meant to be a neutral term, but skeptics complained that the words "flying" and "objects" implied both craft and intelligent guidance. Everyone could agree, though, that this phrase was better than the silly-sounding "flying saucers," which described only some of the aerial oddities people were reporting in the United States and around the world. Some of these phenomena looked like big metal cigars or fire-spewing torpedoes; others were spheres, triangles, or V shapes; and many were simply bright lights zigzagging across the night sky.

For the next 45 years, UFOs would be the focus of ceaseless controversy, wonderment, weirdness, fabrication, derision, mystification and, once in a while, serious investigation. Throughout this publication, many UFO phenomena are discussed; each story is presented from the perspective of the witness who experienced the event.

EARLY UFOs: FACT OR FAIRIES?

In A.D. 1211 Gervase of Tilbury, an English chronicler of historical events and curiosities, recorded this bizarre story:

There happened in the borough of Cloera, one Sunday, while the people were at Mass, a marvel. In this town is a church dedicated to St. Kinarus. It befell that an anchor was dropped from the sky, with a rope attached to it, and one of the flukes caught in the arch above the church door. The people rushed out of the church and saw in the sky a ship with men on board, floating before the anchor cable, and they saw a man leap overboard and jump down to the anchor, as if to release it. He looked as if he were swimming in water. The folk rushed up and tried to seize him; but the Bishop forbade the people to hold the man, for it might kill him, he said. The man was freed, and hurried up to the ship, where the crew cut the rope and the ship sailed out of sight. But the anchor is in the church, and has been there ever since, as a testimony.

A Nuremberg broadsheet tells of an April 14, 1561, aerial battle involving a variety of strange objects—globes, crosses, and tubes—that turned to steam upon hitting the ground (lower right). People viewed the event as a divine warning.

On November 4, 1697, two glowing wheels sailed over Hamburg, Germany,
according to one account. Early reports such as these are difficult to evaluate
and may or may not be related to the modern UFO phenomenon.

This tale—unrelated to any other British legend or supernatural tradition—is, according to folklorist Katharine Briggs, "one of those strange, unmotivated and therefore rather convincing tales that are scattered through the early chronicles."

In a 9th-century Latin manuscript, *Liber contra insulam vulgi opinionem,* the Archbishop of Lyons complained about the French peasantry's insistent belief in a "certain region called Magonia from whence come ships in the clouds." The occupants of these vessels "carry back to that region those fruits of the earth which are destroyed by hail and tempests; the sailors paying rewards to the storm wizards and themselves receiving corn and other produce." The archbishop said he had even witnessed the stoning to death of "three men and a woman who said they had fallen from these same ships." Jakob Grimm, a 19th-century folklorist, speculated, "'Magonia' takes us to some region where Latin was spoken, if we may rely on it referring to Magus, i.e., a magic land."

Are these early references to UFOs and aliens? Possibly. But references of this sort are

The appearance of black and white globes over Basel,
Switzerland, in 1566 was noted in a broadsheet.

9

A VICTORIAN HUMANOID?

The attacker was tall and thin, had pointed ears and fiery eyes, and wore a cloak. He tore at his female victims' clothes and ripped their flesh with hands that felt like iron. When he escaped, he did not run; he bounced away. Those who saw his feet swore he had springs in his boot heels.

At first, the authorities had a hard time believing what victims were telling them. But by January 1838 so many Londoners had seen the figure that the Lord Mayor formed a vigilance committee to capture "Spring Heeled Jack."

In one especially notorious incident, he tried to snatch 18-year-old Jane Alsop right out of her own house. According to the London *Times* (February 22, 1838), he "presented a most hideous and frightful appearance, and vomited forth a quantity of blue and white flame from his mouth, and his eyes resembled red balls of fire. . . . [H]e wore a large helmet, and his dress, which appeared to fit him very tight, seemed to her to resemble white oil skin." The young woman was saved by family members.

An imaginative rendering of Springheel Jack at Aldershot, England, 1877.

One day in 1845, in full view of frightened onlookers, Jack tossed a prostitute off a bridge; she drowned in the open sewer below. Sightings of a comparable figure were recorded elsewhere in England in 1877. In 1904 more than 100 residents of Everton saw a man in a flowing cloak and black boots making great leaps over streets and rooftops.

Who—or what—was Springheel Jack? Some suspected that he was a rowdy nobleman, Henry, Marquis of Waterford, who died in 1859. Doubters countered that Jack-like leaps are physically impossible. During World War II German paratroopers who put springs in their boot heels got broken ankles for their efforts. Was Jack an extraterrestrial being? In July 1953, three Houston residents reported seeing a tall, bounding figure "wearing a black cape, skintight pants, and quarter-length boots." For a few minutes he remained visible in the pecan tree into which he had jumped. He disappeared shortly before a rocket-shaped UFO shot upward from across the street.

Some writers claim that traditional beliefs about fairies anticipated today's UFO encounters. Shu Rhys, a 19th-century Welsh woman, reputedly went away with fairies and never returned.

few and far between. Although ancient and medieval records are filled with stories of strange shapes and figures in the sky, little in these accounts elicits visions of UFOs as we understand them today. Many eerie aerial phenomena of an earlier time can now be identified as meteors, comets, and auroral displays.

Still other accounts of UFOs are rooted in culture, perhaps the result of visions or hallucinations. Just before sunset on April 16, 1651, two women in rural England supposedly witnessed a battle between armies. At the conclusion of the battle there appeared, according to a contemporary account, blue angels "about the bigness of a capon, having faces (as they thought) like owls." Neither wars nor angels in the sky

were uncommon "sights" from Roman times to the early modern era. In A.D. 793 the *Anglo-Saxon Chronicle* reported "fiery dragons . . . flying in the air," and almost a thousand years later, in 1762, a "twisting serpent" supposedly cavorted over Devonshire.

Along with this aerial activity were speculations and reports in popular lore of humanoid creatures dwelling in caves, bodies of water, or invisible realms. These humanoids varied widely in appearance; height alone ranged from a few inches to many feet. They possessed supernatural powers and sometimes kidnapped adults and children. These creatures, unpredictable and easily offended, were so feared that it was considered unwise to even speak their name. They were believed to be, according to one 17th-century account, "of a middle nature between man and angels." To see these humanoids, a person usually had to be in "fai-erie," meaning a state of enchantment. The traditional Anglo-Saxon name for these entities was "elves," now supplanted by "fairies."

Since 1947 some writers, notably Jacques Vallée in *Passport to Magonia*, have tried to link fairies to modern UFO encounters with humanoids. But this connection is speculative at best. The reader must be willing to assume that fairies were "real" and then overlook many dissimilarities between fairies and UFO humanoids. Fairy beliefs really have more in common with ghosts, monsters, and fabulous beasts than modern accounts of encounters with UFOs.

Popular author Jacques Vallée, who rejects ufology's extraterrestrial hypothesis, emphasizes occult phenomena and conspiracy theories in his own exotic solution to the UFO mystery.

Other writers, such as Desmond Leslie, George Hunt Williamson, M. K. Jessup, Yonah Fortner, and Brinsley le Poer Trench, also tried to find evidence of aliens visiting Earth before 1800, but their arguments are weak. Supposedly, extraterrestrials had been here for many thousands of years, leaving traces of their presence in legends and Biblical chapters as well as in such archaeological monuments as Stonehenge, the Great Pyramid, and Peru's Nazca plains. These ideas were picked up and elaborated upon in the late 1960s and 1970s by a new school of writers (most famously Erich von Daniken of Switzerland), referring to "ancient astronauts."

Serious UFO researchers—not to mention astronomers, archaeologists, and historians—rejected these speculations, which in their view grew out of ignorance and distortion. Critics charged that there was no evidence to support so radical a revision of history and that such speculations deliberately slighted the role of human intelligence. Still, von Daniken's books had an enormous impact on impressionable readers.

THE ARRIVAL OF UFOs

In the 19th century, however, accounts of UFOs took on a more believable tone.

As day dawned June 1, 1853, students at Burritt College in Tennessee noticed two luminous, unusual objects just to the north of the rising sun. One looked like a "small new moon," the other a "large star." The first one slowly grew smaller until it was no longer visible, but the second grew larger and assumed a globular

In the 1950s George Hunt Williamson (left) allegedly received radio communications from extraterrestrials. He was one of the most influential figures in the contactee movement.

The Earl of Clancarty (inset), who, as Brinsley le Poer Trench, has written books on flying saucers, ancient astronauts, and the hollow Earth, heads the UFO Select Committee in the House of Lords. Main Image: A frame from a classic UFO film taken in Utah in 1952.

shape. (Probably the objects were moving in a direct line to and from the witnesses or remaining stationary but altering their luminosity.) Professor A. C. Carnes, who interviewed the students and reported their sighting to *Scientific American*, wrote, "The first then became visible again, and increased rapidly in size, while the other diminished, and the two spots kept changing thus for about half an hour. There was considerable wind at the time, and light fleecy clouds passed by, showing the lights to be confined to one place."

Carnes speculated that "electricity" might be responsible for the phenomena. *Scientific American* believed this was "certainly" not the case; "possibly," the cause was "distant clouds of moisture." As explanations go, this was no more compelling than electricity. It would not

be the last time a report and an explanation would make a poor match.

Unspectacular though it was, the event was certainly a UFO sighting, the type of sighting that could easily occur today. It represented a new phenomenon astronomers and lay observers were starting to notice with greater frequency in the Earth's atmosphere. And some of these sights were startling indeed.

On July 13, 1860, a pale blue light engulfed the city of Wilmington, Delaware. Residents looked up into the evening sky to see its source: a 200-foot-long something streaking along on a

Extraterrestrial lore claims England's Stonehenge has alien origins and supernatural powers.

level course 100 feet above. Trailing behind it at 100-foot intervals cruised three "very red and glowing balls." A fourth abruptly joined the other three after shooting out from the rear of the main object, which was "giving off sparkles after the manner of a rocket." The lead object turned toward the southeast, passed over the Delaware River, and then headed straight east until lost from view. The incident—reported in

In Peru lie vast designs—fully visible only from the air—depicting animal shapes. Ancient-astronaut theorists speculate the lines were signals to space "gods." Archaeologists reject that notion, but the function of the lines remains a mystery.

Mysterious "crop circles"—some of elaborate design—have sparked wonder in England. Theories as to their source range from natural phenomena to extraterrestrials. The only area of agreement is that a significant number are hoaxes.

the Wilmington *Tribune*, July 30, 1860—lasted one minute.

During the 1850s and 1860s in Nebraska, settlers viewed some rather unnerving phenomena. Were they luminous "serpents"? Apparently not, but instead elongated mechanical structures. A Nebraska folk ballad reported one such unusual sighting:

> Twas on a dark night in '66
> When we was layin' steel
> We seen a flyin' engine
> Without no wing or wheel
> It came a-roarin' in the sky
> With lights along the side
> And scales like a serpent's hide.

Something virtually identical was reported in a Chilean newspaper in April 1868 (and reprinted in *Zoologist*, July 1868). "On its body, elongated like a serpent," one of the alleged witness-

es declared, "we could only see brilliant scales, which clashed together with a metallic sound as the strange animal turned its body in flight."

Lexicographer and linguist J.A.H. Murray was walking across the Oxford University campus on the evening of August 31, 1895, when he saw a:

> brilliant luminous body which suddenly emerged over the tops of the trees before me on the left and moved eastward across the sky above and in front of me. Its appearance was, at first glance, such as to suggest a brilliant meteor, considerably larger than Venus at her greatest brilliancy, but the slowness of the motion . . . made one doubt whether it was not some artificial firework. . . . I watched for a second or two till [sic] it neared its culminating point and was about to be

A close-up of one of the many crop circles found in southern England.

hidden from me by the lofty College building, on which I sprang over the corner . . . and was enabled to see it through the space between the old and new buildings of the College, as it continued its course toward the eastern horizon. . . . [I]t became rapidly dimmer . . . and finally disappeared behind a tree. . . . The fact that it so perceptibly grew fainter as it receded seems to imply that it had not a very great elevation. . . . [I]ts course was slower than [that of] any meteor I have ever seen.

Some 20 minutes later, two other observers saw the same or a similar phenomenon, which they viewed as it traversed a "quarter of the heavens" during a five-minute period.

But in 1896 events turned up a notch: The world experienced its first great explosion of sightings of unidentified flying objects. The beginning of the UFO era can be dated from

SAUCERS FROM WITHIN?

In the early 19th century an American eccentric, John Cleves Symmes (1779-1829), sought funding for an expedition to enter the Earth through one of two 4,000-mile wide polar holes. Inside the Earth, he was convinced, a benevolent advanced civilization existed. Though an object of derision to most people, some took him seriously, and the idea of a hollow Earth was championed in a number of books throughout the rest of the century and right into the next.

Today, hollow-earthers believe flying saucers zip in and out of the polar holes. The people inside are descendants of Atlantis and its Pacific equivalent, Lemuria. There is even a strong Nazi wing of the movement. According to Canadian neo-Nazi Ernst Zundel, the principal advocate of this theory, Hitler and his elite troops escaped with their saucer technology into the hole at the South Pole.

Ancient-astronaut lore believes that the Great Pyramids and the Sphinx are creations of superior extraterrestrial technology. Such theories have no real basis in fact.

this year. Although sightings of UFOs had occurred in earlier decades, they were sporadic and apparently rare. Also, these earlier sightings did not come in the huge concentrations ("waves" in the lingo of ufologists, "flaps" to the U.S. Air Force) that characterize much of the UFO phenomenon between the 1890s and the 1990s.

Between the fall of 1896 and the spring of 1897 people began sighting "airships," first in California and then across most of the rest of the United States. Most people (though not all) thought the airships were machines built by secret inventors who would soon dazzle the world with a public announcement of a break-

through in aviation technology leading to a heavier-than-air flying machine.

More than a few hoaxers and sensation-seeking journalists were all too happy to play on this popular expectation. Newspaper stories quoted "witnesses" who claimed to have seen the airships land and to have communicated with the pilots. The pilots themselves were quoted word for word boasting of their aeronautical exploits and, in some instances, of their intention to drop "several tons of dynamite" on Spanish fortresses in Cuba. Any reader with access to more than one newspaper account could have seen that the stories conflicted wildly and were inherently unbelievable. We now know that no

CLOSE ENCOUNTER, 1897 STYLE

*The UFO at Lake Elmo was just one of many "airships"
seen between November 1896 and May 1897.*

Late on the evening of April 13, 1897, as they were passing through Lake Elmo, Minnesota, on their way to Hudson, Wisconsin, Frederick Chamberlain and O. L. Jones spotted a shadowy figure in a clearing two blocks away. The figure carried a lantern and seemed to be looking for something. Thinking there might be some emergency, Chamberlain and Jones turned toward the clearing, but the figure and lantern disappeared into the trees. Moments later they heard the crackling of twigs and branches, followed by a "rushing noise . . . like the wind blowing around the eaves of a house," Chamberlain told the St. Paul *Pioneer Press* (April 15). "A second later and we distinguished a long, high object of a gray white color."

Although the two men could not get a clear view of it in the darkness, the object, which had two rows of red, green, and white lights on each side, looked like "most of the top of a 'prairie schooner,'" Chamberlain said. It rose at a sharp angle, then headed south just above the treetops.

At the clearing, the two witnesses found, impressed in the wet ground, 14 two-foot-long prints, six inches wide, and arranged in an oblong pattern seven on a side. Apparently, these were traces left by the craft.

Around that same time Adam Thielen, a farmer in the Lake Elmo area, heard a buzzing sound above him. When he looked up, he saw a dark object with red and green lights sailing overhead.

such ships existed in human technology, and no standard history of aviation ever mentions these tall tales.

But other sightings appear to have been quite real. Most descriptions were of a cylindrical object with a headlight, lights along the side, and a brilliant searchlight that swept the ground. Sometimes the objects were said to have huge wings. An "airship" was observed over Oakland, California, just after 8 P.M. on November 26. One witness said the object resembled "a great black cigar. . . . The body was at least 100 feet long and attached to it was a triangular tail, one apex being attached to the main body. The surface of the airship looked as if it were made of aluminum, which exposure to wind and weather had turned dark. . . . The airship went at tremendous speed" (Oakland *Tribune*, December 1, 1896). Witnesses in California numbered in the thousands, partly due to the objects' appearances—sometimes in broad daylight—over such major cities as Sacramento and San Francisco.

By February 1897 meandering nocturnal lights were also sighted in rural Nebraska. One of these lights swooped low over a group of worshippers leaving a prayer meeting: It turned out to be a cone-shaped structure with a headlight, three smaller lights along each side, and two wings. Such reports became the subject of newspaper articles around the state, leading the Kearney *Hub* on February 18 to remark that the "now famous California airship inventor is in our vicinity." In short order sightings were

Archaeologist Henri Lhote discovered these painted figures (circa 6000 B.C.) on Algerian Sahara rock. Erich von Daniken suggested the large upright figure may be an alien in a space suit. Lhote said the figure, one of many known to archaeologists, is a man wearing ritual costume.

logged in Kansas, and by April across a broad band of middle America—from the Dakotas and Texas in the west to Ohio and Tennessee in the east—the skies were full of UFOs.

But the skies were also full of planets, stars, lighted balloons, and kites, which impressionable observers mistook for airships. Newspapers were full of outrageous yarns: A Martian perished in an airship crash in Texas. "Hideous" creatures lassoed a calf and flew off over Kansas with it. A "bellowing" giant broke the hip of a farmer who got too close to his airship after it landed in Michigan. These stories reflect a powerful undercurrent of speculation about extraterrestrial visitors.

RUSTLERS FROM MARS

On April 23, 1897, a Kansas newspaper, the Yates Center *Farmer's Advocate*, reported an incredible story. On the evening of April 19, local rancher Alexander Hamilton, his son, and a hired man saw a giant cigar-shaped ship hovering above a corral near the house. Hamilton claimed that in a carriage underneath the structure were "six of the strangest beings I ever saw." Just then, the three men heard a calf bawling and found it trapped in the fence, a rope around its neck extending upward. "We tried to get it off but could not," Hamilton said, "so we cut the wire loose to see the ship, heifer and all, rise slowly, disappearing in the northwest."

Kansas farmer Alexander Hamilton's 1897 tall tale of calfnapping aliens fooled the world for decades.

The next day, Hamilton went looking for the animal. He learned that a neighbor had found the butchered remains in his pasture. The neighbor, according to Hamilton, "was greatly mystified in not being able to find any tracks in the soft ground."

Hamilton's statement was followed by an affidavit signed by a dozen prominent citizens who swore that "for truth and veracity we have never heard [Hamilton's] word questioned." In the following days, his story was published in newspapers throughout the United States and even in Europe.

Ufologists rediscovered the account in the early 1960s, and the story rebounded to life through books and magazines. In 1976, however, an elderly Kansas woman came forward to say that shortly before the tale was reported in the *Farmer's Advocate*, she had heard Hamilton boast to his wife about the story he had made up. Hamilton belonged to a local liars' club that delighted in the concoction of outrageous tall tales. According to the woman, "The club soon broke up after the 'airship and cow' story. I guess that one had topped them all."

Aerial phenomena—such as Halley's Comet in 1910—have always fascinated, enthralled, and frightened human beings. Much traditional folklore about objects in the sky has resurfaced in the UFO era.

The wave had run its course by May 1897, but cylindrical UFOs with searchlights would continue to be seen periodically for decades to come. A worldwide wave of sightings took place in 1909 in Australia, New Zealand, Great Britain, and the eastern United States. As late as 1957 an "airship" was seen over McMinnville, Oregon.

Witnesses reported other kinds of UFOs, too. One such report came from U.S. Navy Lieutenant Frank H. Schofield, who served as the Pacific Fleet's commander-in-chief in the 1930s. Standing on the deck of the USS *Supply* on February 28, 1904, Schofield and two other sailors watched "three remarkable meteors," bright red in color, as they flew beneath the clouds toward their ship. The objects then "appeared to soar, passing above the broken clouds . . . moving directly away from the Earth. The largest had an apparent area of about six suns. It was egg-shaped, the larger end forward. The second was about twice the size of the sun, and the third, about the size of the sun. . . . The lights were in sight for over two minutes." (*Monthly Weather Review*, March 1904)

Far eerier stories lurked in the background. Only years later, when it was possible to talk about such things, did they come to light. One account surfaced more than 70 years later. In the summer of 1901, a 10-year-old Bournbrook, England, boy encountered something that looked like a box with a turret. Two little men clad in "military" uniforms and wearing caps with wires sticking out of them emerged through a door to wave him away. They then reentered the vehicle and flew away in a flash of light.

Similar events seem to have been occurring regularly over the early decades of the 20th century along with the less exotic sightings of strange aerial phenomena. These pre-1947 "close encounters of the third kind" were remarkably identical to the post-1947 reports in that the creatures who figured in the encounters were almost always held to be human or humanoid in appearance. In Hamburg, Germany, in June 1914, several "dwarfs" about four feet tall were seen milling around a cigar-shaped vessel with lighted portholes; they then ran into the vessel and flew away. In Detroit during the summer of 1922, through windows along the perimeter of a hovering disc-shaped object, 20 bald-headed figures stared intently at a suitably bewildered young couple. At Christchurch, New Zealand, in August 1944, a nurse at a train station noticed an "upturned saucer" nearby. She approached it, looked through a rectangular window, and spotted two humanoid figures not quite four feet tall. A third figure stood just outside an open door. When this humanoid saw her, the being "drift-ed" through an open hatchway, and the "saucer" shot straight upward.

The UFO wave of 1896 and 1897 sparked great interest as well as many hoaxes. A Chicago newspaper noted an April 11 report, based on what proved to be a faked photograph.

Early on the morning of March 23, 1909, a Peterborough, England, police officer saw a craft with a searchlight flying rapidly at 1,200 feet above the city. In the following weeks many others saw similar objects.

THE FIRST UFOLOGIST

Although these strange sky objects were reported with increasing frequency, the press and the scientific community treated each sighting as a one-time occurrence. There was no sense that such events, far from being isolated, were part of a larger phenomenon. Even the airship wave of 1896 and 1897 quickly passed out of the public's memory. But an eccentric American writer, Charles Fort (1874-1932), finally put it all together, becoming the world's first ufologist.

FOO FIGHTERS

A little remembered cartoon character named Smokey Stover used to declare, "Where there's foo, there's fire." So when enigmatic aerial phenomena kept pace with airplanes and ships in both the European and Pacific theaters during World War II, someone called them "foo fighters." The name stuck. Nobody knew for sure what the foo fighters were, but it was usually assumed that the other side—either the Allies or the Axis powers—had developed a secret weapon. After the war's conclusion, it soon became clear that this was not the explanation.

With the arrival of "flying saucers" in the summer of 1947, memories of foo fighters were revived. Like UFOs after them, foo fighters came in assorted shapes and descriptions, from amorphous nocturnal lights—which gave them their name—to silvery discs.

A typical sighting of foos took place in December 1942 over France. A Royal Air Force pilot in a Hurricane interceptor saw two lights shooting from near the ground toward his 7,000-foot cruising altitude. At first he took the lights to be tracer fire. But when they ceased ascending and followed

This rare photograph of "foo fighters" shows UFOs of the World War II era. Reports of these objects were kept secret until 1944.

him, mimicking every evasive maneuver he made, the pilot realized they were under someone's intelligent control. The lights, which kept an even distance from each other all the while, pursued him for some miles.

In August of that same year, Marines in the Solomon Islands were startled to see a formation of 150 "roaring" silvery objects. Their color, one witness said, was "like highly polished silver." They had neither wings nor tails and moved (as later UFO witnesses would often remark) with a slight wobble.

Official censorship kept reports of these phenomena out of the newspapers until December 1944. All during the war, however, similar objects were sighted by both military and civilian observers in the United States.

Born in Albany, New York, Fort was working as a newspaper reporter before age 20. Determined to become a writer, he traveled the world searching for experiences to write about. In South Africa Fort contracted a fever that followed him back to the United States. He married his nurse, Anna Filing, and embarked on a career as a freelance writer. Fort spent hours on end in the library pursuing his interests in nature and behavior. While paging through old newspapers and scientific journals, he began to notice, among other repeatedly chronicled oddities of the physical world, reports of strange aerial phenomena. Taking voluminous notes, he eventually turned out four books. The first three—*The Book of the Damned* (1919), *New Lands* (1923), and *Lo!* (1931)—dealt in part with UFO reports.

An intellectual with an impish sense of humor, Fort was fond of constructing outrageous "hypotheses" that could "explain" his data. But beneath the humor Fort was trying to make a serious point: Scientists were refusing to acknowledge that the world was full of weird phenomena and occurrences that did not fit with their theories. "Scientific" attempts to explain away such strange events as UFO sightings were laughably inadequate; their explanations, Fort wrote, were no less crazy than his own. "Science is established preposterousness," he declared. "Science of today—superstition of tomorrow. Science of tomorrow—superstition of today."

Charles Fort, the first ufologist, wrote the first UFO book: The Book of the Damned, *published in 1919.*

Behind the joking, however, Fort suspected that sightings of craftlike objects in the air indicated extraterrestrial visits to the Earth. Yet he also understood humanity's resistance to such a fantastic, even threatening notion. In a letter published in the September 5, 1926, issue of *The New York Times*, Fort offered some prescient observations. Extraterrestrial beings would not have to hide their activities, he wrote, because if "it is not the conventional or respectable thing upon this earth to believe in visitors from other worlds, most of us could watch them a week and declare that they were something else, and likely enough make things disagreeable for anybody who thought otherwise."

UFOs: THE OFFICIAL STORY

A lenticular cloud floats above Mount Shasta in northern California. These clouds can be mistaken for UFOs by impressionable viewers. Mount Shasta also plays an important role in New Age philosophy: Mount Shasta supposedly harbors survivors from the lost Pacific continent of Lemuria. When the Lemurians are not engaged in spiritual studies, they transport themselves elsewhere via flying saucer.

From the beginning, society—in the persons of prominent scientists, government officials, military officers, journalists, and ordinary citizens—would make things disagreeable for those who insisted they had seen strange flying objects and those who believed them. Wherever there were "flying saucers," there was also ridicule, dished out in generous portions to anyone courageous or foolish enough to defy the reigning orthodoxy.

A 1951 *Cosmopolitan* article, prepared with Air Force cooperation and encouragement, lashed out at the "screwballs" and "true believers" who thought they were seeing flying saucers. In the decades to come, others would accuse UFO observers of every conceivable social crime or mental disorder. As a result, only a small minority of witnesses would ever report their sightings, and many who did soon lived to regret it. In 1977 a group of professional debunkers warned *The New York Times* that belief in UFOs is not only irrational but also dangerous; if sufficiently widespread, civilization itself could collapse.

Yet in the face of jeering derision and inflated rhetoric, the sightings continued. The great majority of sightings would be by individuals who would have been implicitly believed had they been testifying to anything less outrageous. Of course, these witnesses were not always right. Even sympathetic investigators found that most reports could be explained conventionally. Few of the reports were outright hoaxes (around one

BUBBLES FROM OUTER SPACE

What could be the official explanation of these lights photographed at a Massachusetts Coast Guard station in 1952?

Not all unidentified flying objects are potential alien spacecraft. Some are much stranger. Consider, for example, the strange phenomena that passed over Biskopsberga, Sweden, early in the 19th century.

It was a cloudless afternoon on May 16, 1808, and a hard wind blew from the west; the sun over the village suddenly grew dim. At the western horizon a great number of spherical bodies appeared. They were heading toward the sun and changed from dark brown to black as they got closer to the sun. As they approached, they lost speed but sped up again after passing in front of the sun. They moved in a straight procession across the sky to the eastern horizon. According to *Transactions of the Swedish Academy of Sciences* (1808), "The phenomenon lasted uninterruptedly, upwards of two hours, dur-

ing which time millions of similar bodies continually rose in the west, one after the other irregularly, and continued their career in exactly the same manner."

Some of the balls fell out of the sky, several landing not far from K. G. Wettermark, secretary of the Swedish Academy of Sciences. Seen just before they hit the ground, they resembled "those air-bubbles which children use to produce from soap-suds by means of a reed. When the spot, where such a ball had fallen, was immediately after examined, nothing was to be seen, but a scarcely perceptible film or pellicle, as thin and fine as a cobweb, which was still changing colors, but soon entirely dried up and vanished."

The balls still in the air continued their passage until all disappeared in the east.

This lenticular cloud was photographed over Kepala Batas, Malaysia, in November 1984. Many UFO sightings can indeed be explained via natural occurrences.

percent, according to the Air Force's estimate), but sane and sober eyewitnesses often mistook weather balloons, stars and planets, advertising planes, and other ordinary objects for extraordinary objects. Still, some sightings stubbornly resisted explanation.

In the summer of 1947, the Air Materiel Command (AMC) was asked to study the situation and make recommendations about what should be done. On September 23 Lt. Gen. Nathan F. Twining, the AMC head, wrote his superior with this analysis: "The phenomenon reported is something real and not visionary or fictitious." Three months later the Air Force established Project Sign under AMC command, which is headquartered at Wright Field, soon to be Wright-Patterson Air Force Base (AFB), Dayton, Ohio, to investigate UFO reports.

AN "ESTIMATE OF THE SITUATION"

By late July 1948 Project Sign investigators had come to an incredible conclusion: Visitors

from outer space had arrived. They had begun with suspicions. Now they now had the proof. The proof was . . . well, it depends on which of two versions of the story is to be believed.

In the better-known version, the proof arrived in the sky southwest of Montgomery, Alabama, at 2:45 A.M. on July 24, 1948. To Clarence S. Chiles and John B. Whitted, pilot and copilot respectively of an Eastern Airlines DC-3, the object at first looked like a distant jet aircraft to their right and just above them. But it was moving awfully fast. Seconds later, as it streaked past them, they saw something that Whitted thought looked like "one of those fantastic Flash Gordon rocket ships in the funny papers." It

In September 1947 Lt. Gen. Nathan Twining, head of the Air Materiel Command, said UFOs were "something real and not visionary" and urged an official investigation.

ELINT VS. UFO

Possessing the most sophisticated electronic intelligence (ELINT) gear available to the U.S. Air Force, the RB-47 could handle anything. Unfortunately, in the morning hours of July 17, 1957, over the southern United States, an RB-47 came across something it was unprepared for.

In the first hint of what was to come, one of the three officers who operate the electronic countermeasures (ECM) equipment detected an odd signal. Moving up the radar screen, the blip passed some distance in front of the RB-47, then over Mississippi. Though puzzled, he said nothing. However, a few minutes later, at 4:10 A.M., the sudden appearance of an intense blue light bearing down on the aircraft shook the pilot and copilot. Even more unnerving, the object changed course in the blink of an eye and disappeared at the two o'clock position. The aircraft radar picked up a strong signal in the same spot. The UFO maintained this position even as the RB-47 continued toward east Texas.

The pilot then observed a "huge" light, attached, he suspected, to an even bigger something that the darkness obscured. When the electronics gear noted the presence of another UFO in the same general location as the first, the pilot turned the plane and accelerated toward it. The UFO shot away. By now the crew had alerted the Duncanville, Texas, Air Force ground radar station, and it was soon tracking the one UFO that remained (the second had disappeared after a brief time). At 4:50 radar showed the UFO abruptly stopping as the RB-47 passed under it. Barely seconds later it was gone.

This incredible case—considered one of the most significant UFO encounters ever—remained classified for years. When it became known years later, the Air Force declared that the RB-47 crew had tracked an airliner. Physicist Gordon David Thayer, who investigated the incident for the University of Colorado UFO Project, called this explanation "literally ridiculous."

*Eastern Airlines pilot Clarence S. Chiles (right) and copilot John B. Whitted
encountered a huge cigar-shaped object over Alabama in the
early morning hours of July 24, 1948.*

was a huge, tube-shaped structure, its fuselage three times the circumference of a B-29 bomber, and with two rows of square windows emanating white light. It was, Chiles would remember, "powered by some jet or other type of power shooting flame from the rear some 50 feet." The object was also glimpsed by the one passenger who was not sleeping. After it passed the DC-3, it shot up 500 feet and was lost in the clouds at 6,000 feet altitude.

Although Chiles and Whitted didn't know it at the time, an hour earlier a ground-maintenance crewman at Robins AFB, Georgia, had seen the same or an identical object. On July 20, observers in The Hague, the Netherlands, watched a comparable craft move swiftly through the clouds.

It took investigators little time to establish that no earthly missile or aircraft could have been responsible for these sightings. Moreover, with independent verification of the object's appearance and performance, there seemed no question of the witnesses' being mistaken about what they had seen. In the days following the sighting, Project Sign prepared an "estimate of the situation"—a thick document stamped TOP SECRET—that argued that this and other reliably observed UFOs could only be otherworldly vehicles. But when the estimate landed on the desk of Air Force Chief of Staff Gen. Hoyt S. Vandenberg, he promptly rejected it on the grounds that the report had not proved its case.

This not-quite-accurate sketch of the Chiles-Whitted UFO—witnesses reported two rows of windows—shows an object of structured appearance and extraordinary speed.

In short order Project Sign's advocates of extraterrestrial visitation were reassigned or encouraged to leave the service. The Air Force then embarked on a debunking campaign interrupted only for the brief period between 1951 and 1953 when Capt. Edward J. Ruppelt, who took an open-minded approach, headed the official UFO project. Project Sign was succeeded by Project Grudge (1949-1952); Project Blue Book,

(Continued on page 32)

MR. MOORE GOES TO WASHINGTON

Driving near Montville, Ohio, late on the evening of November 6, 1957, Olden Moore was startled to see a glowing disc, 50 feet high and 50 feet in diameter, come down along the roadside. He got out of his car and watched the landed UFO for the next 15 minutes. It was still there when he left to get his wife, but it was gone when they returned. Police and Civilian Defense investigators found both "footprints" and radioactivity at the site.

A few days later Moore disappeared. When he resurfaced, he would not say where he had been. But in private conversations with ufologist C. W. Fitch, Moore claimed that Air Force officers had flown him to Washington, D.C., and hidden him away while they repeatedly interviewed him. Toward the end of his stay, the officers showed him a UFO film, apparently taken from a military plane, and said UFOs seemed to be of interplanetary origin. Moore then signed a document swearing him to secrecy.

A ROARING UFO AND FIGURES
AT SOCORRO

Officer Lonnie Zamora was chasing a speeder south of Socorro, New Mexico, late on the afternoon of April 24, 1964, but he was about to enter UFO history. No less than the head of Project Blue Book would later tell a CIA audience that Zamora's experience was the most puzzling UFO case he had ever dealt with.

At Socorro, New Mexico—the site where Lonnie Zamora saw a UFO—investigators found burn marks and impressions in the ground that indicated the presence of strange craft.

New Mexico police officer Lonnie Zamora, witness to a UFO landing

All Zamora knew at first was that a roar was filling his ears and a flame was descending in the southwestern sky. Breaking off the chase, Zamora sped to the site, where he expected to find that a dynamite shack had exploded. Instead, as he maneuvered through the hilly terrain, he glimpsed a shiny car-size object resting on the ground about 150 yards away. Near it stood two small figures clothed in what looked like white coveralls.

Zamora briefly lost sight of the object and figures as he passed behind a hill. Zamora thought he had witnessed a car accident, but when he got out of his car to

Air Force investigators from Kirtland Air Force Base, including
Maj. William Connor (center) and Sgt. David Moody (right) of
Project Blue Book, use a geiger counter to check the Socorro
landing site. Witness Lonnie Zamora looks on.

investigate, he suddenly realized otherwise. Egg-shaped and standing on four legs, the object displayed a peculiar insignia on its side, something like an arrow pointing vertically from a horizontal base to a half-circle crown. The two figures had disappeared, and the object was emitting an ominous roar again. Frightened, Zamora charged back to his car. At one point he glanced over his shoulder to see the UFO, now airborne, heading toward a nearby canyon.

Project Blue Book investigators found that Officer Zamora had a reputation for integrity. The investigators also examined what looked like landing marks found on the desert floor. In the middle of these marks was a burned area, apparently from the spacecraft's exhaust.

At a July 1952 Washington, D.C., conference Gen. Roger Ramey and Gen. John Samford (both seated), along with Project Blue Book head Capt. Edward Ruppelt (standing behind the two generals), plotted strategy to defuse UFO hysteria.

(Continued from page 29)

established in March 1952, succeeded Project Grudge. Practically until the day the Air Force closed down Project Blue Book in December 1969, it denied that such a document had ever existed, even when former UFO-project officers swore they had seen or heard of it. No one could produce a copy of the document, however, because the Air Force had all copies burned.

At least one source disputes this account, on the authority of Capt. Ruppelt, who tells it in his memoir of his Project Blue Book years, *The Report on Unidentified Flying Objects* (1956). Years after the original incidents, a retired AMC-assigned officer (now deceased) claimed that Project Sign prepared two drafts of the estimate. The first draft referred to what the officer remembered as a "physical evidence" case in

New Mexico. When Vandenberg saw this reference, he demanded its removal. The second draft, with the offending paragraphs deleted, argued its case solely from eyewitness testimony—of which the Chiles/Whitted encounter was an impressive example. Vandenberg could now claim that, in the absence of physical evidence, no proof existed.

A long time would pass before civilian investigators learned of this New Mexico physical-evidence case. It would turn out to be one of the most important incidents—perhaps the most important incident—in UFO history. With these revelations would come the belated realization that ufology has two histories: a public one and

Another official explanation for UFOs: hoaxers. During the summer of 1947, many people capitalized on the "flying disc" craze. One prankster in Williamsport, Pennsylvania, manufactured a small saucer and informed authorities that it had dropped out of the sky.

DON'T JUDGE A BOOK BY ITS COVER

Judging from the Air Force's press notices, Project Blue Book had the UFO problem well in hand. But in reality, for almost all of its nearly 20-year existence, it was a low-priority operation headed by a lower-ranking officer. A well-funded but highly classified project (even now its name is not known) handled sensitive UFO cases. The staff for Project Blue Book was small and, according to astronomer J. Allen Hynek (Project Blue Book's scientific adviser), less than hardworking. Nonetheless, the Air Force regularly assured reporters, who then uncritically passed the line to newspaper readers, that thorough, scientific investigations had proved the nonexistence of UFOs. In a 1968 letter to the project, Hynek leveled several charges against Project Blue Book: It lacked the trained personnel necessary for the job, had conducted "virtually no dialogue" with the "outside scientific world," and employed statistical methods that were "nothing less than a travesty."

a hidden one. But we're getting ahead of our-
selves. . . .

THE INVADERS

Flying saucers were supposed to be a fad.
Pundits tied these strange shapes in the sky to
"war nerves," a sort of delayed-response reaction
to the traumas of World War II. They were also
supposed to be a peculiarly American delusion.
Unidentified flying objects, however, have sur-
vived longer than war memories and remain an
eerie, discomforting presence the world over.

As military and civilian researchers scrambled
to make sense of all this, anything seemed possible—even attack by hostile aliens.

On January 7, 1948, Kentucky Air National
Guard Capt. Thomas F. Mantell, Jr., died when

*National Guard pilot Thomas Mantell, Jr., died in a plane
crash while pursuing a "UFO" that was later identified
as a Skyhook balloon.*

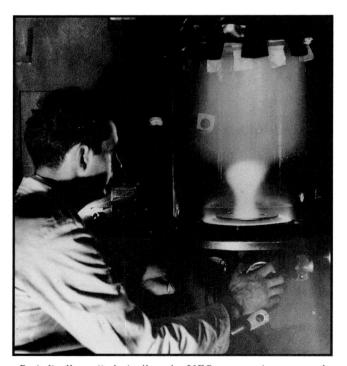

*Periodically, a "solution" to the UFO mystery is announced.
In this instance ionized particles generated in a laboratory
were said to indicate UFOs are natural phenomena.*

his F-51 crashed after chasing what he called, in
one of his last radio transmissions, "a metallic
object of tremendous size." The official Air
Force line was that Mantell saw Venus.
Unofficially, many officers feared that a spaceship had shot down Mantell's plane with a
frighteningly superior extraterrestrial weapon.

Neither answer, it turned out, was correct.
Declassified documents eventually disclosed that
the Navy had been conducting secret balloon
experiments as part of its Skyhook project,
which sought to measure radiation levels in the
upper atmosphere. As Mantell pursued what he

*The Air Force was hard-pressed to explain the reports of such reputable people
as missile engineer James Stokes (left), whose close encounter
on November 4, 1957, resulted in a "sunburn."*

apparently thought was a spaceship, he had foolishly ascended to 25,000 feet—a dangerous altitude for the aircraft he was piloting—and blacked out from lack of oxygen. His F-51 spun out of control and crash-landed in the front lawn of a farmhouse near Franklin, Kentucky. But in the days that followed the tragedy, sensational headlines fueled everyone's worst fears about flying saucers, and the Mantell incident entered UFO legend.

Just as frightening, though more bizarre and less publicized, was a fatal encounter that occurred on November 23, 1953, over Lake Superior. That evening, as Air Defense Command radar tracked an unidentified target moving at 500 miles per hour over the lake, an F-89C all-weather jet interceptor from Kinross AFB took off in hot pursuit. Radar operators watched the aircraft close in on the UFO, and then something fantastic happened: The two blips merged and then faded on the screen, and all communication with the interceptor ceased. An extensive land and water search found not a trace of the craft nor the two men aboard it: pilot Lt. Felix Moncla, Jr., and radar observer Lt. R. R. Wilson.

Unlike the Mantell incident, the Kinross case attracted minimal newspaper coverage; also unlike Mantell, Kinross has never been satisfactorily explained. Later, after aviation writer Donald E. Keyhoe broke the story in his best-selling *The Flying Saucer Conspiracy* (1955), the Air Force insisted that the "UFO" had proved on investigation to be a Royal Canadian Air Force C-47. The F-89C had not actually collided with the Canadian transport plane, but something unspecified had happened, and the interceptor crashed. Aside from implying woeful incompetence on the radar operators' part, this "explanation"—still the official one—flies in the face of the Canadian government's repeated denials that any such incident involving one of its aircraft ever took place.

In 1958 Keyhoe got hold of a leaked Air Force document that made it clear that officialdom considered the Kinross incident a UFO

In 1950 engineers of the Canadian government set up Project Magnet. This semiofficial operation allowed participants to use equipment and facilities during their off hours to monitor UFO activity.

encounter of the strangest kind. The document quoted these words from a radar observer who had been there: "It seems incredible, but the blip apparently just swallowed our F-89." The following year, in conversations with civilian ufologists Tom Comella and Edgar Smith, M. Sgt. O. D. Hill of Project Blue Book confided that such incidents—he claimed Kinross had not been the only one—had officials worried. Many, he said, believed UFOs to be of extraterrestrial origin and wanted to prevent an interplanetary Pearl Harbor. Comella subsequently confronted Hill's superior, Capt. George T. Gregory, at Blue Book headquarters. Gregory looked

In an official picture taken in September of 1957, what appears to be a small UFO follows a Martin B-57 aircraft as it flies over Edwards Air Force Base in California. The exact nature of the UFO remains an object of controversy to this day.

KEYHOE PRESSES
THE AIR FORCE

*Donald Keyhoe battled the Air Force
over UFO secrecy.*

In the 1950s the Air Force's most forceful critic, retired Marine Corps Maj. Donald E. Keyhoe, caused Pentagon UFO debunkers no end of consternation. A respected aviation journalist, Keyhoe wrote an explosive article, "The Flying Saucers Are Real," for the widely read men's magazine *True* (January 1950 issue). Not only did intelligent beings from elsewhere have the Earth under scrutiny, Keyhoe claimed, but the Air Force knew it and was conspiring to cover up the truth. From his Washington

contacts Keyhoe gathered leaked information about encounters between military interceptor aircraft and fast-moving discs as well as documents suggesting concern about these events.

In 1957, after writing three best-selling books on the UFO cover-up, Keyhoe became director of the National Investigations Committee on Aerial Phenomena (NICAP). Though Keyhoe had powerful allies, including former CIA chief R. H. Hillenkoetter, the Air Force had him outgunned. Keyhoe retired from the fray in 1969. When he died 19 years later, the battle against official secrecy had passed to other, younger hands. His pioneering efforts are still remembered.

*Donald Keyhoe was the most famous ufologist
of the 1950s.*

Glimpsing a "dark ball"—possibly a meteorite—Donella Banning of Dayton, Texas, heard something strike her car one night in March 1966 and found two dents on the roof of her car.

shocked, left the room for a short period, and returned to state, "Well, we just cannot talk about those cases."

THE INTELLIGENCE COMMUNITY TAKES CONTROL

A few minutes before midnight on Saturday, July 19, 1952, an air traffic controller at National Airport in Washington, D.C., noticed some odd blips on his radar screen. Knowing that no aircraft were flying in that area—15 miles to the southwest of the capital—he rushed to inform his boss, Harry G. Barnes. Barnes recalled a few days later, "We knew immediately that a very strange situation existed. . . . [T]heir movements were completely radical compared to those of ordinary aircraft." They moved with

THE SENATOR'S
SOVIET SAUCERS

Georgia Senator Richard Russell was a major figure in the U.S. Senate. As head of the Senate Armed Services Committee, he exerted enormous influence over the American defense establishment. When he spoke, the military listened. So when Russell reported what he had seen while traveling through the Soviet Union, no one laughed—and hardly anyone outside official circles knew of his remarkable experience until years later.

Just after 7 P.M. on October 4, 1955, while on a train in the Transcaucasia region, the senator happened to gaze out a window to the south. To his considerable astonishment his eyes focused on a large disc-shaped object slowly ascending as a flame shot from underneath it. The object then raced north across the tracks in front of the train. Russell scurried to alert his two companions, who looked out to see a second disc do what the first had just done. At that moment Soviet trainmen shut the curtains and ordered the American passengers not to look outside.

As soon as they arrived in Prague, Czechoslovakia, the three men went to the United States embassy and sat down with Lt. Col. Thomas S. Ryan, the air attaché. Russell's associate, Lt. Col. E. U. Hathaway, told Ryan that they were about to report something extremely important—"but something that we've been told by your people [the U.S. Air Force] doesn't exist."

Soon rumors about the senator's sighting reached America, but when a reporter for the Los Angeles *Examiner* tried to obtain details, Russell said only, "I have discussed this matter with the affected agencies and they are of the opinion that it is not wise to publicize this matter at this time." The report was not declassified until 1985. Interestingly, one of the "affected agencies" was not Project Blue Book, which never received the report. Apparently, the event was too sensitive for so lowly a project.

During the second half of July 1952, radar screens in the Washington, D.C.,
area tracked fast-moving unknown objects, sparking concerns about
national security. The trackings and accompanying visual sightings
have yet to be satisfactorily explained.

such sudden bursts of intense speed that radar could not track them continuously.

Soon, National Airport's other radar, Tower Central (set on short-range detection, unlike Barnes' Airway Traffic Control Central [ARTC]), was tracking unknowns. At Andrews AFB, ten miles to the east, Air Force personnel gaped incredulously as bright orange objects in the southern sky circled, stopped abruptly, and then streaked off at blinding speeds. Radar at

Andrews AFB also picked up the strange phenomena.

The sightings and radar trackings continued until 3 A.M. By then witnesses on the ground and in the air had observed the UFOs, and at times all three radar sets had tracked them simultaneously.

Exciting and scary as all this had been, it was just the beginning of an incredible episode. The next evening radar tracked UFOs as they performed extraordinary "gyrations and reversals," in the words of one Air Force weather observer. Moving at more than 900 miles per hour, the objects gave off radar echoes exactly like those of aircraft or other solid targets. Sightings and trackings occurred intermittently during the week and then erupted into a frenzy over the following weekend. At one point, as an F-94 moved on targets ten miles away, the UFOs turned the tables and darted en masse toward the interceptor, surrounding it in seconds. The

badly shaken pilot, Lt. William Patterson, radioed Andrews AFB to ask if he should open fire. The answer, according to Albert M. Chop, a civilian working as a press spokesperson for the Air Force who was present, was "stunned silence. . . . After a tense moment, the UFOs pulled away and left the scene."

As papers, politicians, and public clamored for answers, the Air Force hosted the biggest press conference in history. A transcript shows that the spokesperson engaged in what amounted to

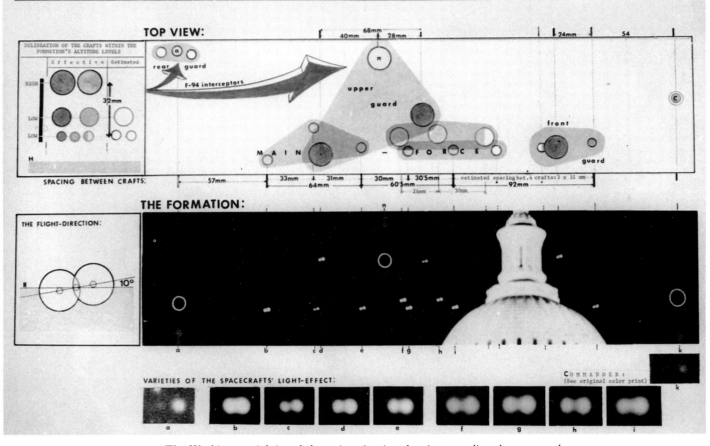

The Washington sightings led one imaginative theorist to outline the command structure of the "intergalactic task force" allegedly responsible. The scare attracted President Truman's personal attention. During the time of the sightings, all intelligence channels into and out of the capital were jammed, leaving the city defenseless if an Earth-bound adversary had chosen to attack.

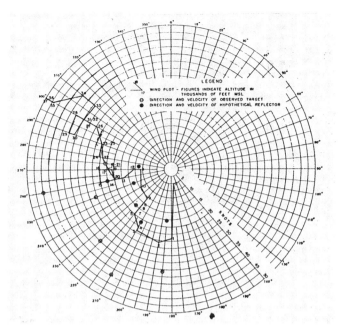

Though the major Washington sightings occurred over the weekends of July 19-20 and July 26-27, 1952, sporadic reports and trackings were recorded into mid-August. Here, the black dots indicate unidentified targets tracked on the radar screen at Washington National Airport on August 15.

double-talk, but the reporters, desperate for something to show their editors, picked up on Capt. Roy James' off-the-cuff suggestion that temperature inversions had caused the radar blips. James, a UFO skeptic, had arrived in Washington only that morning and had not participated in the ongoing investigation.

Nonetheless, headlines across the country echoed the sentiments expressed in the Washington *Daily News:* "SAUCER" ALARM DISCOUNTED BY PENTAGON; RADAR OBJECTS LAID TO COLD AIR FORMATIONS. This "explanation" got absolutely no support from those who had seen the objects either in the air or on the radar screens, and the U.S. Weather Bureau, in a little-noted statement, rejected the theory. In fact, the offi-

cial Air Force position, which it had successfully obscured, was that the objects were "unknowns."

But while the nation's opinion makers, satisfied that all was well, went on to other stories, the aftershocks of the Washington UFO invasion reverberated throughout the defense establishment. H. Marshall Chadwell, assistant director of the CIA's Office of Scientific Intelligence, warned CIA director Gen. Walter Bedell Smith, "At any moment of attack [from the Soviet Union], we are now in a position where we can-

Gen. Walter Bedell Smith, CIA head from 1950 to 1953, was rumored to be a member of a supersecret UFO cover-up group.

This is one of many photographs in which a lens flare, sometimes mistaken for a UFO, appears.

not, on an instant basis, distinguish hardware from phantom, and as tension mounts we will run the increasing risk of false alerts and the even greater danger of falsely identifying the real as phantom." Chadwell feared that the Soviets could plant UFO stories as a psychological warfare exercise to sow "mass hysteria and panic." In fact, as *The New York Times* noted in an August 1, 1952, analysis, the Washington sightings and others across the country in July were so numerous that "regular intelligence work had been affected."

In fact, during the Washington events traffic related to the UFO sightings had clogged all intelligence channels. If the Soviets had chosen to take advantage of the resulting paralysis to launch an air or ground invasion of the United

States, there would have been no way for the appropriate warnings to get through.

Determined that this would never happen again, the CIA approached Project Blue Book and said it wanted to review the UFO data accumulated since 1947. In mid-January a scientific panel headed by CIA physicist H. P. Robertson briefly reviewed the Air Force material, dismissed it quickly, and went on to its real business: recommending ways American citizens could be discouraged from seeing, reporting, or believing in flying saucers. The Air Force should initiate a "debunking" campaign and enlist the services of celebrities on the unreality of UFOs. Beyond that official police agencies

(Continued on page 46)

In the wake of the Washington sightings, the CIA convened a scientific panel under physicist H. P. Robertson (standing) to orchestrate a UFO debunking campaign.

"BALL LIGHTNING"
IN LEVELLAND

Ball lightning, such as this representation seen during a storm in France in 1845, is a rare and poorly understood natural phenomenon that may explain some reports of small, luminous UFOs.

On November 2, 1957, the Soviet Union launched Sputnik II into orbit. Within hours, coincidentally or otherwise, a UFO wave erupted in the United States. At first the wave appeared to be concentrated in a small backwater area of west Texas, where a series of remarkable UFO encounters took place.

The sheriff's office in the town of Levelland scoffed that evening when a frightened man called to report that he and a friend, driving on a country highway four miles west of town, had seen a 200-foot-long "rocket" rise up from a field and rush toward their truck. Terrified of an imminent collision, the two flew out of the cab and hurled themselves into the ditch. As the UFO passed just above the truck, rocking it with a blast as loud as thunder, the vehicle's engine died and its lights went out, only to resume a few seconds later when the mysterious object disappeared from view.

An hour later, another caller recounted his experience with an identical UFO that had also interfered with the electric functioning of his car. The scoffing stopped, and sheriff's officers soon found themselves handling comparable stories from frightened observers who had seen a giant, light- and engine-killing UFO at locations west, east, and north of Levelland. At 1:30 A.M.

Lens flare or ball lightning? A 1972 British photo.

Christian Lynggaard photographed ball lightning at an air force base in Denmark.

Sheriff Weir Clem and a deputy saw the UFO themselves. A few minutes later Ray Jones, Levelland's fire marshal, experienced motor difficulty when the same or a similar phenomenon was in view.

The official Air Force explanation: "ball lightning." But ball lightning never exceeds more than a few feet in diameter and is usually only inches around. Project Blue Book claimed an electrical storm was in progress during the sightings; there was no storm. By 1957 Project Blue Book's "investigations" were perfunctory at best. Even its chief scientific adviser, astronomer J. Allen Hynek, would later remark on the "absence of evidence that ball lightning can stop cars and put out headlights."

(Continued from page 43)

should monitor civilian UFO research groups "because of their potentially great influence on mass thinking. . . . The apparent irresponsibility and the possible use of such groups for subversive purposes should be kept in mind."

The panel's existence and its conclusions remained secret for years, but the impact on official UFO policy was enormous. In short order Project Blue Book was downgraded, becoming little more than a public-relations exercise. In 1966 the Air Force sponsored a project, directed by University of Colorado physicist Edward U. Condon, to conduct what was billed as an "independent" study. In fact it was part of an elaborate scheme to allow the Air Force, publicly anyway, to get out of the UFO business.

Edward U. Condon, head of the University of Colorado UFO Project, urged no further scientific investigation of UFO phenomena.

The official text of the controversial Condon Report, billed in 1969 as the last (and negative) word on UFOs.

The Condon committee was to review or reinvestigate Project Blue Book data and decide if further investigation was warranted. As an internal memorandum leaked to *Look* magazine in 1968 showed, Condon and his chief assistant knew before they started that they were to reach negative conclusions. Condon sparked a fire storm of controversy when he summarily dismissed two investigators who, not having gotten the message, returned from the field with positive findings. In January 1969, when the committee's final report was released in book form, readers who did not get past Condon's introduction were led to believe that "further extensive study of UFOs probably cannot be justified on the expectation that science will be advanced thereby." Those who bothered to read the book found that fully one-third of the cases examined remained unexplained, and scientist-critics would later note that even some of the "explained" reports were unconvincingly accounted for.

But that did not matter; Condon and his committee had done their job, and the Air Force closed down Project Blue Book at the end of the year.

Some years later a revealing memo came to light through the Freedom of Information Act.

Despite the U.S. government's attempts at a cover-up, the UFO controversy would not disappear. Astronomer and Project Blue Book adviser J. Allen Hynek (left)—here investigating UFO reports in Michigan—questioned the treatment UFO reports were given by the Air Force.

In 1951 Urner Liddel of the Office of Naval Research announced the "solution" to the UFO mystery: Skyhook balloons plus "mass hysteria" related to fears of atomic war.

It amounted to confirmation of a long-standing suspicion: Project Blue Book served as a front for a classified project that handled the truly sensitive reports. The memo, prepared on October 20, 1969, by Brig. Gen. C. H. Bolender, the Air Force's Deputy Director of Development, noted that "reports of UFOs which could affect national security should continue to be handled through the standard Air Force procedure designed for this purpose." He did not explain what this "standard Air Force procedure" was, and the 16 pages attached to his memo—which presumably would have shed some light on this curious assertion—are missing from the Air Force files.

The Bolender memo was the first whiff from the cover-up's smoking gun. There would be more—a lot more—in the years to come.

THE DIMENSIONS OF A PHENOMENON

Clyde Tombaugh, discoverer of the planet Pluto, saw UFOs two times. In 1957 he suggested such objects may emanate from the "hundreds of thousands of habitable worlds" in the galaxy. In 1975, in his last public statement on the subject, Tombaugh said the nature of what he had seen was "still a very open question."

OF SAUCERS AND SCIENTISTS

"Have We Visitors from Space?" *Life* magazine asked in an article in its April 7, 1952, issue. It was a question people all over the world were asking in wonder or fear or both. What, short of intruders from other worlds, could explain the presence in the Earth's atmosphere of objects that looked like structured craft but which performed in ways unimaginably beyond the capacity of earthly rockets and airplanes?

Astronomer Clyde Tombaugh—who had discovered the planet Pluto in 1930—was numbered among those who had seen flying saucers. On the evening of August 20, 1949, he, his wife, and his mother-in-law saw a "geometrical group of faint bluish-green rectangles of light" apparently attached to a larger "structure." He said of the experience, "I have done thousands of hours of night sky watching, but never saw a sight so strange as this."

In 1952, in an informal survey of 44 of his fellow astronomers, J. Allen Hynek of Project Blue Book learned that five had seen UFOs. "A higher percentage than among the public at large," Professor Hynek noted in an internal Air Force memorandum. Fear of ridicule kept most scientists silent about their sightings, however. In a 1976 survey of members of the American Astronomical Society, 62 admitted to having had UFO experiences; only one of the scientists made a public report of his sighting.

One astronomer more than any other would be associated with the UFO phenomenon:

Professor Hynek. In 1948 the Air Force asked Hynek—as a faculty member at Ohio State University, he was the astronomer closest to Dayton, Ohio, the location of the UFO project's headquarters at Wright-Patterson Air Force Base (AFB)—to look at the UFO reports it was gathering to determine which of them resulted from misidentification of astronomical phenomena such as meteors, comets, planets, and stars. To the extent he had given the subject any thought, Hynek was deeply skeptical of flying saucers. Yet four years later, he confessed in a lecture to colleagues that some reports were indeed "puzzling." The "steady flow of reports, often made in concert by reliable observers," merited scientific attention, not ridicule. "Ridicule is not a part of the scientific method," Hynek said, "and the public should not be taught that it is."

Yet Hynek, cautious, even plodding, by nature, did not surrender his skepticism easily. By the late 1950s he was urging his Air Force employers to jettison the term "unidentified flying objects." Reports of UFOs continued to flow in simply because science had failed to educate people to think critically and to recognize mundane aerial phenomena. Nonetheless, deep down the puzzling cases continued to rankle Hynek, and he watched with growing dismay the clear incompetence of the Project Blue Book "investigation."

By this time Hynek was head of Northwestern University's astronomy department and one of America's best known and most respected astronomers. He had no reason to voice his quiet, heretical concerns that the UFO question had not been satisfactorily answered. But in the early 1960s a graduate student of his, a young Frenchman named Jacques Vallée (who would go on to write a number of UFO books), urged Hynek to give vent to these suspicions, looking

Astronomer J. Allen Hynek served as the Air Force's chief scientific adviser for its three public projects investigating UFOs: Sign, Grudge, and Blue Book.

at the evidence with an open mind and without fear.

Within a few short years no one could doubt that, even as Hynek remained Project Blue Book's chief scientific adviser, he and the Air Force were now operating on different wavelengths. While the Air Force continued to parrot the same old line—all UFO reports were

BURNED BY A UFO

Stephen Michalak was searching for minerals along Falcon Lake, 80 miles east of Winnipeg, Manitoba, on May 20, 1967, when he heard the cackling of geese. Looking up into the early-afternoon sky, he saw two glowing oval-shaped objects on a steep, swift descent. One abruptly stopped its downward flight while the other continued, landing on a flat rock outcropping 160 feet away.

Michalak carefully approached the strange craft, which looked like a bowl with a dome on top. Forty feet wide and 15 feet high, it emitted a humming sound and a sulphur stench. On the bottom half, just below the rim of the bowl, was a doorlike opening from which muffled voices emanated. "They sounded like humans," he reported.

Michalak's cap was burned and his glove melted in a dramatic Manitoba close encounter in 1967.

"I was able to make out two distinct voices, one with a higher pitch than the other."

Thinking he was dealing with a terrestrial craft, he addressed the speakers in several languages, asking if he could help. He got no answer. He poked his head through the opening into the interior, seeing only a "maze of lights." At that moment three panel doors slid across and sealed the opening. As Michalak stepped back, he touched the vehicle's exterior: It was so hot that it burned his gloves.

Suddenly, the object rose, expelling hot air through a gridlike vent and causing Michalak's shirt to erupt into flames. An attack of nausea overtook him.

When doctors examined Michalak in a Winnipeg hospital a few hours later, they noted a dramatic burn pattern all across his chest—exactly like the grid Michalak had described on the UFO's underside. Michalak's health problems continued and brought him to Minnesota's Mayo Clinic the next year. Investigations by official and civilian bodies uncovered no evidence of a hoax. As late as 1975 a member of the Canadian Parliament complained that the government had not released its findings.

*In October 1973, two Pascagoula, Mississippi, men claimed they were abducted
by UFO beings. Investigation convinced scientists James Harder (left) and J.
Allen Hynek the witnesses were telling what they believed to be the truth.*

explainable, and only fools and charlatans thought otherwise—Hynek boldly advocated a new study. With each pronouncement Hynek made less secret his conviction that a new study would show UFOs to be something extraordinary, in all probability the product of a nonhuman intelligence.

In 1972 Hynek put his thoughts into a book, *The UFO Experience*, that eloquently criticized Project Blue Book's as well as science's neglect of the issue. The book concluded: "When the long awaited solution to the UFO problem comes, I believe that it will prove to be not merely the next small step in the march of science but a mighty and totally unexpected quantum leap."

NOCTURNAL LIGHTS TO CLOSE ENCOUNTERS

Hynek classified UFO reports into six categories: nocturnal lights, daylight discs, radar/visual cases, close encounters of the first kind, close encounters of the second kind, and close encounters of the third kind.

Nocturnal lights. Near midnight on the evening of August 30, 1951, during a spate of sightings of boomerang-shaped lights in

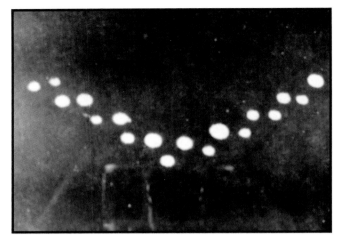

The "Lubbock lights"—a classic example of Hynek's UFO category of nocturnal lights. Other witnesses saw the same V-shaped formation of lights as photographer Carl Hart, Jr., who took this and four additional pictures.

Lubbock, Texas, college student Carl Hart, Jr., glimpsed a formation of 18 to 20 white lights through his bedroom window. Forming a perfect V configuration in two rows, they were passing silently over his parents' house from the north. Grabbing a 35mm camera, Hart raced outside, hoping they would return. A minute later the lights reappeared, and though they were visible for less than five seconds, he was able to snap two pictures. When the lights returned once more, Hart got three more pictures.

The local newspaper as well as the Air Force subjected Hart's photographs of the "Lubbock lights"—as they are known in UFO lore—to intensive investigation. No evidence of a hoax emerged then or later, and no conventional explanation could be found.

Daylight discs. From mid-morning to mid-afternoon on July 8, 1947, silvery disc-shaped objects bedeviled Muroc Air Base (later renamed Edwards AFB). Two discs first showed up at

9:30 A.M; they moved at 300 miles per hour at 8,000 feet altitude on a level flight path against the wind. A third disc, flying in tight circles, then appeared and headed toward the Mojave Desert with the first two. Some 40 minutes later a test pilot warming up an XP-84 aircraft saw another object, again flying into the wind. At noon, as a pilot was conducting a seat-ejection test at 20,000 feet, observers saw a UFO underneath it. The object was descending rapidly; it then headed north. Witnesses told Air Force investigators that "it presented a distinct oval-shaped outline, with two projections on the upper surface which might have been thick fins or knobs. They crossed each other at intervals, suggesting either rotation or oscillation of a slow type. . . . The color was silver, resembling an aluminum-painted fabric." At 4 P.M. an F-51

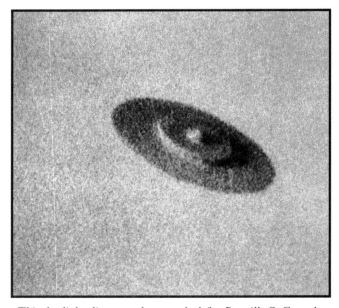

This daylight disc was photographed for Brazil's O Cruzeiro *on May 7, 1952, over Barra Da Tiguca. Critics have pointed out that the shadow pattern on the structure contradicts witnesses' claims about its position in the sky. The shadows should have been on the left side, not the right.*

A UFO FOR THE PRESIDENT-TO-BE

A wide range of people have seen UFOs, including Ronald Reagan when he was governor of California.

One night in 1974, from a Cessna Citation aircraft, one of America's most famous citizens saw a UFO.

There were four persons aboard the plane: pilot Bill Paynter, two security guards, and the governor of California, Ronald Reagan. As the airplane approached Bakersfield, California, the passengers called Paynter's attention to a strange object to their rear. "It appeared to be several hun-

dred yards away," Paynter recalled. "It was a fairly steady light until it began to accelerate. Then it appeared to elongate. Then the light took off. It went up at a 45-degree angle—at a high rate of speed. Everyone on the plane was surprised. . . . The UFO went from a normal cruise speed to a fantastic speed instantly. If you give an airplane power, it will accelerate—but not like a hot rod, and that's what this was like."

A week later Reagan recounted the sighting to Norman C. Miller, then Washington bureau chief for the *Wall Street Journal*. Reagan told Miller, "We followed it for several minutes. It was a bright white light. We followed it to Bakersfield, and all of a sudden to our utter amazement it went straight up into the heavens." When Miller expressed some doubt, a "look of horror came over [Reagan]. It suddenly dawned on him . . . that he was talking to a reporter." Immediately afterward, according to Miller, Reagan "clammed up."

Reagan has not discussed the incident publicly since.

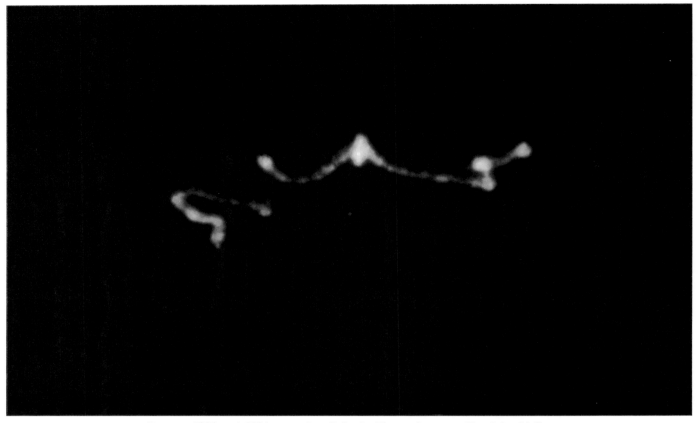

*Between 1981 and 1986 mysterious lights in Norway's remote Hessdalen Valley,
alternately hovering or streaking at incredible speeds, puzzled residents as well as
scientists and ufologists who came to investigate.*

pilot encountered a "flat object of a light-reflecting nature" without wings or fins.

These sightings, Hynek wrote, caused the Air Force to "take a deep interest in UFOs."

Radar/visual. While driving east of Corning, California, near midnight on August 13, 1960, state police officers Charles Carson and Stanley Scott saw a lighted object drop out of the sky. Fearing the imminent crash of an airliner, they screeched to a halt and jumped out of their car. The object continued to fall until it reached about 100 feet altitude, at which point it abruptly reversed direction and ascended 400 feet, then stopped. "At this time," Carson wrote in his

official report, "it was clearly visible to both of us. It was surrounded by a glow making the round or oblong object visible. At each end, or each side of the object, there were definite red lights. At times about five white lights were visible between the red lights. As we watched, the object moved again and performed aerial feats that were actually unbelievable."

The two officers radioed the Tehama County Sheriff's Office and asked it to contact the nearest Air Force base (at Red Bluff). Radar there confirmed the object's presence.

The UFO remained in view for more than two hours. During that time two deputy sheriffs

ANGEL HAIR

UFOs over Oloron, France, dropped a cottony substance likened to "angel hair."

It was the strangest sight to ever grace the sky over Oloron, France. In the early afternoon of October 17, 1952, according to one of the many witnesses, high school superintendent Jean-Yves Prigent, there appeared a "cottony cloud of strange shape. . . . Above it, a narrow cylinder, apparently inclined at a 45-degree angle, was slowly moving in a straight line toward the southwest. . . . A sort of plume of white smoke was escaping from its upper end."

In front of this "cylinder" were 30 smaller objects that, when viewed through opera glasses, proved to be red spheres, each surrounded by a yellow ring. "These 'saucers' moved in pairs," Prigent said, "following a broken path characterized in general by rapid and short zigzags. When two saucers drew away from one another, a whitish streak, like an electric arc, was produced between them."

But this was only the beginning of the strangeness. A white, hairlike substance rained down from all of the objects, wrapping itself around telephone wires, tree branches, and the roofs of houses. When observers picked up the material and rolled it into a ball, it turned into a gelatinlike substance and vanished. One man, who had observed the episode from a bridge, claimed the material fell on him, and he was able to extract himself from it only by cutting his way clear—at which point the material collected itself and ascended.

A nearly identical series of events occurred in Gaillac, France, ten days later.

Such "angel hair" is reported from time to time. Laboratory analysis of authentic material (airborne cobwebs are sometimes mistaken for angel hair) is impossible because the material always vanishes. In the summer of 1957, when Craig Phillips (director of the National Aquarium from 1976 to 1981) witnessed a fall off the Florida coast, he collected samples and placed them in sealed jars. But by the time he got to his laboratory, they were gone.

Hannah McRoberts did not notice this disc-shaped structure as she photographed a mountain on Vancouver Island in October 1981. After an investigation scientist and photoanalyst Richard F. Haines concluded this is an authentic photograph.

and the county jailer saw it from their respective locations. According to Carson:

> On two occasions the object came directly towards the patrol vehicle; each time it approached, the object turned, swept the area with a huge red light. Officer Scott turned the red light on the patrol vehicle towards the object, and it immediately went away

from us. We observed the object use the red beam approximately six or seven times, sweeping the sky and ground areas. The object began moving slowly in an easterly direction and we followed. We proceeded to the Vina Plains Fire Station where it was approached by a similar object from the south. It moved near the first object and both stopped, remaining in that position for some time, occasionally emitting the red beam. Finally, both objects disappeared below the eastern horizon.

Carson noted, "Each time the object neared us, we experienced radio interference."

Close encounters of the first kind. Hynek defines this as "a close-at-hand experience without tangible physical effects." A couple was driving north on Highway 45 north of Bristol, Wisconsin, at 11 P.M. on October 14, 1986. They saw flashing red and white lights that they took to mean that a car accident had occurred on the road just ahead of them. Approaching cautiously, they were stunned to find the real cause: an enormous triangular-shaped object hovering just above the concrete. The lights ran along the object's outer edge. "It was the size of a two-story house and spanned the width of the road," the husband told Don Schmitt of the Center for UFO Studies (CUFOS), the organization Hynek founded in 1973.

ALASKA MOTHERSHIP

Airline pilot Kenju Terauchi

When he first saw them, Japanese Airlines officer Kenju Terauchi, who was piloting a Boeing 747 cargo plane, thought they were lights from a military aircraft. He soon learned otherwise. During the next half hour he and his crew realized that things of a decidedly unearthly character had joined them in the skies over Alaska. It was November 17, 1986, at 5:10 in the afternoon.

The pilot, first officer, and flight engineer saw two lighted structures, "about the same size as the body of a DC-8 jet" in Terauchi's words, moving about 1,000 feet in front of the cargo craft. Terauchi's radio communications to Anchorage flight control were strangely garbled, but enough got through that Anchorage urgently contacted a nearby Air Force radar station to see what it was picking up. At various times during the event the UFOs were tracked by the 747 on-board radar and by the Air Force ground radar.

As the sky darkened, the UFOs paced the 747 and were finally lost in the distant horizon. Then, a pale white light appeared behind the aircraft. Silhouetted against lights on the ground, it looked like an immense Saturn-shaped object—the size, Terauchi estimated, of "two aircraft carriers." He thought it was a "mothership" that had carried the two "smaller" objects, themselves of no inconsequential size. The Anchorage radar was recording the object's presence. For the first time the crew felt fear.

By now the aircraft was running low on fuel, and the captain requested permission to land. The UFO vanished suddenly at 5:39 P.M.

The couple stepped out of the car and gazed up at the structure, no more than 20 feet above them. On its bottom they could make out a grid structure. Two minutes later the object drifted off to the southeast and was lost to view. They told Schmitt, "It was so low that if we would have stood on the roof of the car, we could almost have touched it."

Close encounters of the second kind. In this encounter "a measurable physical effect on either animate or inanimate matter is manifested." Late on the afternoon of January 8, 1981, at Trans-en-Provence, France, a whistling sound disturbed Renato Nicolai as he worked in his garden. When he saw a lead-colored "ship" moving toward him from two pine trees at the edge of his property, he fled to a small cabin on

Two Toulouse men describe an encounter with a "Martian" humanoid in a "diving suit"—one of many such reports from France in the fall of 1954.

OVER THE RAINBOW

In *UFO Reality* (1983) British ufologist Jenny Randles noted that some UFO witnesses experience a "sensation of being isolated, or transported from the real world into a different environmental framework. . . . I call this the 'Oz Factor,' after the fairytale land of Oz."

In one instance on a late-summer evening in 1978, a Manchester, England, couple watched a UFO as it hovered above a well-traveled street almost inexplicably devoid of its customary brisk vehicular and pedestrian traffic. On the afternoon of April 15, 1989, a father and son watched a metallic, gold-colored, dumbbell-shaped object, accompanied by four smaller discs, maneuvering low in the sky near their home in Novato, California. As puzzling to the witnesses as the UFOs themselves was the absence of other humans at a time of day when people would ordinarily be out.

In Randles' view such reports suggest that in some way the "consciousness of the witness [is] the focal point of the UFO encounter."

*On April 21, 1967, at South Hill, Virginia, a warehouse manager driving home
from work saw an object like a large water tank resting on the road. When he
put his lights on it, the object abruptly ascended with a blast of white flame. The
road burned for a few seconds, leaving an imprint for police to examine.*

a nearby hill. From there Nicolai saw the object, shaped like "two saucers upside down, one against the other," descend to the ground. Shortly thereafter it rose up and shot off toward the northeast. On its bottom Nicolai observed "two kinds of round pieces which could have been landing gear or feet."

Not long afterward the gendarmerie appeared on the scene and wrote in their official report: "We observed the presence of two concentric circles, one 2.2 meters in diameter and the other 2.4 meters in diameter. The two circles form a sort of corona 10 centimeters thick on this corona, one within the other. There are two parts clearly visible, and they also show black striations." Groupe d'Étude des Phénomènes Aerospatiaux Non-Identifiés (GEPAN), France's

official UFO-investigative agency, took soil and plant samples to the nation's leading botanical laboratory.

After a two-year study GEPAN determined that a "very significant event . . . happened on

*Betty Andreasson Luca of Connecticut claims to have had
repeated encounters with extraterrestrials. At the 12th annual
Mutual Unidentified Flying Object Symposium in 1981,
Luca presented two representations of extraterrestrial creatures
she claimed to have encountered.*

LANDING AND TRACES AT VALENSOLE

One morning in July 1965 Maurice Masse of Valensole, France, encountered figures and a UFO in a field.

Near the French village of Valensole, farmer Maurice Masse was smoking a cigarette just before starting work at 5:45 A.M. on July 1, 1965, when an object came out of the sky and landed in a lavender field 200 feet away. Annoyed and assuming that a helicopter had made an unauthorized landing, he walked toward it. However, he soon saw it was no helicopter but an oval-shaped structure resting on four legs. In front of it stood two figures, not quite four feet tall, dressed in tight gray-green clothes. Their heads were oversize and with sharp chins, their eyes were large and slanted, and they were making a "grumbling" noise.

One of the beings pointed a pencillike device at Masse, paralyzing him in his tracks. The figures entered the UFO and flew away, and the witness needed 20 minutes to recover his mobility. In its wake the object left a deep hole and a moist area that soon hardened like concrete. Plants in the vicinity decayed, and analysis found a higher amount of calcium at the landing site than elsewhere.

The Valensole case is considered one of the classic UFO incidents. Investigations by official and civilian agencies confirmed Masse's sincerity and good character. Laboratory study of the affected soil and plants confirmed the occurrence of an unusual event. Subsequently, Masse confided that in the course of the encounter he experienced some sort of communication with the entities.

The Valensole UFO left behind a deep hole and other traces and affected the surrounding plant life.

Four badly frightened people reported seeing a mushroom-shaped UFO land and glimpsing a strange figure on the night of July 31, 1966. Upon investigation Presque Isle, Pennsylvania, police found a series of unusual markings in the sand. The U.S. Air Force conducted a brief inquiry and declared that bears were responsible, although no bears live in the area.

this spot." GEPAN head Jean-Jacques Velasco wrote, "The effects on plants in the area can be compared to that produced on the leaves of other plant species after exposing the seeds to gamma radiation." In its 66-page technical monograph on the case, GEPAN cautiously acknowledged that the incident amounted to proof that a UFO had landed: "For the first time we have found a combination of factors which conduce us to accept that something similar to what the eyewitness has described actually did take place."

Close encounters of the third kind. In this occurrence "the presence of animated creatures is reported" inside or in the vicinity of UFOs. As he drove to work at 5:50 A.M. on August 25, 1952, William Squyres, a musician at a Pittsburg, Kansas, radio station, encountered a

On January 6, 1958, from the deck of the Brazilian Navy ship Almirante Saldanha, *Almiro Barauna took four remarkable photographs of a Saturn-shaped UFO as it passed over Trindade Island off the coast of Bahia, Brazil.*

large disc hovering 10 feet above the ground about 250 yards away. He quickly brought his car to a stop, jumped out, and began walking toward the UFO. It looked, he would tell Project Blue Book investigators, like two bowls placed end on end, 75 feet long and 40 feet wide, with a 15-foot-high midsection. Along the side was a row of windows.

Through these windows Squyres detected movement of some sort, but he could not detect its cause. In one window he could see the head and shoulders of a motionless humanlike figure who seemed to be leaning forward and watching

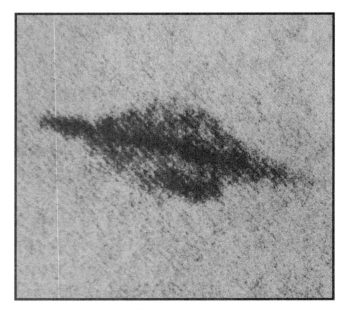

A close-up of one of Barauna's photographs. The pictures continue to defy conventional explanation.

him. The UFO departed before Squyres could get any closer to it. As it ascended, according to the Project Blue Book report on the incident, "it made a sound like a large covey of quail starting to fly at the same time."

This incident is among the few UFO reports Project Blue Book acknowledged it could not explain.

CLOSEST ENCOUNTERS

On the evening of September 19, 1961, while driving home to Portsmouth through rural New Hampshire, Barney and Betty Hill sighted a pancake-shaped UFO with a double row of windows. At one point they stopped their car, and Barney got out for a better look. As the UFO tilted in his direction, he saw six uniformed

Barney and Betty Hill's 1961 New Hampshire encounter is the most famous case of UFO abduction.

"SPACE BROTHERS," MUFON, AND CUFOS

Because most scientists have been apathetic to UFO reports and official government agencies have treated them with indifference or wrapped them in secrecy, we owe most of our UFO knowledge to the efforts of private organizations of varying credibility. At one extreme are quasi-religious groups advocating contact with godlike "Space Brothers." At the other are sober, scientifically grounded efforts that carefully gather and document evidence while keeping speculation to a minimum.

The three most influential groups in the United States have been the Aerial Phenomena Research Organization (now defunct), the Mutual UFO Network (103 Oldtowne Road, Seguin, Texas 78155), and the Center for UFO Studies (2457 W. Peterson Avenue, Chicago, Illinois 60659). MUFON and CUFOS both publish magazines (*MUFON UFO Journal* and *International UFO Reporter*) that cover a wide range of UFO matters.

HOT ENCOUNTERS

During the great sighting outbreak of early November 1957, a number of close encounters had a disturbing consequence: burns and related injuries to witnesses. One of the most dramatic occurrences took place at an army base at Itaipu along Brazil's Atlantic coast. At 2 A.M. on November 4 two guards saw a luminous orange disc coming in over the ocean at a low altitude and an alarming rate of speed. As it passed above the soldiers, the disc came to an instant stop. The two witnesses suddenly felt a wave of heat and a horrifying sensation as if they had burst into flame. Their screams brought other soldiers stumbling out of their barracks just in time to see the UFO streak away. At that moment the fort's entire electrical system failed. Amid

great secrecy the two men were rushed to a military hospital and treated during the next few weeks for first- and second-degree burns to ten percent of their bodies.

A green beam from a UFO struck Denise Bishop on the hand as she stood outside her Plymouth, Devonshire, home on September 10, 1981.

But there were other burn cases as well. In the afternoon of the same day as the Itaipu incident, the engines of several cars along a rural highway near Orogrande, New Mexico, ceased to function as an egg-shaped object maneuvered close by. A witness who stood particularly close to it contracted a "sunburn." In the early morning hours of November 6, outside Merom, Indiana, a hovering UFO, which bathed his farm in light, also seriously burned René Gilham's face. He ended up spending two days in the hospital. At around 1:30 A.M.

This map and accompanying pictures depict the startling UFO incident at Fort Itaipu, Brazil.

More than three months later, the burn on Denise Bishop's hand could still be seen.

on November 10 a Madison, Ohio, woman saw an acorn-shaped UFO hovering just behind her garage. She watched it for half an hour. In the days afterward she developed a body rash and vision problems that her doctor believed suggested radiation poisoning. Subsequent medical tests uncovered no apparent cause for her injuries.

The green beam emanated from a large, disc-shaped object. Many similar cases have been reported.

beings inside. Suddenly frightened, the Hills sped away, but soon a series of beeps sounded, their vehicle started to vibrate, and they felt drowsy. The next thing they knew, they were hearing beeps again. The UFO was gone. When they arrived home, it was two hours later than they expected; somehow, the Hills had lost two hours.

A series of disturbing dreams and other problems led the Hills to seek psychiatric help. Between January and June 1964, under hypnosis, they recounted the landing of the UFO, the emergence of its occupants, their abduction into the craft, and separately experienced medical examinations. In 1965 a Boston newspaper reported the story, which in 1967 became the subject of a best-selling book, John G. Fuller's *The Interrupted Journey*. On October 20, 1975, NBC television broadcast a docudrama, *The UFO Incident*, about the experience.

Most everyone has heard of the UFO abduction of the Hills. At the time it shocked even

The Interrupted Journey *by John G. Fuller recounted the Hills' abduction.*

*One of three photographs taken by Rex Heflin near Santa Ana, California,
on August 3, 1965, this picture—if accepted at face value—indicates that UFOs
are real. Not surprisingly, Heflin's photographs have sparked controversy.
To date, no evidence of a hoax has emerged.*

hard-core ufologists. Nothing quite like it had ever been recorded. Ufologists did know of a bizarre December 1954 incident from Venezuela: Four hairy UFO beings allegedly tried to drag a hunter into their craft, only to be discouraged when his companion struck one of them on the head with the butt of his gun. In any case, ufologists traditionally viewed with suspicion claims of on-board encounters with UFO crews. Those kinds of stories were associated with "contactees," who were regarded, with good reason, as charlatans who peddled long-winded tales of meetings with godlike "Space Brothers." The Hills, however, had a sterling personal reputation, and they returned from their experience with no messages of cosmic uplift.

Investigators collected more and more accounts of such abductions, usually, though not always, elicited through hypnosis. In most cases witnesses told of seeing a UFO or even humanoid beings, then suffering amnesia for a period of anywhere from a few minutes to a few hours. Some witnesses claimed repeated experiences that started when they were children.

THE LITTLE MEN OF
NORTH HUDSON PARK

*Budd Hopkins has pioneered research in
UFO abduction.*

At around 2:45 A.M. on January 12, 1975, George O'Barski was driving home through North Hudson Park, New Jersey, just across the Hudson River from Manhattan, when static filled his radio. Leaning forward to fiddle with the dial, he noticed a light to his left. A quick glance, followed by an astonished stare, revealed its source: a dark, round object with vertical, brilliantly lit windows. It was heading in the same direction as the car and emitted a humming sound.

O'Barski slowed down for a better view. The UFO entered a playing field and hovered a few feet off the ground. A panel opened between two windows, and a ladder emerged. Seconds later about ten identically clad little figures—they wore white one-piece outfits with hoods or helmets that obscured their facial features—came down the ladder. Each figure dug a hole in the soil with a spoonlike device and dumped the contents into a bag each carried. The figures then rushed back into the ship, which took off toward the north. The entire incident had lasted less than four minutes.

Months later O'Barski confided the story to a long-time customer and acquaintance, Budd Hopkins, who was interested in UFOs. Hopkins and two fellow investigators subsequently found independent witnesses who verified the presence of a brightly lit UFO in the park at the time of O'Barski's sighting, although only O'Barski was close enough to see the little figures. One witness, a doorman at an apartment complex bordering the park, said that as he watched the object, he heard a high-pitched vibration, and the lobby window broke just as the UFO departed.

DAMAGED CAR IN MINNESOTA

Studying the brilliant light in the stand of trees two and a half miles south of him, Marshall County Deputy Sheriff Val Johnson wondered if drug smugglers had flown over the Canadian border into the flat, isolated terrain of far northwestern Minnesota. The light was close to the ground, suggesting that the plane had either landed or crashed. Or maybe there was some simpler explanation. Johnson headed down the county highway to investigate. It was 1:40 A.M. on August 27, 1979.

The next thing Johnson knew, the light was shooting directly toward him, moving so fast that its passage seemed almost instantaneous. The last thing he heard was the sound of breaking glass.

At 2:19 A.M. a weak voice crackled over the radio in the sheriff's dispatcher's office at Warren, Minnesota. It was Johnson, who had just regained consciousness. His car had skidded sideways and now was stretched at an angle across the northbound lane, its front tilting toward the ditch. Asked what happened, Johnson could only reply, "I don't know. Something just hit my car."

Officers who arrived on the scene found the car had sustained strange damage, including a seriously cracked windshield, a bent antenna, smashed lights, and other damage. Both the car clock and Johnson's wristwatch were running 14 minutes slow, though both had been keeping correct time until the UFO incident. Johnson's eyes hurt badly as if, an examining physician declared, from "welding burns."

Allan Hendry of the Center for UFO Studies along with experts from Ford and Honeywell conducted an extensive investigation. Their conclusion: The windshield damage was caused by stones apparently carried in the wake of the unknown object. The Honeywell expert thought the bent antenna probably resulted from a "high-velocity air blast superimposed on the air movement over the fast-moving car."

As a UFO passed over his farm near McMinnville, Oregon, on May 11, 1950, Paul Trent snapped two pictures. The photographs are considered a major piece of evidence supporting the reality of UFOs. Withstanding four decades of investigation and analysis, these pictures are the genuine article.

The clear implication was that UFO beings (typically described in these instances as little gray humanoids with oversize heads, slanted eyes, two holes for a nose, and a slit for a mouth) had a long-term interest in certain human beings. Some abductees even reported that the abductors had put small implants—usually said to be tiny balls inserted through the nose and (apparently) into the brain via a long needle—inside their bodies.

In time new and even more unsettling dimensions to the abduction experience came to light.

(Continued on page 72)

A close-up of a Trent photo. A government report called this "one of the few UFO reports in which all factors investigated . . . [are] consistent with the assertion that an extraordinary flying object . . . flew within sight of two witnesses."

Above: *A close-up of one of two photographs of a UFO taken by George Stock of Passaic, New Jersey, on July 29, 1952, as the UFO hovered about 200 feet above the ground.* Right: *The photograph first appeared in the Paterson* Morning Call *on August 1. The photograph has never been investigated, so no conclusions about its authenticity can be reached. If there is such a thing as a typical flying saucer, George Stock's picture comes pretty close.*

EVIDENCE IN THE TREES

An odd "thrashing sound" brought James Richard, 41, and his 16-year-old daughter, Vanea, to the north window of their Columbia, Missouri, mobile home at 12:30 A.M. on June 28, 1973. Some 50 feet away and five feet apart, two brilliant silvery white beams of light shone. When these lights suddenly faded away, an oval-shaped object, about 15 feet in diameter, became visible near the ground. It was so bright that Richard had to look away. The entire area was "lit up as bright as day," he reported.

The trees in the UFO's vicinity swayed as if caught in a powerful wind. One almost touched the ground, and a limb snapped off. All the while, Richard's dogs lay quiet-

ly inside the house; their behavior seemed oddly out of character. Unnerved, Richard went for a gun, which he kept close as the UFO continued to hover by the trees. Richard then called the trailer park switchboard and asked that the police be notified. As he spoke, the lights in his house dimmed twice.

The UFO headed off toward the north, its color dimming slightly and revealing a silvery surface with blue and orange bands of light. At one point it moved toward Richard's residence, then retreated and after a few minutes was gone altogether.

Investigators subsequently found broken tree limbs, crushed foliage, and on some trees burned leaves as high as 35 feet above the ground. In the days ahead more leaves wilted and died. The UFO left imprints two feet deep in the hard ground.

A UFO is said to have left this triangular mark after landing in a Norwegian fjord. Cases in which UFOs reportedly interact with the environment in some way are called close encounters of the second kind.

(Continued from page 69)

Some female abductees reported sexual experiences followed by pregnancies that would be terminated in a follow-up abduction some months later. During later abductions the UFO entities would show the women strange-looking children, apparently human/alien hybrids, whom they would sense were their own.

Not surprisingly, such reports gave rise to furious controversy. Even many ufologists rejected them, preferring, in common with UFO skeptics, to believe "abductions" were fantasies generated by the process of hypnosis itself. Contrary to popular understanding, hypnosis is no royal road to the truth. Hypnotic subjects are in a highly suggestible state and may seek to please the hypnotist. Thus, if the hypnotist asks leading questions, the subject will be led to provide the desired answers. Moreover, purely imaginary events can seem real under hypnosis (confabulation), as testified to in the phenomenon of "past lives" recounted while in a hypnotic state.

HIGHWAY HIJACK

....

Sandy Larson, her 15-year-old daughter, Jackie, and Jackie's boyfriend, Terry O'Leary, awoke early that morning, August 26, 1975. Mrs. Larson, who lived in Fargo, North Dakota, was planning to take a real-estate test in Bismarck, 200 miles away. At 4 A.M., 45 miles west of Fargo on Interstate 94, they encountered an unexpected, unimaginable unknown.

First they saw a flash and heard a rumbling sound. Then, in the southern sky, heading east, they saw eight to ten glowing objects with "smoke" around them. One was notably larger than the others, and the witnesses had the impression that in some fashion the other objects had come out of it. The UFOs descended until they were above a grove of trees 20 yards away. Then half of them shot away. The three witnesses suddenly felt an odd sensation, as if they had been frozen or "stuck" for a second or two. Then the UFOs were departing. Even more weirdly, Jackie, who had been sitting in the middle of the front seat between

Larry and her mother, now sat in the middle of the back seat with no idea how she had gotten there. Moreover, the time now was an hour later.

The following December, Sandy and Jackie separately underwent hypnosis under the direction of University of Wyoming psychologist R. Leo Sprinkle. (Though Terry confirmed the sighting and the peculiar feelings associated with it, he declined the offer to explore the incident further.) Jackie remembered being outside the car in a state of paralysis. Her mother told of being floated into the UFO with Terry. A six-foot-tall robotlike being with glaring eyes put her on a table, rubbed a clear liquid over her, and inserted an instrument up her nose, then performed other medical procedures. Dizzy and nauseous, she felt as if her head would explode. After a period of time she and Terry (whom she did not recall seeing inside the UFO) were returned to their car, and all conscious memory of the incident vanished immediately.

Thomas E. Bullard, Ph.D., studies the relationship between traditional folklore and modern UFO beliefs. He is a widely respected scholarly authority on the UFO phenomenon.

To test the confabulation hypothesis, folklorist Thomas E. Bullard collected all available abduction accounts. He found that as many as one-third of the informants had full conscious recall of their experiences and had never resorted to hypnosis to elicit the details. These non-hypnotic reports proved identical in all significant particulars to those told under hypnosis. Bullard also learned that the identity of the individual hypnotist made no difference. The stories remained consistent down to details that even those most familiar with the phenomenon had failed to notice. In short, Bullard concluded, whatever its ultimate cause, the abduction phenomenon was not the product of hypnosis. "The skeptical argument needs rebuilding from the ground up," he wrote.

A growing number of mental-health professionals have conducted their own investigations

THE CASE OF THE MISSING WATER

The sounds of frightened cattle woke a rancher from a sound sleep in the early morning of September 30, 1980, near Rosedale, Victoria, Australia. When he went outside, he was astonished to see a domed disc with orange and blue lights gliding about ten feet above the ground. It rose slightly in the air, hovered briefly above an open 10,000-gallon water tank, and then landed 50 feet away. The rancher jumped on a motorbike and sped toward the object, which was making a "whistling" sound. Suddenly, an "awful scream" sounded as a black tube extended from the UFO's base. With an ear-splitting bang the strange craft rose into the air. A blast of hot air almost knocked the witness down.

The sounds ceased as the object slowly moved to a position about 30 feet away and

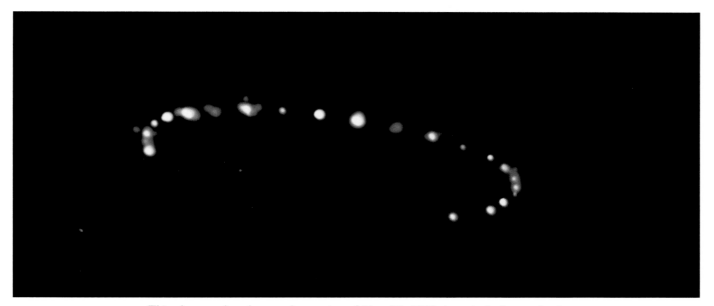

This photograph, taken on the evening of May 26, 1988, is typical of several taken in recent years of enormous, slow-moving structures with lights along the perimeter.

of the abduction phenomenon. In the early 1980s psychological testing of a small group of abductees in New York indicated that they suffered from post-traumatic stress disorder (PTSD). Dr. Elizabeth Slater, a psychologist with a private practice in New York City, remarked that these findings are "not inconsistent with the possibility that reported UFO abductions have, in fact, occurred." Other studies since then have come to similar conclusions, and the scientific investigation of the abduction phenomenon continues.

eight feet above the ground. Hovering briefly, it dropped debris—stones, weeds, cow dung—from underneath it, then flew away, disappearing in the east.

Where the disc had landed could be found a ring of black, flattened grass 30 feet in diameter. When he examined it in the daylight, the witness discovered that all the yellow flowers within the circle had been removed. Only green grass remained. But even more bizarre, the water tank was empty, with no evidence of spillage. Only the muddy residue at the bottom of the tank was left, and there was something peculiar about even this: It had been pulled into a two-foot-high cone shape. The witness was sick with headaches and nausea for more than a week afterward.

A similar ring was found the following December at Bundalaguah, not far from Rosedale. The water in a nearby reservoir was also mysteriously missing.

INTO THE WILD BLUE

While visiting Hawaii on April 25, 1974, a Japanese news photographer took a picture that, when developed, showed a "UFO" not seen at the time the photograph was taken. Other such pictures of "invisible UFOs" can be explained as flaws in the photographic process.

MENACE OF THE UNDEREARTHERS

Before there were little green Martians and tall blond Venusians, there were deros.

In the 1930s a Pennsylvania man named Richard Sharpe Shaver overheard them speaking through his welding equipment. And the voices—singularly unpleasant ones, obsessed with torture and sexual perversion—would not shut up. Their incessant chatter drove Shaver to desperate acts that landed him in mental hospitals and prisons. While Shaver was serving time in a prison, a woman materialized and whisked him away to a cavern underneath the Earth where she and her fellow teros, though badly outnumbered, battled the dero hordes.

Deros, Shaver explained, were "detrimental robots." The teros were "integrative robots." But neither deros nor teros were actually robots. As with much else, Shaver was vague on the question of why these beings were called robots at all. They were the remnants of a super race of giants, the Atlans and the Titans, the rest of whom had fled Earth in spaceships 12,000 years ago when the sun began emitting deadly radiation. Those few remaining had retreated to vast caves; during the centuries many degenerated into sadistic idiots (deros) and used the advanced Atlan technology to wreak havoc on the good guys, the teros, who had managed to keep their brains and dignity intact. Other Atlans either stayed on or returned to the Earth's surface, adjusted to the new solar radiation, and became our ancestors. To this day

THE SAUCERS OF S-4

On November 11 and 13, 1989, viewers of KLAS-TV in Las Vegas, Nevada, heard an incredible story from news reporter George Knapp: A scientist had come forth to reveal that the U.S. government possesses the remains of extraterrestrial vehicles. From these vehicles have come extraordinary technological breakthroughs.

The scientist, Robert Scott Lazar, said he had worked in the S-4 section of Area 51, a corner of the Nevada Test Site. There, he had read documents indicating the existence of ongoing research on an "anti-gravity reactor" for use in propulsion systems. He was astonished, he said, but he was even more shocked to be shown nine flying discs "of extraterrestrial origin" stored in a hangar. As part of the gravity-harnessing propulsion, the craft used an element, 115, unknown on Earth, because it is "impossible to synthesize an element that heavy here on Earth. . . . The substance has to come from a place where super-heavy elements could have been produced naturally." From the recovered craft the U.S. government had collected some 500 pounds of the stuff.

Robert Lazar claims to have studied extraterrestrial hardware.

Adding apparent credibility to Lazar's testimony were persistent reports (chronicled even in the respected *Aviation Week & Space Technology*) of bizarre lights over the test site—craft maneuvering in ways beyond the capacity of known aviation technology. These reports are almost certainly genuine.

Lazar's tales, on the other hand, are almost certainly bogus. Investigations raised serious questions about his reliability. His claims about his education and employment could not be verified, and his character proved to be questionable. In 1990 he was arrested for his involvement with the operation of a Nevada brothel.

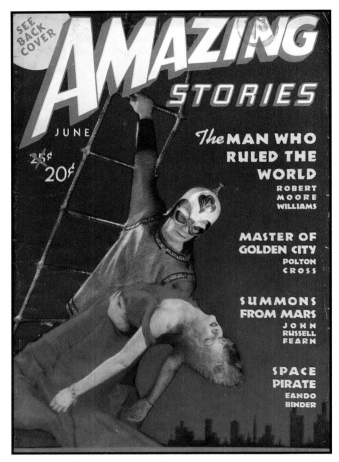

Amazing Stories was the first science-fiction magazine. In the mid-1940s it promoted the bizarre—and supposedly true—"Shaver mystery," which anticipated some themes of later UFO lore.

Ray Palmer, editor of Amazing Stories, introduced the magazine to articles on "true mysteries." Even before 1947, contributors to Amazing Stories speculated about extraterrestrial visitation, drawing on the writings of Charles Fort.

deros kidnap and torture surface humans, shoot airplanes out of the sky, and commit other evil acts.

These lurid fantasies enthralled readers of two popular pulp science-fiction magazines, *Amazing Stories* and *Fantastic Adventures*, between 1944 and 1948. Just about anyone else would have pegged Shaver as a complete nut case and paid no more attention, but he intrigued senior editor Ray Palmer, who snatched Shaver's initial letter out of a wastebasket into which another editor had tossed it with a sneering remark about

"crackpots." Soon, as the most intense controversy in the history of science-fiction fandom swirled around him, Palmer vigorously promoted the "Shaver mystery." To many readers it was lunatic nonsense. To others it was the secret of the ages.

Believers who sought "evidence" for dero activity filled the magazines' pages with material gleaned from Charles Fort's writings and from occult lore. Some of this concerned reports of strange ships in the Earth's atmosphere. In fact, the June 1947 issue of *Amazing Stories* featured

The COMING of the SAUCERS

By Kenneth Arnold & Ray Palmer

In The Coming of the Saucers, *Kenneth Arnold and Ray Palmer hailed the dawning of the UFO age. Arnold recounted his own celebrated sighting as well as his involvement with the notorious Maury Island incident, a hoax Arnold naively participated in.*

an article on mysterious flying objects that it linked to extraterrestrial visitation. The magazine was on the newsstands when Kenneth Arnold's sighting brought "flying saucers" into world consciousness.

The Shaver episode, which started just before the UFO age and faded from all but fringe view after its first year, set a standard for tall tales that others would have to scramble to match. Some proved up to the challenge.

"ETHER SHIPS"?

In a 1950 monograph California occultist N. Meade Layne proposed that UFOs and their occupants come here not from other planets but from another order of reality. Layne called this place Etheria and declared that it surrounds us yet is usually invisible. Psychically inclined individuals are most attuned to it, but some of its manifestations, such as flying saucers, can be seen by anyone. The saucers can materialize and dematerialize; at certain stages they are "jellylike," enabling them to "change in shape and apparent size." Layne's theory, at least in general, would survive to be championed by ufologists (most notably John Keel and Jacques Vallée).

John Keel, controversial UFO theorist

As editor of Amazing Stories *and* Fate, *Ray Palmer was the first major commercial exploiter of flying saucers. He promoted some rather exotic theories, notably that saucers were based inside a hollow Earth.*

THE DIRTIEST HOAX OF ALL

From the beginning the urge to spin yarns proved irresistible to some. Like weeds in saucerdom's fertile ground, hoaxes, tall tales, rumors, and other silliness sprouted and spread.

One of the most notorious—and successful— liars, the late Fred L. Crisman, actually bridged the gap between the Shaver mystery and the UFO mystery. Crisman first surfaced in a letter published in the May 1947 issue of *Amazing Stories*, in which he claimed to have shot his way out of a cave full of deros with a submachine gun. Palmer next heard from him the fol-

lowing July. This time Crisman said he had actual physical evidence of a flying saucer.

Palmer passed the story on to Kenneth Arnold, who was investigating reports in the Pacific Northwest. Arnold interviewed Crisman and an associate, Harold Dahl, who identified themselves as harbor patrolmen (they were not). Crisman, who did most of the talking, reported that Dahl had seen doughnut-shaped craft dump piles of slaglike material on the beach of Maury Island in Puget Sound. The next morning a mysterious man in black threatened Dahl. "I know a great deal more about this experience of yours than you will want to believe," the man said cryptically.

The two men showed the material to Arnold. In a state of high excitement Arnold contacted an Army Air Force intelligence officer of his acquaintance, Lt. Frank M. Brown, who quickly flew up from Hamilton Field in California in

Most photographs of alleged UFOs are of dubious origin; "hoax" may be too strong a word. Many are simply jokes, such as this one in which a prankster dressed in outlandish garb passes himself off as a visitor from another world.

MON-KA OF MARS

Mon-Ka is many people's favorite Martian. According to one chronicler, he "has a wisdom that is light years beyond the most intelligent person on our planet."

Mon-Ka first communicated with earthlings in April 1956 at the Giant Rock Spacecraft Convention in Southern California, when contactee Dick Miller played recordings that he said had mysteriously appeared on tapes in sealed cans. On the tapes Mon-Ka asked a favor and made a promise: "On the evening of November 7, of this your year 1956, at 10:30 P.M. your local time, we request that one of your communications stations remove its carrier signal from the air for two minutes. At that time we will speak from our craft, which will be stationed at an altitude of 10,000 feet over your great city of Los Angeles."

In September Miller went to London and played the tapes for impressionable British saucer fans. The Associated Press' tongue-in-cheek treatment afforded the story international attention. A subsequent Los Angeles *Mirror-News* account revealed that Miller had once faked a radio communication from a saucer in his native Detroit. Nonetheless, Southern California succumbed to Mon-Ka mania. Two mass rallies were held in Los Angeles in late October, and organizer Gabriel Green enthusiastically talked up the Martian on Art Linkletter's popular *House Party* television show.

When the evening of November 7 rolled around, the faithful climbed to the rooftops and scanned the skies. As publicity gimmicks two radio stations went off the air at the appointed hour, and a television station sent out a plane to look for the Martian spaceship. Mon-Ka did not show up.

He was not, however, gone for good. Since then Mon-Ka has channeled psychic communications to numerous contactees. Today he is beloved as a tireless (and garrulous) "soldier for the cause of peace," in the words of one admirer.

To poke fun at the excitement about flying saucers, Reed O'Hanlon, editor of a Blair, Nebraska, weekly newspaper, took this picture of "Zuergla Wbshpt," a "Martian" sent to Earth to peddle extraterrestrial trinkets.

the company of another officer. The moment they saw the material, their interest in it evaporated: It was ordinary aluminum. Embarrassed for Arnold, the officers left without telling him their conclusions.

While flying back to Hamilton, their B-25 caught fire and crashed, killing both officers. Though Crisman and Dahl subsequently confessed to other Air Force investigators that they had made up the story, the legend would live on for decades afterward. Some writers—including

Arnold and Palmer, who wrote a book about the case—hinted that the officers died because they knew too much. But to Capt. Edward Ruppelt of Project Blue Book, the Maury Island incident was the "dirtiest hoax in UFO history."

Years later Crisman's name would reemerge in another contentious context. In December 1968, while investigating what he believed to be a high-level conspiracy to murder President John F. Kennedy, New Orleans district attorney Jim Garrison called Crisman to testify before a grand jury. Some early assassination-conspiracy theorists would identify Crisman (falsely) as one of the three mysterious "hoboes" arrested and photographed shortly after the shooting in Dallas.

Before his death Crisman was peddling a new, improved, UFO-less version of the Maury Island story. He now claimed that the "truth" involved, not flying doughnuts dropping slag, but something even more dangerous: illegal dumping by military aircraft of radioactive waste into the harbor. Though this tale was no less tall than his earlier one, it has already entered UFO literature as the "solution" to the Maury Island "mystery."

Four "UFO" pictures taken in 1967 by Michigan teenagers Dan and Grant Jaroslaw were reprinted all over the world. The two eventually admitted that the object was a model suspended from the branches of a tree.

DEVILS OR ANGELS?

To fundamentalist Christians UFO beings are either demons or angels. Most fundamentalist writers favor the first interpretation. Kelly L. Segraves, for example, holds that these beings are "fallen angels and followers of Satan" who seek to lead us into "depravity and rejection of God." Clifford Wilson believes Satan's agents have abducted human beings into UFOs and turned them into agents as part of "some great super-plan of a spiritual counterattack to reach its culmination in Armageddon." But to the most famous evangelist of all, Billy Graham, UFOs are "astonishingly angel-like." He believes, they are here to prepare us for Jesus' return.

Billy Graham

*The most celebrated contactee of the 1950s was George Adamski. New York
radio and television personality Long John Nebel provided
Adamski with a forum to promote his books and photographs, though
Nebel did not hide his personal skepticism.*

FROM OUTER SPACE TO YOUR WALLET

Consider the case of George Adamski. Born in Poland in 1891, Adamski came to America in his infancy. He received a spotty education and developed an early interest in occultism. By the 1930s Adamski had established a niche as a low-rent guru in Southern California's mystical scene. He founded the Royal Order of Tibet, whose teachings drew on his psychic channelings from "Tibetan masters." In the late 1940s "Professor" Adamski produced pictures of what

he said were spaceships he had photographed through his telescope.

The pictures attracted wide attention. But the events that began on November 20, 1952, would make Adamski a saucer immortal. Responding to channeled directions from extraterrestrials (who had replaced the Tibetan masters, though their messages were identical), Adamski and six fellow occult seekers headed out for the desert. Near Desert Center, California, he separated from the others and met a landed spaceship. Its pilot was a friendly fellow named Orthon, a handsome, blond-haired Venusian.

Serious UFO investigators scoffed, but other people all over the world believed, even as Adamski's tales grew ever more outrageous. Adamski's 1955 book *Inside the Space Ships* recounted his adventures with Venusians, Martians, and Saturnians, who had come to Earth out of concern for humanity's self-destructive ways. These "Space Brothers," as Adamski and his disciples called them, proved a long-winded lot, fond of platitudes and full of tedious metaphysical blather.

In Adamski's wake other "contactees" emerged to spread the interplanetary gospel and

(Continued on page 88)

Though reviled by conservative ufologists and ridiculed in the press, Adamski preached an occult-based interplanetary gospel to a worldwide following of believers.

MASTER OF THE UNIVERSE

As galactic heavyweights go, few tip the scales as impressively as Ashtar, the commander of the 24,000,000 extraterrestrials involved in the Earth project. According to one of his Earth friends, Ashtar is sponsored by "Lord Michael and the Great Central Sun government of this galaxy. . . . Second only to the Beloved Commander Jesus-Sananda in responsibility for the airborne division of the Brotherhood of Light," Ashtar beams his channeled messages from a colossal starship, or space station, that entered the solar system on July 18, 1952.

The first to hear from him was California contactee George Van Tassel, but since then dozens, and possibly hundreds, all over the world have heard from him and communicated his sermons. Asked what he looks like, Ashtar replied modestly, "I am seven feet tall in height, with blue eyes and a nearly white complexion. I am fast of movement and considered to be an understanding and compassionate teacher."

THE STATE DEPARTMENT AND
THE VENUSIANS

George Adamski was one of the most famous—or notorious—figures on the fly-ing-saucer scene from 1952 until his death in 1965. In books and lectures he recounted his meetings with friendly Venusians, Martians, and Saturnians. He also claimed that high government officials—themselves in contact with "Space Brothers"—secretly knew he was telling the truth.

Nonetheless, Adamski was shocked one day in December 1957 to receive a letter

In his first book Adamski told of his conversation with a Venusian in the California desert.

An avid amateur astronomer, "Professor" Adamski claimed to have photographed spaceships through his telescope.

written on U.S. State Department sta-tionery with a stamped department seal and a Washington, D.C., postmark. Signed by "R. E. Straith, Cultural Exchange Commit-tee," it stated, "The Department has on file a great deal of confirmatory evidence bear-ing out your own claims. . . . While cer-tainly the Department cannot publicly con-firm your experiences, it can, I believe, with propriety, encourage your work."

The Straith letter electrified Adamski's followers. They charged the department

*West Virginia writer and publisher Gray Barker, a gleeful promoter
of outlandish tall tales, was the source of the Straith letter.*

with covering up the truth when the department denied, as it did repeatedly, that it knew anything of an "R. E. Straith" or a "Cultural Exchange Committee." All the while Straith proved elusive; despite repeated efforts, Adamski's supporters could not find him. Undaunted, they concluded that his committee must be so highly classified that the government would never admit to its existence.

Ufologists skeptical of Adamski's claims were sure the letter was a forgery—perhaps, as analyst Lonzo Dove suspected, composed on the typewriter of Gray Barker, a saucer publisher and practical joker. When Dove submitted an article on the subject to *Saucer News* editor Jim Moseley, Moseley rejected it on the grounds that Dove had not proved his case. But years later, after Barker's death in December 1984, Moseley confessed that he and Barker had written the letter on official stationery provided by a friend of Barker's, a young man with a relative high in the government.

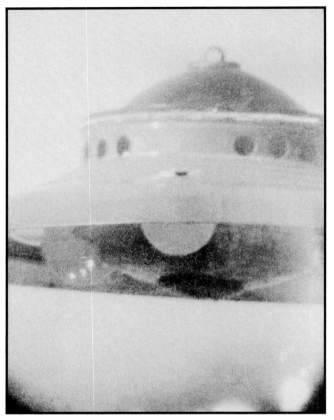

George Adamski photographed this Venusian "scoutship"—in actuality a small model patterned after a craft proposed by space-travel theorist Mason Rose—at his Palomar Garden, California, home on December 13, 1952.

(Continued from page 85)

to count the take at gatherings of the faithful. The principal gathering was held every summer at Giant Rock, near Twentynine Palms, California. The driving force behind the Giant Rock gatherings was George Van Tassel, who had established psychic contact with extraterrestrial starships ("ventlas") in early 1952. A few months later he rushed into print the first modern contactee book, the misleadingly titled *I Rode a Flying Saucer!* The following year, Van Tassel would get to do just that when his pal Solganda invited him inside a spaceship for a quick spin.

At the space people's direction, Van Tassel established the College of Universal Wisdom and solicited donations for the construction of the "Integratron," a rejuvenation machine. When completed, Van Tassel told his supporters, it would handle as many as 10,000 persons a day. People would emerge looking no younger, but their cells would be recharged. Untold tens of thousands of dollars later, the Integratron languished unfinished in February 1978 when Van Tassel died—from the ravages of old age.

Reincarnated Saturnian and space communicant Howard Menger held forth from his farm in New Jersey, where followers would come to witness—well, something. Followers would see lights and even figures but always in the dark and never up close. Once, when Menger led a follower into a dark building to speak with a spacewoman, a sliver of light happened to fall on the face of the "extraterrestrial." It was, the fol-

Sober ufologists disparaged Adamski's yarns and photographs. At a 1966 press conference astronomer and Project Blue Book consultant J. Allen Hynek cited one such picture as an example of a particularly blatant hoax.

At Giant Rock in the Southern California desert, contactees and their followers convened every summer from 1953 to 1977 to prepare themselves for a glorious New Age brought by flying saucers.

lower could not help noticing, identical to the face of a young blond woman who happened to be one of Menger's closest associates.

After releasing a book, *From Outer Space to You* (1959), and a record album, *Music from Another Planet*, Menger would virtually recant

In the late 1950s followers of New Jersey contactee Howard Menger called him the "East Coast Adamski" because his story was so similar to his California counterpart's.

NAKED SPACE PEOPLE?

Two outlandish yet similar tales told half a century apart seem to indicate that extraterrestrial beings may at times appear nude. On April 19, 1897, the St. Louis *Post-Dispatch* printed a letter from one W. H. Hopkins. Three days earlier, near Springfield, Missouri, Hopkins encountered a beautiful nude woman standing outside a landed "airship." As he approached, a similarly clad man stepped up to protect her. Though neither being spoke English, Hopkins convinced them of his peaceful intentions. Asked where they came from, they "pointed upwards, pronouncing a word which sounded like Mars." On March 28, 1950, Samuel Eaton Thompson reportedly met up with nude Venusian men, women, and children in a forest outside Mineral, Washington. Friendly but childlike, they spoke "uneducated" English. Whereas Hopkins' Martians were sweating in the spring temperatures, Thompson's Venusians were cold because of the respective distances of the two planets from the sun.

his story, vaguely muttering about a CIA experiment. In the late 1980s he withrew his recantation and marketed a new book detailing his latest cosmic adventures.

Most contactees have managed to stay out of legal trouble, though law-enforcement and other official agencies look into their activities from time to time. Reinhold Schmidt was not so lucky. In the course of contacts with German-speaking Saturnians, Schmidt's space friends showed him secret stores of quartz crystals in the mountains of California. Armed with this information and a gift for (so the prosecutor charged) "loving talk," he persuaded several elderly women to invest their money in a crystal-mining venture. The money went, however, into his own pocket. He went on trial for grand theft and from there to jail.

Howard Menger tried to market a "free energy" device based, he claimed, on extraterrestrial science.

SPACESHIP CRASH IN 1884?

On June 6, 1884, as a band of cowboys rounded up cattle in remote Dundy County, Nebraska, a blazing object streaked out of the sky and crashed some distance from them, leaving (according to a contemporary newspaper account) "fragments of cog-wheels and other pieces of machinery . . . glowing with heat so intense as to scorch the grass for a long distance around

each fragment." The light was so intense that it blinded one of the witnesses.

This incredible event was recorded two days later in Lincoln's *Daily State Journal,* which printed a dispatch from Benkelman, Nebraska, by an anonymous correspondent. The correspondent wrote that prominent local citizens had gone to the site, where the metal now had cooled. He reported, "The aerolite, or whatever it is, seems to be about 50 or 60 feet long, cylindrical, and

Still, not all contactees are con artists, by any means. In 1962 Gloria Lee, who chronicled her psychic contacts with "J.W." of Jupiter in *Why We Are Here* (1959), starved to death in a Washington motel room after a two-month fast for peace ordered by her space friends. In 1954, in the face of massive press ridicule, followers of Dorothy Martin, who communicated with extraterrestrials through automatic writing, quit jobs and cut all other ties as they awaited a prophesied landing of a flying saucer that would pick them up just before geological upheavals caused massive destruction.

The charlatan contactees typically claim physical encounters, nearly always have photographs and other artifacts (in one especially brazen instance, packets of hair from a Venusian dog) to "prove" it, and in general behave more like

After persuading investors to buy into quartz mines shown him by Saturnians, Reinhold Schmidt was jailed for fraud.

about 10 or 12 feet in diameter." A *State Journal* editor remarked that this must have been an "air vessel belonging originally to some other planet."

But on June 10 an anticlimactic dispatch came from Benkelman. In a heavy rainstorm the remains had "melted, dissolved by the water like a spoonful of salt." The obvious message: Take the story with a grain of sodium chloride. The *State Journal*, red-faced, dropped it then and there.

In the 1960s a copy of the first newspaper article resurfaced, and reporters, historians, and ufologists rushed to Dundy County. Lifelong residents of the area assured them no such thing had ever happened. Later, even after the telltale follow-up dispatch was uncovered, one humorless author theorized that the "storm was artificially created so that a UFO concealed within the clouds could retrieve the wreckage of the crashed UFO."

Dorothy Martin (right) of Chicago communicated psychically with extraterrestrials. Her space friends urged her to warn the world of geological upheavals that would occur on December 20, 1954. The failed prophecy made her the butt of international ridicule.

profiteers than prophets. The psychic contactees, on the other hand, tend to be quiet, unflamboyant, and almost painfully sincere. They can best be described as Space Age religious visionaries. In another century their messages would have been from gods or angels or spirits. These messages, generally inane and rarely profound, are manifestly not from true extraterrestrials. Psychologists who have studied contactees believe these individuals are not crazy, just unusually imaginative; their communicators come from inner, not outer, space, via a nonpathological form of multiple-personality disorder.

ARE YOU A STAR PERSON?

Contactee chronicler Brad Steiger says you may be a Star Person if you are physically attractive, have a magnetic personality, require little sleep, hear unusually well, work in the healing or teaching profession, and harbor the suspicion that this world is not your home. Steiger discovered this while working on a book on space channeling. When he announced his discovery in the May 1, 1979, issue of the *National Enquirer*, he was inundated with letters from people who recognized themselves.

According to Steiger, there are four kinds of Star People—Refugees, Utopians, Energy Essences, and reincarnated E.T.'s—all of whom have been placed on Earth to prepare it for the great changes that will come in the wake of worldwide disasters that will precede mass landings by the Star People's off-world relatives. In his 1981 book, *The Star People*, Steiger predicted a pole shift and worldwide famine in 1982, World War III in the mid-1980s, and Armageddon in 1989.

Laramie, Wyoming, psychologist R. Leo Sprinkle sponsors a yearly conference at
the University of Wyoming, where contactees gather to share experiences.
Sprinkle's interest is more than academic: He believes himself to be a
communicant with extraterrestrials.

Though only a few professional contactees of the 1950s are still alive or active today, the contactee movement is as big and vibrant as ever. This is due in part to the efforts of a Laramie, Wyoming, psychologist, R. Leo Sprinkle, who sponsors an annual summer conference on the University of Wyoming campus. Those attending are mostly individuals convinced that the Galactic Federation—a sort of extraterrestrial United Nations—has placed them on Earth to spread the cosmic gospel. In a sense these conferences function as revival meetings in which the faith is renewed even as the larger world continues to scoff.

THE DARK SIDE

While contactees offer a rosy picture of the UFO phenomenon, other, darker visions have obsessed some saucer enthusiasts. In fact, even contactees agree that all is not well. Sinister forces oppose the Space Brothers' benevolent mission. Some of these are extraterrestrial and others terrestrial, and they work together to thwart the emergence of the truth.

Among the early victims of this evil "Silence Group" was Albert K. Bender of Bridgeport, Connecticut. In 1952 Bender formed the International Flying Saucer Bureau (IFSB), which met with immediate success, but he shut it down the next year under mysterious circumstances. In due course Bender confided that three men in black had imparted to him the ter-

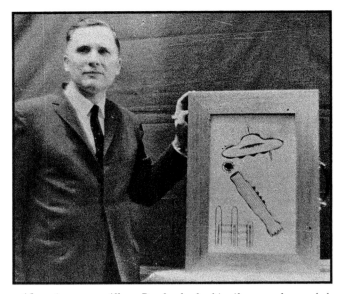

After nine years Albert Bender broke his silence and revealed the "truth" in Flying Saucers and the Three Men. *According to Bender, the men in black were monsters from the distant plant Kazik.*

The central figure in a UFO legend, Albert Bender supposedly was silenced by menacing men in black because he had discovered the answer to the UFO mystery.

rifying answer to the UFO mystery and turned his life into a nightmare. He would say no more. Three years later an IFSB associate, Gray Barker, wrote a book about the episode; the title perfectly captured the paranoia abroad in UFO-land: *They Knew Too Much About Flying Saucers.*

Through the "Bender mystery" the legend of the "men in black" (MIB) came into the world—even though, as Barker observed, a man in black had played a villainous role in the Maury Island incident. According to Barker, the MIB were ranging as far afield as Australia and New Zealand, scaring still more UFO buffs into silence.

By the late 1980s MIB tales had become sufficiently ubiquitous that the august *Journal of American Folklore* took note of them in a long article. Just who the MIB were remained unclear. To saucerians enamored with conspiracy theories, they were enforcers for the Silence Group, associated with international banking interests that sought to stifle the technological advances and moral reforms the Space Brothers wanted to bestow on Earthlings. To others, they were alien beings—perhaps, some speculated, Shaver's deros. In 1962 Bender came down on the side of the alien school. Breaking his nine-year silence in *Flying Saucers and the Three Men*, which he insisted was not a science-fiction novel, Bender revealed that the men in black

Albert Bender drew this sketch of one of the men in black. The "Bender mystery" provided endless fodder for UFO buffs of a paranoid disposition.

A MAN IN BLACK

In 1987, writing in the respected *Journal of American Folklore*, Peter M. Rojcewicz examined "folk concepts and beliefs in 'other worlds'" as they related to "men in black" (MIB) legends. One classic tale of an MIB involved a man with the pseudonym "Michael Elliot." One afternoon, as Elliot sat in a university library immersed in UFO literature, a thin, dark-featured man approached him. Speaking in a slight accent, the man asked Elliot what he was reading about. Flying saucers, Elliot replied, adding that he had no particular interest in their reality or unreality, just in the stories told about them. The stranger shouted, "Flying saucers are the most important fact of the century, and you're not interested!?" Then the man stood up "as if mechanically lifted"; spoke gently, "Go well in your purpose"; and departed. When Elliot went to follow the man, he found the library eerily deserted. A year or two after his article appeared, Rojcewicz confessed that he was "Michael Elliot."

In a particularly preposterous—and ghoulish—hoax, a Maryland man circulated a photograph that he said depicted the body of an alien who had died in a spaceship crash in the Southwest. In fact, the wreckage was of an American aircraft that crashed in an eastern state, and the "alien" was its human pilot.

who drove him out of ufology were monsters from the planet Kazik. Even Barker, the book's publisher and a relentless Bender promoter, remarked privately and out of customers' hearing, that maybe it had all been a "dream."

Fear of the MIB was generated in part by worries about the possibly hostile motives of UFOs. A popular early book, *Flying Saucers on the Attack* by Harold T. Wilkins (1954), fretted that a "Cosmic General Staff" could even now be plotting a real-life war of the worlds. But next to demonologist-ufologist John A. Keel, author of *UFOs: Operation Trojan Horse* (1970) and other writings, Wilkins sounded like an optimist. In Keel's rendering UFO intelligences are not simply extraterrestrials but "ultraterrestrials"—entities from unimaginable other dimensions of reality. Worse, they definitely do not like us at all. Human beings, Keel thunders, are "like ants, trying to view reality with very limit-

ed perceptive equipment. . . . We are biochemical robots helplessly controlled by forces that can scramble our brains, destroy our memories and use us in any way they see fit. They have been doing it to us forever."

In recent years new and even wilder strains of paranoia have sprouted along ufology's fringes. Inspiration comes not just from UFO rumors but from conspiracy theories associated with the far right end of the political spectrum. The two major figures in what has been called the "dark side movement" are John Lear, a pilot who once flew aircraft for a CIA-linked company, and

John Lear, spinner of nightmarish conspiracy theories concerning UFOs

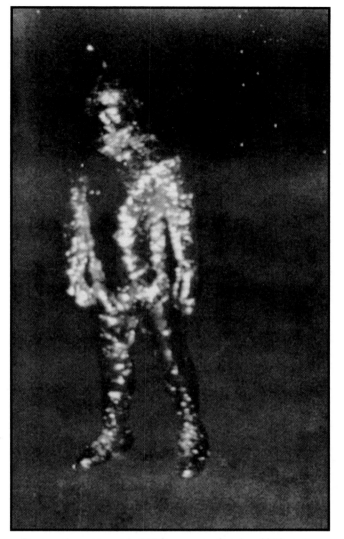

During the nationwide UFO wave in October 1973, police officer Jeff Greenhaw of Falkville, Alabama, photographed this figure, supposedly an alien but widely suspected of being a young colleague in a fire-protection garment.

Milton William Cooper, a retired Navy petty officer.

According to dark siders, a ruthless "secret government" controls the world. Among other nefarious activities, it runs the international drug trade and has unleashed AIDS and other deadly diseases as population-reducing measures. Its ultimate goal is to turn the Earth and surrounding planets into slave-labor camps. For some

PSYCHOLOGICAL DISORDERS?

According to a 1972 paper by two psychiatrists associated with the Harvard Medical School, flying saucers are almost certainly misperceptions of sex organs. Lester Grinspoon and Alan D. Persky wrote that most UFO witnesses are persons suffering from untreated psychological disorders. They have reverted to "primal modes of thinking" and lapsed back into childhood. This includes dreams and hallucinations that are mistaken for reality. In this state of ambulatory schizophrenia, victims recall their "earliest infantile perceptions." They may see an approaching flying saucer—in fact an hallucination of a mother's breast. Or conversely, they may see a cigar-shaped object—a phallic symbol if ever there was one. "The flying objects," Grinspoon and Persky pronounced, "are representations, symbols, of highly libidinized primary objects in the development of the individual. They are symbols of extremes of gratification and of omnipotence."

*A Venezuelan airline pilot photographed this "UFO" but later
confessed that it was nothing more than a button. Investigators had
doubted the picture's authenticity for other reasons, especially the
artificial-looking "shadow" on the ground.*

time this secret government has been in contact with alien races, allowing the aliens to abduct human beings in exchange for advanced alien technology.

The aliens, known as the "grays" (because of their gray skin color), do more than abduct human beings. They mutilate and eat them as well, using the body parts to rejuvenate themselves. The secret government and the aliens labor together in vast underground bases in New Mexico and Nevada, where they collect human and animal organs, drop them into a chemical soup, and manufacture soulless android creatures. These androids, who are then unleashed to do dirty work for the government/alien conspiracy, are best known to the rest of us as the men in black.

With each retelling, with the appearance of each new and expensive book, video, or tape, the dark-side story gets crazier. In one version the

SALVATION FROM SPACE

Contactees who once gathered at Giant Rock, California (above), now meet in Laramie, Wyoming.

Every summer contactees—people who believe they have communicated with god-like space people—flock to the Rocky Mountain Conference on UFO Investigation, held on the University of Wyoming campus in Laramie. All these people have remarkable stories to tell: stories of personal transformation that sound like classic religious experiences in Space Age guise.

One of the stories is told by Merry Lynn Noble, by her own admission once "one of the leading call girls in the western United States." She was also an alcohol and drug addict seeking to change her life through spiritual studies. In February 1982, exhausted and depressed, she visited her parents in Montana. One evening, as they were driving in the country, a flying saucer appeared, bathing the car in light.

Noble's parents, who "were just frozen there," seemed unaware of the UFO's presence. Meanwhile, Merry Lynn in her astral body was being drawn into the craft, where she felt "absolute ecstasy, total peace, womblike warmth. . . . 'I'm so glad to leave that body,' I thought." She communicated telepathically with a "presence" who gave her a "new soul, with new energy, new humility." The next thing she knew, she was jolted back into her physical body.

From that moment her life began to change for the better. She found a good job and joined Alcoholics Anonymous, where she met the man whom she would marry. Her psychic contact with the extraterrestrial she met aboard the saucer continues, and she has written an unpublished autobiography, *Sex, God and UFOs*.

TO THE MOON, OTIS!

To hear him tell it, Otis T. Carr was the smartest man since Isaac Newton, Albert Einstein, and Nikola Tesla. Not only that but Tesla, the great electrical genius and Thomas Edison contemporary, had confided some of his deepest secrets to Carr when the latter worked as a young hotel clerk in New York City in the 1920s.

In the mid-1950s, with Tesla long gone, Carr was ready to tell the world and collect the rewards. He founded OTC Enterprises, hired a fast-talking business manager named Norman Colton, and set out to secure funding for a "fourth dimensional space vehicle" powered by a "revolutionary Utron Electric Accumulator." The saucer-shaped OTC-X1 would undergo its first flight in April 1959 and the following December go on all the way to the moon.

Carr and Colton secured hundreds of thousands of dollars from wealthy investors and contactee-oriented saucer fans, including Warren Goetz, who claimed to be an actual space person, having materialized as a baby in his (Earth) mother's arms while a

Otis T. Carr—founder of OTC Enterprises—ended up in prison after soliciting money to build a "free-energy-driven" spaceship that, he told investors, would fly to the moon in December 1959.

saucer hovered overhead. Another associate, Margaret Storm, wrote a biography of Tesla, who turns out to have been a Venusian. To skeptics Carr was a shameless spouter of double-talk and baffle-gab. As one observer put it, "For all most people know, he might well be a great scientist.

After all, he is completely unintelligible, isn't he?"

On Sunday, April 19, 1959, while crowds gathered at an amusement park in Oklahoma City to watch the OTC-X1's maiden flight, Carr suddenly contracted a mysterious illness and had to be hospitalized. He mumbled something about a "mercury leak," but burly guards kept reporters who wanted to check for themselves out of the plant where the craft supposedly was being constructed. One who managed to catch a glimpse saw only a jumble of disconnected wires and parts—nothing that looked remotely like a functioning aircraft.

The OTC-X1 never went to the moon, but Carr went to prison for selling stock illegally. He died penniless years later in a Pittsburgh slum. Colton, who had skipped out of Oklahoma a step ahead of the authorities, formed the Millennium Agency, which sold stock in machines "operated entirely by environmental gravitic forces." They never flew either.

The "UFO" in this picture (upper right) is actually a lens flare caused by the sun (lower left). The flares are not seen in the sky. Investigators tend to view with suspicion any "UFO" photograph when no one observed anything unusual at the time.

conspirators travel into the future to observe the emergence of the anti-Christ in the 1990s, World War III in 1999, and the Second Coming of Christ in 2011. George Bush oversees the world's drug traffic. The secret government has maintained bases on Mars since the early 1960s. The conspirators employ drugs and hypnosis to turn mentally unstable individuals into mass murderers of schoolchildren and other inno-

*In March 1966 a British teenager photographed these dubious-looking
"UFOs"—apparently superimposed cardboard cutouts—and persuaded many
that they were spaceships from another world.*

cents; the purpose is to spur anti-gun sentiment, resulting in gun-control legislation. Thus, Americans will be disarmed and defenseless when the secret government's storm troopers round them up and herd them into concentration camps.

A small army of fervent believers all around the world has embraced these monstrous yarns, for which—no rational reader will be surprised to learn—not a shred of supporting evidence exists. The true sources of these lurid tales are not hard to find: They are a hodgepodge of elements patched together from saucer folklore, extremist political literature, and a 1977 British mock-documentary, *Alternative 3*. The purpose of this show was to satirize popular credulity and paranoia. Unfortunately, some remain convinced the show was sober fact, ironically serving only to give rise to fresh varieties of mass gullibility and fear.

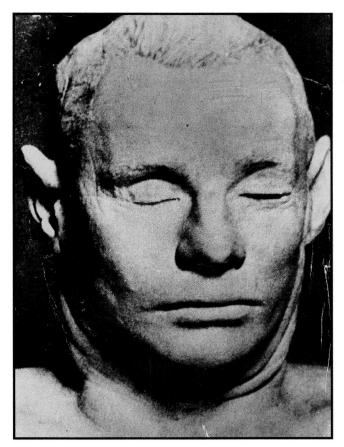

In 1948 a dead man was found on a beach near Adelaide, Australia, and investigating authorities could not identify him. Eventually, a tabloid newspaper picked up the story and spread the news that he was an extraterrestrial. This photograph of the man's death mask regularly appears in fringe UFO literature.

SPACE ANIMALS?

In the late 1940s and 1950s some theorists thought flying saucers might be space animals. The first to suggest this idea, however, was Charles Fort, in his 1931 book *Lo!* where he speculated that unknown objects in the sky could be "living things that occasionally come from somewhere else." A few days after Kenneth Arnold's sighting on June 24, 1947, John Philip Bessor wrote the Air Force to tell it what the flying discs were: A "form of space animal" propelled by "telekinetic energy." These creatures might be carnivorous. "Many falls of flesh and blood from the sky in times past," he declared, could be the leftover remains of unfortunate persons eaten by hungry UFOs. In 1955 Countess Zoe Wassilko-Serecki theorized that UFOs were "vast, luminous bladders of colloidal silicones" that feed on electrical energy. Californian Trevor James Constable claimed to have photographed these "critters," as he called them, on infrared film.

THE ULTIMATE SECRET

Government authorities explained away the wreckage of a mysterious aircraft discovered near Corona, New Mexico, in 1947 as the remains of a weather balloon, but those who participated in the recovery now admit that this was false.

RUMORS OF THE INCREDIBLE

The stories began to circulate in the late 1940s. They were so fantastic that even those willing to seriously consider the possibility of extraterrestrial visitation responded with incredulity.

In fact, no more than a couple of weeks after Kenneth Arnold's sighting ushered in the UFO age, the first such story hit the press. On the afternoon of July 8, 1947, a New Mexico paper, the Roswell *Daily Record,* startled the nation with a report of a flying saucer crash near Corona, Lincoln County, northwest of Roswell, and of the recovery of the wreckage by a party from the local Army Air Force base. Soon, however, the Air Force assured reporters that it had all been a silly mistake: The material was from a downed balloon.

Though this particular incident was quickly forgotten, rumors of recovered saucers and, in addition, the bodies of their alien occupants, became a staple of popular culture—and con games. In 1949 *Variety* columnist Frank Scully wrote that a "government scientist" and a Texas oilman had told him of three crashes in the Southwest. The following year Scully expanded these claims into a full-length, best-selling book, *Behind the Flying Saucers,* which claimed that the occupants of these vehicles were humanlike Venusians dressed in the "style of 1890." But two years later *True* magazine revealed in a scathing exposé that Scully's sources were two veteran confidence men, Silas

Vapor formations from a 1967 NASA rocket launch off Wallops Island, Virginia, filled the sky with colored clouds visible over much of the East Coast, resulting in a flurry of reports of UFO sightings.

Newton and Leo GeBauer. Newton and GeBauer were posing respectively as an oilman and a magnetics scientist in an attempt to set up a swindle involving oil-detection devices tied to extraterrestrial technology.

To serious ufologists, including those who suspected the government wasn't telling everything it knew about UFOs, crash stories were farfetched yarns of "little men in pickle jars." A person with such a story got a chilly reception when he or she passed it on to anyone but

"EXPLAINING" UFOs

Most UFO reports turn out to have conventional explanations. Typically, IFO (identified flying object) sightings are of stars, planets, meteors, balloons, advertising planes, optical illusions, and hoaxes. Skeptics argue that the remainder of the reports could probably be explained if additional information were available. This argument sounds logical but is in fact demonstrably false. Between 1952 and 1955 the Battelle Memorial Institute in Columbus, Ohio, a think tank that does classified analytical work for the U.S. government, studied Project Blue Book's collection of UFO reports. The Institute established that the unexplained sightings were fundamentally different from both explained sightings and those sightings with insufficient information for evaluation. Moreover, the "unknowns" came from the best-qualified observers, the sightings were of longer duration, and the unknown objects seldom bore any resemblance to their conventional counterparts.

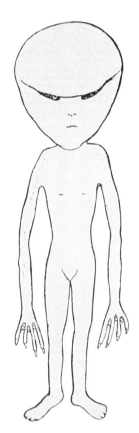

Ufologist Leonard H. Stringfield has collected dozens of stories from persons who claim to be privy to some of the U.S. government's deepest UFO secrets. One informant was a military doctor who said he had performed autopsies on the bodies of large-headed humanoids recovered from a crashed spacecraft.

fringe ufologists. In 1952 Ed J. Sullivan of the Los Angeles-based Civilian Saucer Investigators wrote that such tales "are damned for the simple reason, that after years of circulation, not one soul has come forward with a single concrete fact to support the assertions. . . . We ask you to beware of the man who tells you that his friend knows the man with the pickle jar. There is good reason why he effects [sic] such an air of mystery, why he has been 'sworn to secrecy'— because he can't produce the friend—or the pickle jar."

Nonetheless, rumors persisted. In 1954, after President Dwight Eisenhower dropped out of sight while visiting California (sparking a press-wire report that he had died), it was alleged that he had taken a secret trip to Edwards Air Force Base (AFB) to view alien remains—or, as another version had it, to confer with living aliens. A soldier with the Air Force confided that in 1948 he and other soldiers were dispatched to a New Mexico site to dismantle a nearly intact craft, from which an earlier party had removed the bodies of little men. In Europe it was said that the Norwegian military found a saucer on a remote North Atlantic island of Spitsbergën, or maybe it was the German military and the island was Heligoland. On May 23, 1955, newspaper columnist Dorothy Kilgallen wrote, "British scientists and airmen after examining the wreckage of one mysterious flying ship are convinced that these strange aerial objects are not optical illusions or Soviet inventions but are actual flying saucers which originate on another planet."

Several individuals who say they have seen alien bodies held by the Air Force describe the fingers as long, webbed, and pointed.

From William Nash in a Pan American Airlines DC-3 in 1952 to Gerson
Macial de Britto in a Brazilian airliner in 1982, pilots have often seen UFOs.
De Britto said a large, luminous UFO accompanied his plane for an hour and
20 minutes. He sketched it at a press conference the next day.

Over Chesapeake Bay on the evening of July 14, 1952, the pilot and copilot of a Pan American DC-3 had a much-publicized encounter with eight plate-shaped UFOs. The next morning, as they waited to be interviewed separately by Air Force officers, the two agreed to ask about the crash rumors. Subsequently, the copilot, William Fortenberry, raised the question, and one of the interrogators replied, "Yes, it is true." Pilot William Nash forgot to ask until afterward, when he and Fortenberry met together with the officers. Nash recalled, "They all opened their mouths to answer the question, whereupon Maj. [John H.] Sharpe looked at them, not me, and said very quickly, 'NO!' It appeared as if he were telling them to shut up rather than addressing the answer to me." Later Nash met a New York radio newsperson who claimed the Air Force had briefed him and two

(Continued on page 110)

SAUCER, SICKNESS, SECRECY

Vickie Landrum (left) and Betty Cash fell victim to radiation sickness after a December 1980 close encounter.

A UFO sighting on the evening of December 29, 1980, changed the lives of three Texans forever—and not for the good.

While driving through the southern tip of the east Texas piney woods, north of Houston, Betty Cash, Vickie Landrum, and Vickie's seven-year-old grandson Colby came upon a huge diamond-shaped object just above the trees and 130 feet away. Cash hit the brakes, and she and the elder Landrum stepped outside. Immediately, they noticed intense heat. Their faces felt as if they were burning. When Vickie reentered the car and touched the dashboard to steady herself, she left a handprint.

Blasting fire and heat, the UFO slowly ascended. Suddenly, numerous helicopters—23 in all—appeared from all directions, positioning themselves near the strange craft. By this time the witnesses were back in the car and watching the spectacle from their moving vehicle. (Other motorists saw the object and the helicopters from different, more distant locations.) Eventually, the flying objects were lost to

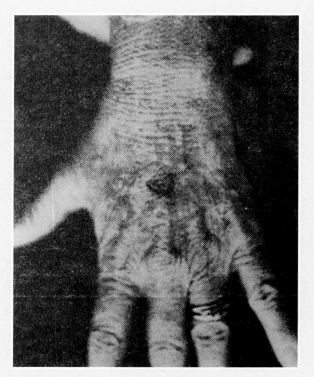

Among other symptoms, Vickie Landrum and Betty Cash suffered festering body sores. The UFO sighting has had a permanent effect on their health.

*A CH-47 Chinook Army helicopter of the type seen during the
Cash-Landrum sighting.*

view. Unfortunately, the episode was only beginning.

Back home the three fell sick, Cash most severely. She suffered blisters, nausea, headaches, diarrhea, loss of hair, and reddening of the eyes. On January 3, unable to walk and nearly unconscious, she was admitted to a Houston hospital. Vickie and Colby were experiencing the same symptoms, though less severely.

The witnesses' health problems continue to this day. In September 1991 Cash's personal physician, Dr. Brian McClelland, told the Houston *Post* that her condition was a "textbook case" of radiation poisoning, comparable to being "three to five miles from the epicenter of Hiroshima." For years the three have pursued their case through the courts, seeking answers and redress, but official agencies deny any knowledge of the incident—even though the helicopters have been identified as twin-rotor Boeing CH-47 Chinooks, used by both the Army and the Marines.

(Continued from page 107)

other reporters (one from *Life* magazine) about its recovery of a crashed UFO.

TESTIMONY OF A SCIENTIST

A remarkable interview occurred in Washington, D.C., on September 15, 1950, but the content did not leak out until the early 1980s, when Canadian ufologist Arthur Bray found a memo by one of the participants, radio engineer Wilbert B. Smith of Canada's Department of Transport. The memo described a conversation with physicist Robert I.

In September 1950 physicist and Department of Defense consultant Robert I. Sarbacher (left) confided to Canadian scientists that the United States possessed remains of UFO humanoids—"the most highly classified subject in the U.S. government."

HOW SECRET IT IS

The late comedian Jackie Gleason's second wife Beverly tells a strange story that she swears is true. One evening in 1973, she writes in an unpublished book on their marriage, Gleason returned to her Florida home badly shaken. After first refusing to tell her why he was so upset, Gleason confided that earlier in the day his friend President Richard Nixon had arranged for him to visit Homestead Air Force Base in Florida. Upon his arrival armed guards took Gleason to a building at a remote location on the site. There, Gleason, who harbored an intense interest in UFOs, saw the embalmed bodies of four alien beings, two feet long, with small bald heads and big ears. He was told nothing about the circumstances of their recovery. He swore his wife to secrecy, but after their divorce Beverly freely discussed the story. In the mid-1980s, when ufologist Larry Bryant sued the U.S. government to get it to reveal its UFO secrets, he tried without success to subpoena Gleason.

Sarbacher, a consultant with the U.S. Department of Defense Research and Development Board (RDB), at one of the regular meetings Sarbacher and other government scientists conducted with their Canadian counterparts.

Asked about the crash rumors, Sarbacher said they were "substantially correct." He said UFOs "exist. . . . We have not been able to duplicate their performance. . . . All we know is, we didn't make them, and it's pretty certain they didn't originate on the Earth." The issue was so sensitive that "it is classified two points higher even than the H-bomb. In fact it is the most highly classified subject in the U.S. government at the present time." Sarbacher refused to say more.

Smith, who died in 1961, mounted a small, short-lived UFO investigation, Project Magnet, for his government. Through official channels he tried unsuccessfully to learn more than

Sarbacher identified nuclear physicist J. Robert Oppenheimer as one of the scientists involved in a top secret UFO project that studied extraterrestrial hardware.

According to Sarbacher, Vannevar Bush, President Truman's chief science adviser, headed a project formed to coordinate research into physical evidence of UFOs. Even the name of the project (if it existed) remains unknown.

Sarbacher's cryptic remarks had revealed. After the memo surfaced, ufologists found a listing for Sarbacher in *Who's Who in America*, citing his impressive scientific, business, and educational credentials.

When interviewed, Sarbacher said he had not personally participated in the UFO project, though he knew those who had, including RDB head Vannevar Bush, John von Neumann, and J. Robert Oppenheimer—three of America's top scientists in the 1940s and 1950s. He had read documents related to the project and on occasion had been invited to participate in Air Force briefings.

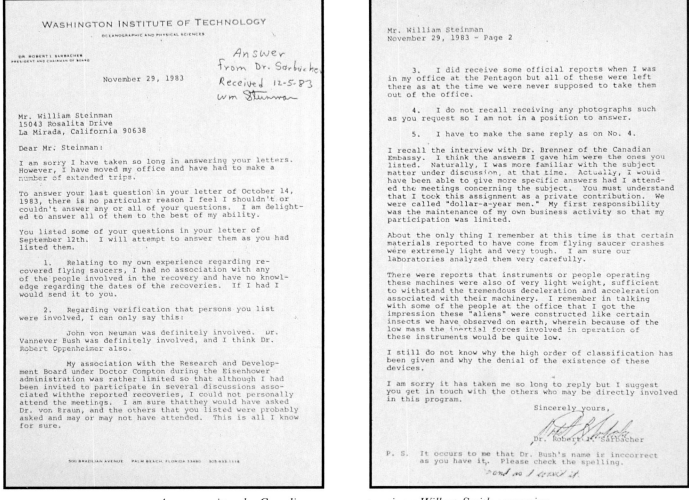

A memo written by Canadian government engineer Wilbert Smith concerning the September 1950 meeting with Sarbacher surfaced three decades later. This led ufologists to Sarbacher for answers. In answer to an inquirer, Sarbacher passed on what he remembered hearing about UFOs during his tenure as a scientific consultant to the Defense Department.

"There were reports that instruments or people operating these machines were also of very light weight, sufficient to withstand the tremendous deceleration and acceleration associated with their machinery," Sarbacher told an inquirer in 1983. "I remember in talking with some of the people at the office that I got the impression these 'aliens' were constructed like certain insects we have observed on Earth, wherein because of the low mass the inertial forces involved in operating of these instruments would be quite low. I still do not know why the high order of classification has been given and why the denial of the existence of these devices." Sarbacher could not recall where the crashes had taken place, but he did remember hearing of "extremely light and very tough" materials recovered from them.

Sarbacher's story never varied, and he resisted the temptation to elaborate or speculate. All who interviewed him were impressed. Still, his story could not be verified, since the persons he named were all dead. Sarbacher himself died in the summer of 1986.

ROSWELL UNRAVELED

On the evening of July 2, 1947, several witnesses in and near Roswell, New Mexico, observed a disc-shaped object moving swiftly in a northwesterly direction through the sky. The following morning Mac Brazel, foreman of a ranch located near tiny Corona, New Mexico, rode out on horseback to move sheep from one field to another. Accompanying him was a young neighbor boy, Timothy D. Proctor. As they rode, they came upon strange debris—various-size chunks of metallic material—running from one hilltop, down an arroyo, up another hill, and running down the other side. To all appearances some kind of aircraft had exploded. In fact Brazel had heard something that sounded like an explosion the night before, but because it happened during a rainstorm (though it was different from thunder), he had not looked into the cause. Brazel picked up some of the pieces. He had never seen anything like them. They were extremely light and very tough.

By the time events had run their course, the world would be led to believe that Brazel had found the remains of a weather balloon. For three decades, only those directly involved in the incident would know this was a lie. And in the early 1950s, when an enterprising reporter sought to reinvestigate the story, those who knew the truth were warned to tell him nothing.

The cover-up did not begin to unravel until the mid-1970s, when two individuals who had been in New Mexico in 1947 separately talked with investigator Stanton T. Friedman about what they had observed. One, an Albuquerque radio station employee, had witnessed the muzzling of a reporter and the shutting down of an in-progress teletyped news story about the inci-

(Continued on page 116)

Physicist and lecturer Stanton T. Friedman—here holding a portrait of a humanoid based on the recollections of a New Hampshire man who claims he was abducted in 1971— pioneered investigation into the Roswell incident.

MAJESTIC MYSTERY

In December 1984 a package with no return address and an Albuquerque postmark arrived in Jaime Shandera's mail in North Hollywood, California. Inside was a roll of 35mm film. When developed, it turned out to contain eight pages of an alleged briefing paper, dated November 18, 1952, in which Vice Adm. Roscoe Hillenkoetter told President-elect Dwight Eisenhower of the recovery of the remains of two crashed spaceships. In the first of these crashes, in early July 1947, authorities recovered the bodies of four humanoid beings. According to the document, which appended a copy of what was supposed to be the actual executive order, President Harry Truman authorized the creation of a supersecret group called "Majestic 12" (MJ-12 for short) to study the remains.

Acting on a tip from sources who claimed to represent Air Force intelligence, Shandera and his associate William Moore (coauthor of *The Roswell Incident*) flew to Washington, D.C. They searched the National Archives looking for references in official documents to MJ-12. They found a July 1954 memo from Gen. Robert Cutler, an Eisenhower assistant, referring to an

In December 1984 this document—allegedly a briefing paper prepared by "Operation Majestic-12"—arrived in the mail to a Los Angeles man researching official UFO secrets. Supposedly, Operation Majestic-12 (MJ-12) comprised 12 prominent men with military, intelligence, and scientific backgrounds. Formed by order of President

TOP SECRET / MAJIC
EYES ONLY
················
· TOP SECRET ·
················

EYES ONLY   COPY ONE OF ONE.

A covert analytical effort organized by Gen. Twining and
Dr. Bush acting on the direct orders of the President, resulted in a preliminary consensus (19 September, 1947) that
the disc was most likely a short range reconnaissance craft.
This conclusion was based for the most part on the craft's
size and the apparent lack of any identifiable provisioning.
(See Attachment "D".) A similar analysis of the four dead
occupants was arranged by Dr. Bronk. It was the tentative
conclusion of this group (30 November, 1947) that although
these creatures are human-like in appearance, the biological
and evolutionary processes responsible for their development
has apparently been quite different from those observed or
postulated in homo-sapiens. Dr. Bronk's team has suggested
the term "Extra-terrestrial Biological Entities", or "EBEs",
be adopted as the standard term of reference for these
creatures until such time as a more definitive designation
can be agreed upon.

Since it is virtually certain that these craft do not originate in any country on earth, considerable speculation has
centered around what their point of origin might be and how
they get here. Mars was and remains a possibility, although
some scientists, most notably Dr. Menzel, consider it more
likely that we are dealing with beings from another solar
system entirely.

Numerous examples of what appear to be a form of writing
were found in the wreckage. Efforts to decipher these have
remained largely unsuccessful. (See Attachment "E".)
Equally unsuccessful have been efforts to determine the
method of propulsion or the nature or method of transmission
of the power source involved. Research along these lines
has been complicated by the complete absence of identifiable
wings, propellers, jets, or other conventional methods of
propulsion and guidance, as well as a total lack of metallic
wiring, vacuum tubes, or similar recognizable electronic
components. (See Attachment "F".) It is assumed that the
propulsion unit was completely destroyed by the explosion
which caused the crash.

················
· TOP SECRET ·
················
EYES ONLY TOP SECRET / MAJIC   TS2-EXEMPT (E)
EYES ONLY

Truman, MJ-12 came into being in the wake of the Roswell incident. When this document was released to the public in May 1987, it sparked massive controversy. The document is now believed to be a hoax, but the identity and motive of the perpetrator remain unknown even after an FBI investigation.

"MJ-12 SSP [Special Studies Project]" to be held at the White House on the 16th of that month.

In the spring of 1987 an unknown individual, allegedly associated with an intelligence agency, gave British writer Timothy Good a copy of the MJ-12 document. Upon learning Good was going to disclose its existence to the press, Moore and Shandera released their copy, along with the Cutler memo. The result was a massive uproar, including coverage in *The New York Times* and *Nightline*, an FBI investigation, and furious controversy that continues to this day.

For various technical reasons most investigators agree that the MJ-12 document is a forgery, but the identity of the forger remains a deep mystery that even the FBI cannot crack. The forger apparently had access to obscure official information, much of it not even in the public record, leading to suspicions that an intelligence agency created the document for disinformation purposes. Whatever the answer, the MJ-12 document is surely the most puzzling hoax in UFO history.

Stanton T. Friedman, an outspoken proponent of extraterrestrial UFOs and critic of official UFO secrecy, maintains—in the face of widespread skepticism among his fellow ufologists—that the MJ-12 document is authentic. He contends it is the smoking gun of the cover-up.

(Continued from page 113)

dent. The other, an Army Air Force intelligence officer, had led the initial recovery operation. The officer, retired Maj. Jesse A. Marcel, stated flatly that the material was of unearthly origin.

The uncovering of the truth about the Roswell incident—so called because it was from Roswell Field, the nearest Air Force base, that the recovery operation was directed—would be an excruciatingly difficult process. It continues to this day, even after publication of three books and massive documentation gleaned from interviews with several hundred persons as well as other evidence. Besides being the most impor-

U.S. GOVERNMENT IN CONTACT WITH E.T.'s?

Former CIA operative Victor Marchetti, coauthor of the best-selling *The CIA and the Cult of Intelligence* (1974), thinks the U.S. government maintains secret contacts with extraterrestrials. He bases his suspicion—he admits he cannot prove it—on stories he heard while working at "high levels of the CIA." These tales alleged that the National Security Agency (NSA), which collects electronic intelligence, had received "strange signals," said by intelligence sources to be of extraterrestrial origin. Marchetti could learn nothing about the content of these communications, which had a level of secrecy that was extraordinary even by the standards of the supersecret NSA. In the 1980s UFO investigators William Moore and Jaime Shandera heard comparable tales from Air Force intelligence sources. No good evidence backs up these tales, but they are undeniably intriguing, if only because of who is telling the tales.

tant case in UFO history—the one with the potential not to settle the issue of UFOs but to identify them as extraterrestrial spacecraft—the Roswell incident is also the most fully investigated. The principal investigators have been Friedman, William L. Moore (coauthor of the first of the books, *The Roswell Incident* [1980]), Kevin D. Randle, and Donald R. Schmitt. Randle and Schmitt, associated with the Chicago-based Center for UFO Studies (CUFOS), authored the most comprehensive account so far, *UFO Crash at Roswell* (1991).

William Moore, the first investigator to document the Roswell UFO crash, maintains a controversial association with Air Force intelligence officers who claim to be cover-up insiders.

Victor Marchetti, a 14-year veteran of the CIA, coauthored The CIA and the Cult of Intelligence; *the CIA attempted to prevent publication of the book. Marchetti has written that official efforts to discount UFOs "have all the earmarkings of a classic intelligence cover-up."*

Friedman's book, written with Don Berliner, will be published in 1992. From this research, the outlines of a complex, bizarre episode have emerged.

Eighth Air Force Commander Brig. Gen. Roger Ramey, acting under orders from Gen. Clements McMullen at the Pentagon, concocted the weather balloon story to "put out the fire," in the words of retired Brig. Gen. Thomas DuBose, who in July 1947 was serving as adjutant to Ramey's staff. The actual material, all who saw it agreed, could not possibly have come from a balloon. For one thing, there was far too much of it. For another, it was not remotely like balloon wreckage. Maj. Marcel described it:

> [We found] all kinds of stuff—small beams about ⅜ or a half-inch square with some sort of hieroglyphics on them that nobody could decipher. These looked something like balsa wood and were of about the same

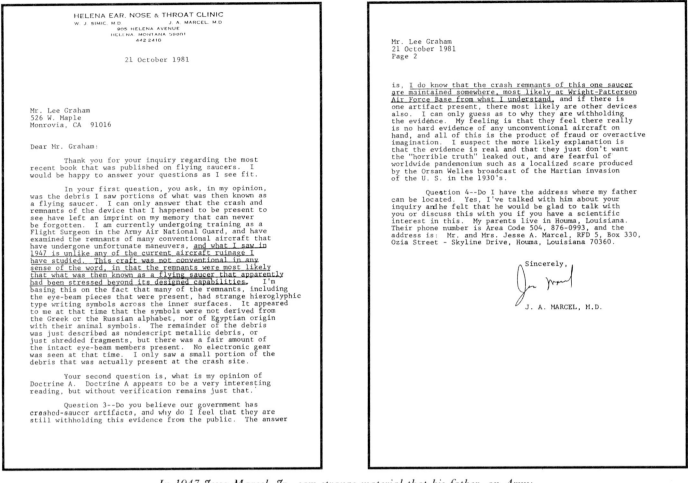

HELENA EAR, NOSE & THROAT CLINIC
W. J. SIMIC, M.D.   J. A. MARCEL, M.D.
905 HELENA AVENUE
HELENA, MONTANA 59601
442-2410

21 October 1981

Mr. Lee Graham
526 W. Maple
Monrovia, CA 91016

Dear Mr. Graham:

Thank you for your inquiry regarding the most recent book that was published on flying saucers. I would be happy to answer your questions as I see fit.

In your first question, you ask, in my opinion, was the debris I saw portions of what was then known as a flying saucer. I can only answer that the crash and remnants of the device that I happened to be present to see have left an imprint on my memory that can never be forgotten. I am currently undergoing training as a Flight Surgeon in the Army Air National Guard, and have examined the remnants of many conventional aircraft that have undergone unfortunate maneuvers, and what I saw in 1947 is unlike any of the current aircraft ruinage I have studied. This craft was not conventional in any sense of the word, in that the remnants were most likely that what was then known as a flying saucer that apparently had been stressed beyond its designed capabilities. I'm basing this on the fact that many of the remnants, including the eye-beam pieces that were present, had strange hieroglyphic type writing symbols across the inner surfaces. It appeared to me at that time that the symbols were not derived from the Greek or the Russian alphabet, nor of Egyptian origin with their animal symbols. The remainder of the debris was just described as nondescript metallic debris, or just shredded fragments, but there was a fair amount of the intact eye-beam members present. No electronic gear was seen at that time. I only saw a small portion of the debris that was actually present at the crash site.

Your second question is, what is my opinion of Doctrine A. Doctrine A appears to be a very interesting reading, but without verification remains just that.

Question 3--Do you believe our government has crashed-saucer artifacts, and why do I feel that they are still withholding this evidence from the public. The answer

Mr. Lee Graham
21 October 1981
Page 2

is, I do know that the crash remnants of this one saucer are maintained somewhere, most likely at Wright-Patterson Air Force Base from what I understand, and if there is one artifact present, there most likely are other devices also. I can only guess as to why they are withholding the evidence. My feeling is that they feel there really is no hard evidence of any unconventional aircraft on hand, and all of this is the product of fraud or overactive imagination. I suspect the more likely explanation is that the evidence is real and that they just don't want the "horrible truth" leaked out, and are fearful of worldwide pandemonium such as a localized scare produced by the Orsan Welles broadcast of the Martian invasion of the U. S. in the 1930's.

Question 4--Do I have the address where my father can be located. Yes, I've talked with him about your inquiry and he felt that he would be glad to talk with you or discuss this with you if you have a scientific interest in this. My parents live in Houma, Louisiana. Their phone number is Area Code 504, 876-0993, and the address is: Mr. and Mrs. Jesse A. Marcel, RFD 5, Box 330, Ozia Street - Skyline Drive, Houma, Louisiana 70360.

Sincerely,

J. A. MARCEL, M.D.

In 1947 Jesse Marcel, Jr., saw strange material that his father, an Army Air Force intelligence officer, recovered in Lincoln County, New Mexico, at what is now known as the Roswell incident site. His father, since deceased, testified to the material's unearthly nature.

weight, although flexible, and would not burn. There was a great deal of an unusual parchmentlike substance which was brown in color and extremely strong, and a great number of small pieces of a metal like tin foil, except that it wasn't tin foil. . . . [The parchment writing] had little numbers and symbols that we had to call hieroglyphics because I could not understand them. . . . They were pink and purple.

They looked like they were painted on. These little numbers could not be broken, could not be burned . . . wouldn't even smoke.

The metallic material not only looked but acted strange. It had memory. No matter how it was twisted or balled up, it would return to its original shape, with no wrinkles. One woman who saw a rolled-up piece tossed onto a table watched in astonishment as it unfolded itself

SHIPS IN THE FOREST

We may never know the full story of what happened between December 26 and 27, 1980, in Rendlesham forest, located between two U.S. Air Force bases, Woodbridge and Bentwaters, on England's east coast. The incidents remain shrouded in secrecy. What we do know—learned through a painstaking, years-long investigation by civilian researchers—is fantastic enough.

Just after midnight on December 26, eyewitnesses and radar screens followed an unidentified object as it vanished into the forest. Soldiers dispatched to the site encountered a luminous triangular-shaped craft, ten feet across and eight feet high, with three legs. The UFO then retracted the legs and easily maneuvered its way through the trees. The soldiers chased it into a field, where it abruptly shot upward, shining brilliant lights down on them. At that moment the witnesses lost consciousness. When they came to, they were back in the forest. Other troops sent to rescue them found tripod landing marks where the object apparently had rested.

The following evening, after observers reported strange lights, the deputy base commander, Lt. Col. Charles Halt, led a larger party into Rendlesham. There, Halt measured abnormal amounts of radiation at the original landing site. Another, smaller group, off on a separate trek through the forest, spotted a dancing red light inside an eerily pulsating "fog." They alerted Halt's group, who suddenly saw the light heading toward them, spewing forth a rainbow waterfall of colors. Meanwhile, the second group now watched a glowing domed object in which they could see the shadows of figures moving about. During the next hour both groups observed these and other darting lights.

Cable News Network learned that films and photographs were taken of these events, despite official denials. According to curiously persistent rumors, never verified but never conclusively disproved, occupants were encountered at some point during the event.

When a constituent told him about the incident, U.S. Sen. James Exon launched an extensive but secret inquiry. He has never revealed his findings, even to staff members. He says only that he learned "additional information" that ties the Rendlesham case to "other unexplained UFO incidents."

Impressionable people believe this widely published photograph shows the body of an extraterrestrial humanoid recovered from the crash site of a flying saucer. In fact, the figure in the picture, taken in 1981, is a wax doll displayed in a museum in Montreal.

until it was as flat, and as wrinkle-free, as the table top. When an acetylene torch was turned on samples of the material, they barely got warm and could be safely handled a moment or two later.

Air Force searchers scoured the recovery site until they had picked up what they thought were all pieces, however minuscule, of the crashed vehicle. Two years later, when Bill Brazel, Mac's son, let it be known he had found a few pieces the soldiers had missed, an Air Force officer called on him and demanded them.

He handed them over without argument. Young Brazel knew how serious the military was about all this. After all, in July 1947 the Air Force had held his father incommunicado for days and made certain (through threats and, it is suspected, a large bribe) that he never again talked about his discovery.

The material was secretly flown out of Eighth Army Headquarters in Fort Worth, Texas, to Wright Field (later Wright-Patterson AFB) in Dayton, Ohio. At Wright Field, according to an officer who was there, Lt. Col. Arthur Exon (who would become commander of the base in the mid-1960s), it underwent analysis in the Air Force's material evaluation laboratories. Some of it, he recalled, was "very thin but awfully strong and couldn't be dented with heavy hammers. . . . It had [the scientists] pretty puzzled. . . . [T]he overall consensus was that the pieces were from space."

EXTRATERRESTRIAL BIOLOGICAL ENTITIES

But it wasn't just metal that had arrived at Wright Field.

As they reconstructed the unknown craft's trajectory, military investigators concluded it had

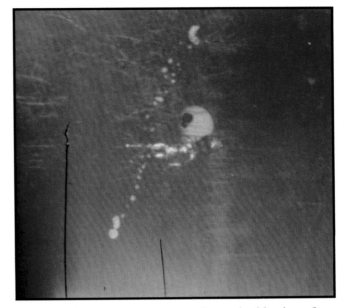

When studying the Roswell incident, a healthy dose of skepticism will help weed out phony information—such as this photograph of a "humanoid."

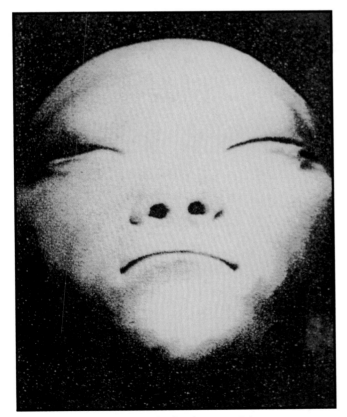

This dubious photograph of unknown origin purports to show the face of a dead alien. Similar pictures have proliferated in the wake of revived interest in stories of crashed UFOs and cover-ups.

come in from the southeast (in other words, from the Roswell area). Two and a half miles southeast of the debris field, looking down from a reconnaissance aircraft, searchers spotted a second, smaller, relatively more intact though undeniably crashed, machine. Sprawled near it were four bodies. They were not the bodies of human beings.

This aspect of the Roswell story is the most fantastic, unbelievable, and difficult to document. The Air Force went to extraordinary lengths to hide it even from some of those who participated in the recovery of the material at the first site. Yet from the meticulous (and ongoing) research of Schmitt and Randle, we get the testimony of credible individuals who were involved, directly or indirectly, with the recovery of extraterrestrial remains. According to Exon, who heard the story from Wright person-

*This comet over New Mexico provides a wondrous sight. Could UFOs be
another wondrous sight the skies have to offer?*

nel who had examined the bodies at the base, "they were all found . . . in fairly good condition," even though they had lain there for six days (they were discovered on July 8) and varmints had chewed on some of the soft organs.

Those who participated in the recovery of the bodies have provided consistent descriptions of what these "extraterrestrial biological entities" (the official designation, according to some unconfirmed accounts) looked like. They were four to five feet tall, humanoid, with big heads, large eyes, and slitlike mouths. They were thin and had long arms with four fingers. An Army nurse who worked on the initial autopsy at Roswell remarked on how fragile the skull and bones were. Within hours the bodies were put into large sealed wooden crates, loaded into the bomb pit of a B-29, and flown to Fort Worth Army Air Field. From there they went almost immediately to Wright Field.

Participants kept silent for years. Finally, as initial reports of the Roswell incident began to appear in the 1980s, they began to confide to close friends or family members what they had seen. Even then they were uneasy, still afraid of getting into trouble. One participant, Capt. Oliver ("Pappy") Henderson, flew the plane that first spotted the bodies. Apparently, judging from what he told his family, he also saw the

This UFO was photographed October 16, 1957, as it hovered over Holloman Test Range in New Mexico.

bodies up close. Sgt. Melvin Brown rode in a truck with the bodies from the crash site to Roswell Field, then stood guard at the hangar where they were first stored.

Several persons who were at Wright Field or who knew individuals who were have testified to the arrival of wreckage and bodies at Wright in July 1947. One of these, retired Gen. Exon, says a top-secret committee was formed to oversee the investigation of this and other highly classified UFO incidents. Nearly 20 years later, when he took command of the base, the committee was still operating. It had nothing to do with Project Blue Book, the poorly funded, inadequate project that apparently served little more than a public relations function. As Brig. Gen. Bolender had indicated in the internal Air Force memorandum quoted earlier (see Chapter 2 "UFOs: The Official Story"), UFO reports "which could affect national security . . . are not part of the Blue Book system."

The pioneering UFO work of Dr. J. Allen Hynek, now deceased, is carried on by many ufologists hoping to uncover the secret of Roswell and other UFO reports.

On November 12, 1954, citizens of Rome tracked the passage of a "disco volante" (flying saucer). From the Middle Ages to the present day, people have always searched the heavens, wondering what lies beyond the solar system.

Echoes of the Roswell incident have been heard for decades in popular folklore about secret rooms and buildings at Wright-Patterson AFB where government personnel study physical and biological proof of alien visitation. Most—but not all—are "friend-of-a-friend" tales. Retired Wright-Patterson employee Norma Gardner claimed before her death ("Uncle Sam can't do anything to me once I'm in my grave.") to have catalogued UFO material, including parts from the interior of a machine that had

been brought to the base some years earlier. She also said she had typed autopsy reports on the bodies of occupants; once, moreover, she saw two of the bodies as they were being moved from one location to another. From her description—if she was telling the truth—she saw the Roswell entities. In the mid-1960s Sen. Barry Goldwater, a brigadier general in the Air Force reserve, asked his friend Gen. Curtis LeMay about the rumors. Goldwater told *The New Yorker* (April 25, 1988) that LeMay gave him "holy hell" and warned him never to bring up the subject again.

INTIMATIONS OF INFINITY

If intelligent life exists elsewhere, according to a view held by many astronomers, it is likely to generally look like us. It is also probable, according to Carl Sagan, Frank Drake, and other specialists in exobiology, that the galaxy teems with extraterrestrial civilizations. Some of these civilizations are older than Earth's and have superior technologies. "It is extremely probable," Michael D. Swords of Western Michigan University writes in a survey of the scientific literature on the subject, "that some, if not all, of these advanced civilizations have the means, albeit with difficulty, of traversing interstellar space. And it is essentially a certainty that these advanced life forms have several instincts/moti-

When he asked Gen. Curtis LeMay about rumors concerning the Roswell incident, Senator Barry Goldwater said he caught "holy hell" and was warned to avoid the subject.

vators/behaviors in common with Homo sapiens, one of which (curiosity) may be particularly germane to such journeys."

In other words, visitation from elsewhere is not just possible, it's something that, given a well-populated galaxy, we should expect. From every indication such visitation is happening now. It remains a secret only to those who have not seen it in operation with their own eyes, read the UFO evidence with an open mind, or examined—at some secure facility somewhere—the metal and the bodies that fell out of the sky one night in 1947 and forever proved we are not alone.

Carl Sagan and other exobiologists speculate that a universe containing uncounted numbers of stars harbors many solar systems that support extraterrestrial life. As much as any motive, curiosity may drive these humanoids to visit Earth.